Notes of an Overland Journey Through France and Egypt to Bombay

Miss Emma Roberts

Contents

MEMOIR. 7
CHAPTER I. LONDON TO PARIS. 16
CHAPTER II. PARIS TO MARSEILLES. 31
CHAPTER III. MARSEILLES TO ALEXANDRIA. 43
CHAPTER IV. ALEXANDRIA TO BOULAK. 57
CHAPTER V. CAIRO. 73
CHAPTER VI. THE DESERT. 89
CHAPTER VII. SUEZ TO ADEN. 104
CHAPTER VIII. ADEN. 116
CHAPTER IX. BOMBAY. 132
CHAPTER X. BOMBAY--(Continued). 148
CHAPTER XI. BOMBAY--(Continued.) 165
CHAPTER XII. BOMBAY--(Continued). 181

NOTES OF AN OVERLAND JOURNEY THROUGH FRANCE AND EGYPT TO BOMBAY

BY
Miss Emma Roberts

MEMOIR.

Experience has, especially of late years, amply refuted the barbarous error, which attributes to Nature a niggardliness towards the minds of that sex to which she has been most prodigal of personal gifts; the highest walks of science and literature in this country have been graced by female authors, and, perhaps, the purity and refinement which pervade our works of imagination, compared with those of former days, may not unjustly be traced to the larger share which feminine pens now have in the production of these works. It would appear to countenance the heretical notion just condemned, to assume that a robust organization is essential to the proper development and exercise of the powers of the understanding; but it is certain that, in several instances, individuals, who have exhibited the most striking examples of female pre-eminence, have not reached the full maturity of their intellectual growth, but have been lost to the world in a premature grave: to the names of Felicia Hemans and Laetitia E. Landon, besides others, is now added that of Emma Roberts, who, although in respect of poetical genius she cannot be placed upon a level with the two writers just named, yet in the vigour of her faculties, and in the variety of her talents, is worthy of being associated with them as another evidence against the asserted mental inequality of the sexes.

Miss Roberts belonged to a Welsh family of great respectability. Her grandfather, who was a gentleman of good property, and served the office of High Sheriff for Denbighshire, North Wales, possessed the fine estate of Kenmell Park in that county, which was disposed of after his death to Colonel Hughes, the present Lord Dinorben, whose seat it continues to be. He had three sons, all of whom entered a military life, which seems to have had peculiar attractions to this gallant family. The eldest, the late General Thomas Roberts, raised a regiment, which became the 111th, and it is said he frequently officiated as Gold Stick in Waiting to George the

Third. A son of General Roberts was aide-de-camp to Sir Arthur Wellesley in Portugal, was taken prisoner by the French, and detained during the war: he afterwards rose to the rank of lieutenant-colonel. The second son, Colonel David Roberts, of the 51st regiment, distinguished himself in the Peninsular war, having, on the 7th January, 1809, during Sir John Moore's retreat, near the heights of Lugo, headed a party which repulsed the French Light Brigade, on which occasion his cloak was riddled with bullets, two of which passed through his right-hand, which was amputated. He was then a major, but afterwards commanded the regiment, in Lord Dalhousie's brigade, and subsequently in Flanders, and was so seriously and repeatedly wounded, that his pensions for wounds amounted to L500 a year. Colonel Roberts was an author, and wrote, amongst other things, the comic military sketch called ***Johnny Newcome***. The youngest son, William (the father of Miss Roberts), in the course of his travels on the continent, in early life, formed some intimacies at the Court of St. Petersburgh (to which he was introduced by the British Ambassador), and eventually entered the Russian service; he was made aide-de-camp to General Lloyd, his countryman, and served with great distinction in several campaigns against the Turks. He afterwards entered the British army, but had not attained a higher rank than that of captain (with the paymastership of his regiment), when he died, leaving a widow, a son (who died a lieutenant in the army), and two daughters.

Emma, the youngest daughter of Captain Roberts, was born about the year 1794. After the death of her father, she resided with her mother, a lady of some literary pretensions, at Bath. Though possessed of a very attractive person, though of a lively disposition, and peculiarly fitted to shine in the gayest circles of social life, her thirst for letters was unquenchable, and the extent of her reading proves that her early years must have been years of application.

Her first literary work was in the grave department of history,--Memoirs of the Rival Houses of York and Lancaster, or the White and Red Roses, which was published in two volumes, 1827. In the preparation of this work, Miss Roberts prosecuted her researches into the historical records at the Museum with so much diligence and perseverance, as to attract the notice of the officers of that institution, who rendered her much assistance. This work did not take hold of public attention; the narrative is perspicuously and pleasingly written, but it throws no additional light upon the events of the time. It is not unusual for young writers, in their first essay, to mistake the bent of their powers.

On the death of her mother and the marriage of her sister to an officer of the Bengal army (Captain R.A. M'Naghten), Miss Roberts accompanied Mrs. M'Naghten and her husband to India, in February 1828, taking her passage in the ***Sir David Scott***, to Bengal. From Calcutta she proceeded with them to the Upper Provinces, where she spent the years 1829 and 1830, between the stations of Agra, Cawnpore, and Etawah. Her active and inquisitive mind was constantly employed in noting the new and extraordinary scenes around her, the physical aspect of the country, the peculiar traits of its population, and the manners of both natives and Anglo-Indians: the strong and faithful impressions they made never faded from a memory remarkably retentive. It is to these favourable opportunities of diversified observation, in her journeys by land and water, along the majestic Ganges, or by the dawk conveyance in a palanquin, and in her residence for so long a period away from the metropolis of British India, which exhibits but a mongrel kind of Eastern society, that the English public owe those admirable pictures of Indian scenery and manners, which have conquered, or contributed to conquer, its habitual distaste for such topics.

Whilst at Cawnpore, Miss Roberts committed to the press a little volume of poetry, entitled ***Oriental Scenes***, which she dedicated to her friend Miss Landon, then rising into eminence under the well-known designation of L.E.L. This volume, which she republished in England, in 1832, contains some very pleasing specimens of glowing description, graceful imagery, and well-turned expression, which show that her powers required only cultivation to have secured to her a respectable rank among modern poets.

Mrs. M'Naghten died in 1831, and about this time (either soon after or shortly before the death of her sister), she exchanged provincial scenes and society for the more cheerful atmosphere of Calcutta, where a new world of observation and of employment opened to her. The sketches she has given of the City of Palaces, and of its inhabitants, prove how accurately she had seized their characteristic features. Here her pen was called into incessant activity; besides various contributions to Annuals and other ephemeral works, Miss Roberts undertook the formidable task (doubly formidable in such a climate) of editing a newspaper, and the ***Oriental Ob-***

server, whilst under her direction, was enriched by some valuable articles written by herself, indicating the versatility of her talents, the extent of her resources, and the large area of knowledge over which her active mind had ranged.

This severe over-employment, however, entailed the inevitable penalty, loss of health, and in 1832, being now bound by no powerful tie to India, and looking forward, perhaps, with innocent ambition, to a less confined theatre for the display of her talents and acquisitions, she quitted the country, and returned to England, the voyage completely repairing the injury which the climate of India had wrought upon her constitution. The reputation she had acquired preceded her to this country, where she had many literary acquaintances, some of whom had reached a high station in public esteem; and her entrance into the best literary circles of the metropolis was thereby facilitated; but the position which she was entitled to claim was spontaneously conceded to talents such as hers, set off by engaging and unaffected manners, warmth and benevolence of heart, equanimity and serenity of temper.

The fruits of her observations in the East were given to the world in several series of admirable papers, published in the **Asiatic Journal**,[1] a periodical work to which she contributed with indefatigable zeal and success, from shortly after her return to England until her death. A selection of those papers was published, in three volumes, in 1835, under the title of **Scenes and Characteristics of Hindostan**, which has had a large circulation, and (a very unusual circumstance attending works on Indian subjects) soon reached a second edition. This work established Miss Roberts's reputation as a writer of unrivalled excellence in this province, which demands a union of quick and acute discernment with the faculty of vivid and graphic delineation. Of the many attempts which have been made in this country to furnish popular draughts of Indian "Scenes and Characteristics," that of Miss Roberts is the only one which has perfectly succeeded.

Her pen now came into extensive requisition, and the miscellaneous information with which she had stored her mind enabled her, with the aid of great fluency of composition and unremitted industry, to perform a quantity and a variety of literary labour, astonishing to her friends, when they considered that Miss Roberts did not seclude herself from society, but mixed in parties, where her conversational talents rendered her highly acceptable, and carried on, besides, a very extensive

---

1 The first appeared in the Journal for December, 1832.

correspondence. History, biography, poetry, tales, local descriptions, foreign correspondence, didactic essays, even the culinary art, by turns employed her versatile powers. Most of these compositions were occasional pieces, furnished to periodical works; to some she attached her name, and a few were separately published. Amongst the latter is a very pleasing biographical sketch of Mrs. Maclean (formerly Miss Landon), one of her oldest and dearest friends.

It was now seven years since she had quitted British India, during which period important events had occurred, which wrought material changes in its political and social aspects. The extinction of the East-India Company's commercial privileges had imparted a new tone to its government, given a freer scope to the principle of innovation, and poured a fresh European infusion into its Anglo-Indian society; steam navigation and an overland communication between England and her Eastern empire were bringing into operation new elements of mutation, and the domestic historian of India (as Miss Roberts may be appropriately termed) felt a natural curiosity to observe the progress of these changes, and to compare the British India of 1830 with that of 1840. With a view of enlarging the sphere of her knowledge of the country, and of deriving every practicable advantage from a twelve-months' visit, she determined to examine India on its Western side, and (contrary to the urgent advice of many of her friends) to encounter the inconveniences of performing the journey overland, through France and Egypt. Previous to her departure, she entered into an arrangement with the *Asiatic Journal* (the depository of most of her papers on Indian subjects) to transmit, on her way, a series of papers for publication in that work, descriptive of the objects and incidents met with in the overland route, and of the "rising presidency," as she termed Bombay. By a singular coincidence, the last paper of this series was published in the very number of the *Asiatic Journal*[2] which announced her death. These papers, which are now before the reader, carry on the biography of Miss Roberts almost to the end of her life.

She quitted England in September, 1839, and, having suffered few annoyances on the journey, except a fever which attacked her in the Gulf, arrived in Bombay in November, where she experienced the most cordial reception from all classes, including the Governor and the most respectable of the native community. Miss Roberts was known to Sir James Carnac, and in his Excellency's family she became

---

2 For December, 1840.

a guest for some time, quitting his hospitable mansion only to meet with a similar cordiality of welcome from other friends, at the presidency and in the interior. Her residence at Parell has enabled her to draw, with her accustomed felicity, in one of the papers published in this volume, a lively sketch of the domestic scenes and public receptions, as well as the local scenery, at this delightful place. It appears from her letters that Miss Roberts meditated a tour into Cutch or Guzerat, which probably was prevented by her subsequent illness. "It is my intention," she wrote from Parell, December 30th, 1839, "to go into the provinces, as I have received numerous invitations; I am at present divided between Guzerat and Cutch: by going to the latter, I might have an opportunity of seeing Scinde, the new Resident, Captain Outram, being anxious that I should visit it." She adds: "I have received much attention from the native gentlemen belonging to this presidency, and have, indeed, every reason to be pleased with my reception." She had projected a statistical work on this part of India, and in her private letters she speaks with grateful enthusiasm of the liberality with which the government records were opened to her, and of the alacrity with which Europeans and natives forwarded her views and inquiries. In a letter dated in February, 1840, she says: "I am very diligently employed in collecting materials for my work; I am pleased with the result of my labours, and think I shall be able to put a very valuable book upon Bombay before the public. I hope to go in a short time to Mahableshwar, and thence to Sattara, Beejapore, &c." Her literary aid was invoked by the conductors of periodical works at Bombay, to which she furnished some amusing pictures of home-scenes, drawn with the same spirit and truth as her Indian sketches. She likewise undertook the editorship of a new weekly paper, the **Bombay United Service Gazette**, and with the benevolence which formed so bright a feature in her character, she engaged with zeal in a scheme for rescuing the native women, who (as her observation led her to believe) impede the progress of improvement, from the indolence in which they are educated, by devising employments for them suited to their taste and capacity. The concluding chapter of this volume contains some very sound and salutary reflections upon native education.

Perhaps too close and unremitting application, in a climate which demands moderation in all pursuits that tax the powers of either mind or body, produced or aggravated a disease of the stomach, with which this lady was seriously attacked when on a visit to Colonel Ovans, the Resident at Sattara. Some indication of disordered health manifested itself whilst she was in the Hills. Writing from thence in April, and adverting to some incident which caused her vexation, she observed: "My health is failing me, and I can scarcely bear any increased subject of anxiety." She experienced in the family of Colonel Ovans all the attention and sympathy which the kindest hospitality could suggest; but her disorder increasing, she removed, in the hope of alleviating it by change of air, to Poona, and arrived at the house of her friend, Colonel Campbell, in that city, on the 16th of September. She expired unexpectedly on the following morning. Her remains are deposited near those of one of her own sex, who was also distinguished for her literary talents, Miss Jewsbury.

The death of Miss Roberts excited universal sorrow amongst all classes, European and native, at Bombay, as well as at the other presidencies, especially Calcutta, where the most cordial and flattering tributes to her memory appeared in the public journals. She had nearly completed her inquiries, and accomplished all the objects for which she had revisited the treacherous clime of India, and one of her latest letters to the writer of this Memoir expressed a cheerful anticipation of her speedy return to England! "I positively leave India next October, and am now looking joyfully to my return."

The person and manners of Miss Roberts were extremely prepossessing. In early life, she was handsome; and although latterly her figure had attained some degree of fulness, it had lost none of its ease and grace, whilst her pleasing features, marked by no lines of painful thought, were open and expressive, beaming with animation and good humour. She had not the slightest tinge of pedantry in her manner and deportment, which were natural and affable, so that a stranger never felt otherwise than at ease in her society. It was not her ambition to make a display of mental superiority, which inspires the other sex with any feelings but those of admiration--which is, indeed, tacitly resented as a species of tyranny, and frequently assigned as the ground of a certain prejudice against literary ladies. "It may safely he said," observes a friend of her's at Calcutta, "that, although devoted to literature as Miss Roberts was, yet in her conversation and demeanour she evinced less of what is known as 'blue' than any of her contemporaries, excepting Miss Landon." Another Calcutta acquaintance says: "Though her mind was deeply interested in subjects connected with literature, her attention was by no means absorbed by them, and she mixed cordially and freely in society without the least disposition to despise persons of less intellectual elevation. She had a true relish of all the little pleasures that promiscuous society affords, and did not underrate those talents which are better fitted for the drawing-room than the study." Her warmth of heart and kindness of disposition, which co-operated with her good sense in thus removing all disagreeable points from her external character, made her the sincerest of friends, and ever ready to engage in any work of charity or benevolence.

It would be affectation to attempt in this slight Memoir to elaborate a picture of the intellectual character of Miss Roberts, cut off, as she has been, before that character had been fully developed. The works, upon which her reputation as a writer principally rests, are not, perhaps, of a quality which calls for any commanding powers of mind. Her business was with the surfaces of things; her skill consisted in a species of photography, presenting perfect fac-similes of objects, animate and inanimate, in their natural forms and hues. Deep investigations, profound reflections, and laboured and learned disquisitions, would have defeated the very object of her lively sketches, which was to make them, not only faithful and exact, but popular. Of her success in this design, the following testimony from a competent authority, the **Calcutta Literary Gazette**, is distinct and decisive; and with this extract we may fitly close our melancholy office: "Nothing can be more minute and faithful than her pictures of external life and manners. She does not, indeed, go much beneath the surface, nor does she take profound or general views of human nature; but we can mention no traveller, who has thrown upon the printed page such true and vivid representations of all that strikes the eye of a stranger. Her book, entitled **Scenes and Characteristics of Hindostan**, is the best of its kind. Other travellers have excelled her in depth and sagacity of remark, in extent of information, and in mere force or elegance of style; but there is a vivacity, a delicacy, and a truth in her light sketches of all that lay immediately before her, that have never been surpassed in any book of travels that is at this moment present to our memory. She had a peculiar readiness in receiving, and a singular power of retaining, first impressions of the most minute and evanescent nature. She walked through a street or a bazaar, and every thing that passed over the mirror of her mind left a clear and lasting trace. She was thus enabled, even years after a visit to a place of interest, to describe every thing with the same freshness and fidelity as if she had taken notes upon the spot. They who have gone over the same ground are delighted to find in the perusal of her pages their own vague and half-faded impressions revived and defined by her magic glass, while the novelty and vividness of her foreign pictures make her home-readers feel that they are nearly as much entitled to be called travellers as the fair author herself."

CHAPTER I.
LONDON TO PARIS.

Departure from London--A French Steam-vessel--Unfavourable Weather--Arrival at Havre--Difficulties at the Custom-house--Description of Havre--Embarkation on the Steamer for Rouen--Appearance of the Country--Inclemency of the Weather--Arrival at Rouen--Description of Rouen--Departure by the Boat for Paris--Scenes and Traditions on the Banks of the Seine--Journey by the Railroad to Paris--The **Douaniers**--Observations on the Journey up the Seine.

A strong predilection in favour of river scenery induced me, at the commencement of an overland journey to Bombay, through France and Egypt, to take a passage from London in a steamer bound to Havre. Accordingly, on the 1st of September, 1839, accompanied by some friends, one of whom was to perform the whole journey with me, I embarked on board the *Phenix*, a French vessel, which left the Tower Stairs at about ten o'clock in the morning.

The weather was showery, but occasional gleams of sunshine encouraged us to hope that it might clear up, and permit us to keep the deck during the greater part of the voyage, which we expected to perform in eighteen hours. To the majority of readers, in these days of universal travelling, it will be superfluous to describe a steam-boat; but there may possibly be some quiet people who are still ignorant of the sort of accommodation which it affords, and to whom the description will not be unacceptable.

The *Phenix* is a fine vessel of its class, five hundred tons burthen, and 160-

horse power. It was handsomely fitted up, and the vases of flowers upon the chimney-piece in the principal saloon, and other ornaments scattered about, gave to the whole a gay appearance, as if the party assembled had been wholly bent upon pleasure. The ladies' cabin was divided by a staircase; but there were what, in a sort of mockery, are called "state-cabins" opening into that appropriated to the general use, around which were sofas, and bed-places upon a sort of shelf above, for the accommodation of the gentlemen. This apartment was handsomely carpeted, and otherwise well furnished; the steward and his assistant having the appearance of the better class of waiters belonging to a well-frequented hotel: all the servants were English, and the whole afforded a most delightful contrast to the sort of packets which many of the party on board were quite old enough to remember.

The passengers were numerous, and apparently inclined to make themselves agreeable to each other; one, an American, objected to the sight of a footman, who came upon the quarter-deck for a few minutes, observing that such a thing would not be permitted in his country.

As soon as the vessel got under weigh, preparations were made for breakfast, which was served, *a la fourchette*, in very excellent style, the cookery being a happy combination of the French and English modes. At the conclusion of the repast, we repaired to the deck, all being anxious to see the **British Queen**, which was getting her steam up, at Gravesend. We were alongside this superb vessel for a few minutes, putting some persons on board who had come down the river in the **Phenix** for the purpose of paying it a visit; and taking advantage of a favourable breeze, we hoisted a sail, and went along at a rate which gave us hope of a speedy arrival at Havre.

After passing the Nore, however, our progress was impeded; and at length, when off Margate, we were obliged to lie-to, in order to wait for the turn of the tide: the wind blowing so strongly as to render it questionable whether we could get round the Foreland. The sun was shining on the buildings at Margate, and the bells knolling for evening service; affording a home-scene of comfort and tranquillity which it was agreeable to carry abroad as one of the last reminiscences of England.

In about three hours, we got the steam up again, and saw the **British Queen** in the distance, still lying to, and apparently, notwithstanding her prodigious power, unable to get down the Channel.

Dinner was served while the ***Phenix*** lay off Margate; but it was thinly attended, the motion of the vessel having sent many persons to their cabins, while others were totally deprived of all appetite. An elderly gentleman, who sate upon my left hand, complained exceedingly of his inability to partake of the good things before him; and one or two left the table in despair. Again we sought the deck, and saw the sun sink behind an ominous mass of clouds; the sky, however, cleared, and the stars came out, reviving our spirits with hopes of a fine night. Unfortunately, soon after nine o'clock, a heavy squall obliged us to go below, and one of my female friends and myself took possession of a state cabin, and prepared to seek repose.

It was my first voyage on board a steamer, and though the tremulous motion and the stamping of the engine are anything but agreeable, I prefer it to the violent rolling and pitching of a sailing vessel. We were certainly not nearly so much knocked about; the vases of flowers were taken off the mantel-piece, and placed upon the floor, but beyond this there were no precautions taken to prevent the movables from getting adrift; every thing remained quiet upon the tables, a circumstance which could not have happened in so heavy a sea in any vessel not steadied by the apparatus carried by a steamer.

The ***Phenix*** laboured heavily through the water; a torrent of rain soon cleared the deck of all the passengers, and the melancholy voices calling for the steward showed the miserable plight to which the male portion of the party was reduced. Daylight appeared without giving hope of better weather; and it was not until the vessel had reached the pier at Havre, which it did not make until after three o'clock P.M. on Monday, that the passengers were able to re-assemble. Many had not tasted food since their embarkation, and none had been able to take breakfast on the morning of their arrival.

And here, for the benefit of future travellers, it may not be amiss to say, that a small medicine-chest, which had been packed in a carpet-bag, was detained at the custom-house; and that the following day we experienced some difficulty in getting it passed, being told that it was contraband; indeed, but for an idea that the whole party were going on to Bombay, and would require the drugs for their own consumption, we should not have succeeded in rescuing it from the hands of the Philistines. The day was too far advanced to admit of our getting the remainder of the baggage examined, a mischance which detained us a day at Havre, the steamer to Rouen starting at four o'clock in the morning.

The weather was too unpropitious to admit of our seeing much of the environs of the town. Like all English travellers, we walked about as much as we could, peeped into the churches, made purchases of things we wanted and things we did not want, and got some of our gold converted into French money. We met and greeted several of our fellow-passengers, for though little conversation, in consequence of the inclemency of the weather, had taken place on board the ***Phenix***, we all seemed to congratulate each other upon our escape from the horrors of the voyage.

The gale increased rather than abated, and we now began to entertain fears of another day's detention at Havre, the steamer from Rouen not having arrived; and though we were very comfortably lodged, and found the town superior to the expectations we had formed of a sea-port of no very great consideration, we had no desire to spend more time in it than we could help.

Havre appears to carry on a considerable commerce with India, several shops being wholly devoted to the sale of the productions of the East, while the number of parrots and monkeys to be seen show that the intercourse must be very extensive. The shops had a very English air about them, and though the houses were taller, and rather more dilapidated in their appearance, than they are usually found at home, they reminded us of familiar scenes. ***Hamlet*** was announced for the evening's performance at the theatre, and but for the novelty of dining at a ***table d'hote***, we might have fancied ourselves still in England.

The Hotel de l'Europe is the best in Havre; there are several others very respectable, and more picturesque, from the ancient style of the building: all were full, intercourse with Havre being on the increase. English carriages were arriving every hour; the steamer from Southampton brought an immense number of passengers, and travellers seemed to flock in from every part of the world. We were amused by seeing a well-dressed and well-mannered Russian lady, at the ***table d'hote***, fill her plate half-full of oil, and just dip the salad into it.

It was the first time that one of my friends and myself had ever visited France, and we endeavoured as much as possible to accommodate ourselves to the manners of a strange country. We could not, however, entirely give up our English habits, and ordered tea in the evening in our private apartments: the French are by this time well accustomed to requisitions of this nature, and few places are now unsupplied with a tea-pot.

On Tuesday morning, we were up at four o'clock, in order to embark on board the steamer for Rouen. It rained heavily, and any hopes, the interposition of the high houses gave, that the wind had abated, were destroyed upon turning the first angle, and after a hasty glance at the threatening sky and surging waters, we went below, intending, if possible, to remain there until the weather should clear.

Passengers now came flocking in; many respectable French families, with their children and neatly dressed **bonnes**, were of the party; but the young folk speedily becoming very sick, we sought the deck, and in spite of the rain, which still continued to fall, established ourselves as well as we were able.

Upon entering the river, the turbulence of the water subsided a little, and a gleam of sunshine, the first that smiled upon us, shewed a chateau and town nestling in the midst of gardens and orchards, and spreading down to the water's edge. The banks on either side were picturesque, presenting the most pleasing pictures of rural enjoyment, and conveying an idea of comfort which we had not previously associated with the smaller classes of country residences in France. The houses were cleanly on the outside, at least, and neither paint nor white-wash was spared in their decoration; the surrounding parterres were gay with flowers, amid which, as with us, dahlias made a very conspicuous appearance. They were not, we thought, quite so large and luxuriant as those which we see in our cottage-gardens at home; and this remark we found afterwards would apply to the more carefully tended plants in the pleasure-grounds of palaces. We are probably more skilful in the adaptation of soil to foreign importations, and therefore succeed in producing a finer flower.

In my baggage I had brought a large basket-full of the roots of our English hearts-ease, as a present to a French gentleman, who had expressed a wish, in the early part of the summer, to take some with him from London, he having been much delighted with the superior beauty of those which he had seen in our English gardens; they were not then in a fit state for transplanting, and having, through the kindness of the secretary of the Royal Botanic Society, been enabled to carry away an extensive and choice collection of roots, I indulge a hope that I may be instrumental in spreading the finest varieties of this pretty flower throughout France.

We lost, of course, many scenes of beauty and interest, in consequence of the inclemency of the weather. Just as we arrived at a most beautiful place, a church of elegant architecture rising in the centre, with gay-looking villas clustered round, the gathering clouds united over our devoted heads, the rain, descending in a cataract, beat down the smoke to the very decks, so that we all looked and felt as if we had been up the chimney, and the whole lovely scene was lost to us in a moment. The rain continued for about an hour after this, and then the sky began to clear.

We reached Rouen at about half-past twelve. The approach is very fine, and the city makes an imposing appearance from the river. We had been recommended to the Hotel d'Angleterre, which is the best, but were so strongly tempted to rush into the hotel immediately opposite, that, trusting to its exterior, we hastened to house ourselves, and found no reason to repent our choice. We were shown into very handsome apartments, and found the staircases, lobbies, and ante-chambers as clean as we could desire. A change of attire and breakfast enabled us to sally forth to see as much of the town and its neighbourhood as our time would admit.

The modern portion of Rouen is extremely handsome; the quay being lined with a series of lofty stone mansions, built in the style which is now beginning to be adopted in London. The public buildings are particularly fine, and there are two splendid bridges, one of stone, and one upon the suspension principle. Very extensive improvements are going on, and it seems as if, in the course of a very few years, the worst portions of the town will be replaced by new and elegant erections. Meantime, imagination can scarcely afford more than a faint idea of the horrors of the narrow, dirty streets, flanked on either side by lofty squalid houses, in the very last stage of dilapidation.

The cathedral stands in a small square, or market-place, where the houses, though somewhat better than their neighbours in the lanes, have a very miserable appearance; they make a striking picture, but the reality sadly detracts from the pleasure which the eye would otherwise take in surveying the fine old church, with which, through the medium of engravings, it has been long familiar. Many workmen are at present employed in repairing the damage which time has inflicted upon this ancient edifice.

The interior, though striking from its vastness, is at first rather disappointing, its splendid windows of stained glass being the most prominent of its ornaments. In pacing the long aisles, and pausing before the small chapels, the scene grows upon the mind, and the monuments, though comparatively few, are very interesting. An effigy of Richard Coeur de Lion, lately discovered while looking for the fiery monarch's heart, which was buried in Rouen, is shown as one of the chief curiosities of the place.

The porter of the cathedral inhabited an extremely small dwelling, built up against the wall, and surrounded by high, dark buildings; but we were pleased to see that he had cheered this dismal place of abode by a gay parterre, several rich-looking flowers occupying pots beneath his windows.

Our next pilgrimage was to the statue of Joan of Arc, which we approached through narrow streets, so dirty from the late heavy rains, as to be scarcely passable. We had, as we might have expected, little to reward us, except the associations connected with the Maid of Orleans, and her cruel persecutors. The spot had been to me, from my earliest years, one which I had felt a wish to visit, my researches, while writing the Memoirs of the Rival Houses of York and Lancaster, materially increasing the interest which an earlier perusal of the history of England and France had created, concerning scenes trodden by the brave, the great, and the good. However mistaken might have been their notions, however impolitic their actions, we cannot contemplate the characters of the Paladins, who have made Rouen famous, without feelings of respect. The murder of Joan of Arc formed the sole blot on the escutcheon of John Duke of Bedford, and the faults and vices of his companions in arms were the offspring of the times in which they lived.

We were surprised by the excellence of the shops, even in the most dilapidated parts of the city of Rouen, the windows in every direction exhibiting a gay assemblage of goods of all descriptions, while the confectioners were little, if at all, inferior to those of Paris. One small square in particular, in which a market was held, was very striking, from the contrast between the valuable products sold, and the houses which contained them. Seven or eight stories in height, weather-stained, and dilapidated, the lower floors exhibited handsome porcelain and other costly articles, which gave an impression of wealth in the owners, that astonished those amongst our party who were strangers to the country. Our hearts absolutely sunk within us as we thought of the wretchedness of the interiors, the misery of being obliged to inhabit any one of the numerous suites of apartments rising tier above tier, and from which it would be absolutely impossible to banish vermin of every description.

The French appear certainly to be beginning to study home comforts, all the modern houses being built upon very commodious plans; still the middling classes, in the towns at least, are miserably lodged, in comparison with the same grades in England, families of apparently great respectability inhabiting places so desolate as to strike one with horror.

After picking our way through the least objectionable of the streets in the heart of the city, we were glad to escape into the open air, and solace ourselves with the views presented on the neighbouring heights. Nothing can be finer than the landscapes round Rouen; every necessary of life appears to be cheap and plentiful, and persons desirous of a quiet and economical residence abroad might spend their time very happily in the outskirts of this picturesque city.

We found the guests at the ***table-d'hote*** chiefly English, travellers like ourselves, and some of our party recognised London acquaintance among those who, upon hearing our intention to proceed the following day up the Seine to Paris, recommended the boat by which they had arrived--the ***Etoile***.

Again we were summoned at four o'clock in the morning, and wended our way, along the banks of the river, to the starting-place, which was just beyond the second bridge. The one large boat, which conveyed passengers from Havre, was here exchanged for two smaller, better suited to the state of the river. We were taught to expect rather a large party, as we had understood that forty persons were going from our hotel.

The bell of the ***Dorade***, the opposition vessel, was sounding its tocsin to summon passengers on board, while ours was altogether mute. Presently, through the grey mist of the morning, we observed parties flocking down to the place of embarkation, who, somewhat to our surprise, all entered the other vessel. A large boat in the centre, in which the baggage is deposited, was speedily filled, carpet bags being piled upon carpet bags, until a goodly pyramid arose, which the rising sun touched with every colour of the prism. The decks of the ***Dorade*** were now crowded with passengers, while two respectable-looking young women, in addition to ourselves, formed the whole of our company.

Our bell now gave out a few faint sounds, as if rather in compliance with the usual forms observed, than from any hope that its warning voice would be heeded;

and getting up our steam, we took the lead gallantly, as if determined to leave the heavier boat behind. Presently, however, the **Dorade** passed us with all her gay company, and speeding swiftly on her way, would have been out of sight in a few minutes, but for the windings of the river, which showed us her smoke like a pennon in the distance. We were now left alone in our glory, and felt assured of what we had more than suspected before, namely, that we had got into the wrong boat. We then, though rather too late, inquired the cause of the extraordinary disproportion of the passengers, and were told that the **Etoile** was the favourite boat going down the river, while the **Dorade** had it hollow in going up.

We now began to consider the circumstances of the case, and the chances of our not arriving time enough at the place of debarkation to get on to Paris by the rail-road that night. Agreeing that the detention would not be of the least consequence, that we should enjoy having the whole boat to ourselves, and the slow method of travelling, which would enable us the better to contemplate the beauties of the river, we made up our minds to a day of great enjoyment. The weather was fine, a cool breeze allaying the heat of the sun, which shone upon us occasionally through clouds too high to afford any apprehension of rain.

The boat was very elegantly fitted up below, the ladies' cabin, in particular, being splendidly furnished. Above, the choice of seats proved very acceptable, since, in consequence of a new-fangled apparatus, we had four chimneys, whence sparks escaped in a constant shower, threatening destruction to any garment that might be exposed to them. Seated, therefore, at the prow, beyond the reach of this fiery shower, after partaking of an excellent breakfast, there being a first-rate **restaurateur** on board, we began to converse with a very intelligent boatman, who amused us with the legends of the river and accounts of the different places which we passed.

At Blossville-Bon-Secours there is an extremely steep hill, with a chapel, dedicated to the Virgin, at the summit; the holy edifice is, upon ordinary occasions, approached by a circuitous winding road, but at Easter and other great festivals, thousands of persons flock from all parts, for the purpose of making a pilgrimage up the steepest portion of the ascent, in order to fulfil vows previously made, and to pay their homage to the holy mother of God. There was a waggery in our friend's eye, as he described the sufferings of the devout upon these occasions, which indicated an opinion that, however meritorious the act, and however efficacious in shortening the path to heaven, he himself entertained no desire to try it. This man had seen something of the world, his maritime occupation having formerly led him to distant places; he had been a sailor all his life, was well acquainted with Marseilles, which he described with great enthusiasm, and gave us to understand that, having had a good offer elsewhere, this would be one of his last voyages in the *Etoile*, since he worked hard in it, without getting any credit.

At the town of Elboeuf, we picked up another passenger; a country woman, with a basket or two, and a high Normandy cap, had come on board at one of the villages; and with this small reinforcement we proceeded, halting occasionally to mend some damage in the engine, and putting up a sail whenever we could take advantage of the breeze.

Arriving at La Roquelle, our *cicerone* pointed out to us the ruined walls of what once had been a very splendid chateau; its former owner being an inveterate gamester, having lost large sums of money, at length staked the chateau to an Englishman, who won it. Upon arriving to take possession, he was disappointed to find that he had only gained the chateau, and that the large estate attached to it was not in the bond. Being unable to keep it up without the surrounding property, he determined that no other person should enjoy it, and therefore, greatly to the annoyance of the people in the neighbourhood, he pulled it down. The present proprietor now lives in an adjacent farm-house, and the story, whether true or false, tells greatly to the prejudice of the English, and our friend, in particular, spoke of it as a most barbarous act.

We found the chateaux on the banks of the Seine very numerous; many were of great magnitude, and flanked by magnificent woods, the greater number being clipped into the appearance of walls, and cut out into long avenues and arcades, intersecting each other at right angles, in the very worst taste, according to the English idea of landscape-gardening. There was something, however, extremely grand and imposing in this formal style, and we were at least pleased with the novelty which it afforded.

At Andelys, perched upon a conical hill, are the picturesque remains of the chateau Gaillard, which was built by Richard Coeur de Lion, and must formerly have been of very great extent, its walls reaching down to the river's brink. We were told that the chateau furnished stabling for a thousand horses, and that there was a subterranean passage which led to the great Andelys. This passage is now undergoing a partial clearing, for the purpose of increasing the interest of the place, by exhibiting it to strangers who may visit the neighbourhood. Our informant proceeded to say, that during several years, an old witch inhabited the ruins, who was at once the oracle and the terror of the neighbourhood.

The sketch-books of the party were here placed in requisition, and though the celerity with which a steamer strides through the water is not very favourable to the artist, a better idea of the scene was given than that which we found in the Guide Book. The banks of the Seine present a succession of pictures, all well worthy of the pencil, and those who are fond of the picturesque, and who have time at their disposal, will find the voyage up the river replete with the most interesting materials.

The first sight of the vineyards, which began to spread themselves up the steep sides of the hills, delighted us all; and our prospects now began to be diversified with rock, which in a thousand fantastic forms showed itself along the heights. The country seemed thickly spread with villages, many at the edge of the water, others receding into winding valleys, and all boasting some peculiar beauty. Whether upon a nearer approach they would have been equally pleasing, it is not possible to say; but, from our position, we saw nothing to offend the eye, either in the cottages or the people; some of the very humblest of the dwellings boasted their little gardens, now gay with sun-flowers and dahlias, while the better sort, with their bright panes of glass, and clean muslin window-curtains, looked as if they would afford very desirable homes.

A present of a bottle of wine made our boatmen very happy. They produced one of those huge masses of bread, which seems the principal food of the lower classes, and sate down to their meal with great content. Our dinner, which we had ordered rather early, was delayed by the arrival of the boat at Vernon, where we were obliged, according to the French phrase, to "mount the bridge." It was built, agreeably to the old mode of construction, with a mill in the centre, and the difficulty, and even danger, of getting through the arch, could not be called inconsiderable. Letting off the steam, we were hauled up by persons stationed for the purpose; and just as we got through, passed the steamers going down to Rouen, the partners of the vessels which went up in the morning; both were full, our *star* being the only unlucky one. However, what might have been a hardship to many others was none to us, it being scarcely possible to imagine any thing more delightful than a voyage which, though comparatively slow, was the reverse of tedious, and in which we could discourse unrestrainedly, and occupy any part of the vessel most agreeable to ourselves. We picked up a very respectable man and his daughter, an interesting little girl, who spoke English very tolerably, and seemed delighted to meet with English ladies; and also an exquisite, dressed in the first style of the Parisian mode, but of him we saw little, he being wholly occupied with himself.

The steam-company are entering into an arrangement at Vernon for the construction of a lock similar to one already formed at Pont-de-l'Arche, which we had passed through in the morning, and which will obviate the inconvenience and difficulty of the present mode of navigating the river.

The next place of interest to which we came was Rosny, a village famous in the pages of history as the residence of the great and good, the friend and minister of Henry IV., the virtuous Sully. Our boatmen, who were not great antiquaries, said nothing about the early occupants of the chateau, exerting all their eloquence in praise of a later resident--the Duchesse de Berri. This lady rendered herself extremely popular in the vicinity, living in a style of princely splendour, and devoting her time to acts of munificence. Every year she portioned off a bride, giving a dowry to some respectable young lady of the neighbourhood, while to the poor she was a liberal and untiring benefactress. The boatmen blessed her as they passed, for to all she sent wine, and upon fete-days gave banquets to the rural population, to whom her remembrance will be ever dear. Our informants pointed out a small chapel, which they described as being very beautiful, which she had built as a depository for her husband's heart; this precious relic she carried away with her when she left Rosny, which she quitted with the regrets of every human being in the neighbourhood.

The chateau has been purchased by an English banker, but is now uninhabited: there was a report of its being about to be pulled down. It is a large, heavy building, not distinguished by any architectural beauty, yet having an imposing air, from its extent and solidity. It is surrounded by fine woods and pleasure-grounds, laid out in the formal style, which is still the characteristic of French landscape-gardening.

Nothing can be more beautiful than the surrounding scenery, the winding river with its vineyards hanging in terraces from the opposite heights, the village reposing beneath sun-lit hills, while corn-fields, pasture-land, and cattle grazing, convey the most pleasing ideas of the comfort of those who dwell upon this luxuriant soil.

The city of Mantes now appeared in the distance, and as we approached it, our guides pointed out, on the opposite heights of Gassicourt, a hermitage and Calvary, which had formerly proved a great source of profit. An ascetic, of great pretensions to sanctity, took up his abode many years ago in this retreat, carrying on a thriving trade, every boat that passed contributing twopence, for which consideration the hermit rung a bell, to announce their arrival at the bridge of Mantes, giving notice to the town, in order to facilitate the transfer of baggage or passengers. This tax or tribute the hermit was not himself at the trouble of collecting, it being scrupulously despatched to him by the donors, who would have deemed it sinful to deprive the holy man of what they considered his just due.

The sort of piety, which once supported so great a multitude of religious mendicants, is greatly on the decline in France. A few crosses on the bridges and heights, and the dresses of the priesthood whom we encountered in the streets, were the only exterior signs of Roman Catholicism which we had yet seen. Our boatmen spoke with great respect of the Sisters of Charity, pointing out a convent which they inhabited, and told us that during illness they had themselves been greatly indebted to the care and attention of these benevolent women.

It was now growing dark, and we very narrowly escaped a serious accident in passing the bridge of Meulan, the boat coming into contact with one of the piers; fortunately, the danger was espied in time. There was now not the slightest chance of reaching Paris before the following morning; but we regretted nothing except the want of light, the gathering clouds rendering it impossible to see any thing of the scenery, which, we were told, increased in beauty at every mile. We consoled ourselves, however, with tea and whist in the cabin; in fact, we played with great perseverance throughout the whole of our journey, the spirits of the party never flagging for a single instant.

We found a good hotel at the landing-place, at which we arrived at a very late hour, and starting the next morning by the early train to Paris, passed by the rail-road through an extremely interesting country, leaving St. Germain-en-Laye behind, and tracking the windings of the Seine, now too shallow to admit of the navigation of boats of any burthen.

The construction of this rail-road was attended with considerable difficulty and great expense, on account of its being impeded by the works at Marli, for the supply of water to Versailles. The building of the bridges over the Seine, which it crosses three times, was also very costly. The carriages of the first class are very inferior to those of the same description upon the rail-roads in England, but they are sufficiently comfortable for so short a distance. We were set down at the barrier of Clichi, an inconvenient distance from the best part of Paris. Here we had to undergo a second inspection of our baggage, and I became somewhat alarmed for the fate of my medicine-chest. We had taken nothing else with as that could be seizable, and this was speedily perceived by the officials, who merely went through the form of an examination.

The divisions in one of my portmanteaus had excited some suspicion at Havre, one of the men fancying that he had made a grand discovery, when he pronounced it to have a false bottom. We explained the method of opening it to his satisfaction, and afterwards, in overhauling my bonnet-box, he expressed great regret at the derangement of the millinery, which certainly sustained some damage from his rough handling. Altogether, we had not to complain of any want of civility on the part of the custom-house officers; but travellers who take the overland route to India, through France, will do well to despatch all their heavy baggage by sea, nothing being more inconvenient than a multitude of boxes. I had reduced all my packages to four, namely, two portmanteaus, a bonnet-box, and a leather bag, which latter contained the medicine-chest, a kettle and lamp, lucifer-matches, &c; my bonnet-box was divided into two compartments, one of which contained my writing-case and a looking-glass; for as I merely intended to travel through a portion of our British possessions in India, and to return after the October monsoon of 1840, I wished to carry every thing absolutely necessary for my comfort about with we.

Another annoyance sustained by persons who take the route through France is, the trouble respecting their passports, which must be ready at all times when called upon for examination, and may be the cause of detention, if the proper forms are not scrupulously gone through. We were not certain whether it would be necessary to present ourselves in person at the Bureau des Passeports, Quai des Orfevres, in Paris, after having sent them to the British embassy; but we thought it better to avoid all danger of delay, and therefore drove to a quarter interesting on account of its being a place of some importance as the original portion of Paris, and situated on the island. In this neighbourhood there are also the famous Hotel Dieu and Notre Dame, to both of which places we paid a visit, looking **en passant** at the Morgue. The gentleman who accompanied us entered a building, with whose melancholy celebrity all are acquainted; but though it did not at that precise moment contain a corpse, the report did not induce us to follow his example: a circumstance which we afterwards regretted. It may be necessary to say, that at other places we sent our passports to the Hotel de Ville; but at Paris there is a different arrangement.

Although the journey up the Seine from Havre proved very delightful to me, I do not recommend it to others, especially those to whom time is of importance. There is always danger of detention, and the length of the sea-voyage, especially from London, may be productive of serious inconvenience. For seeing the country, it is certainly preferable to the diligence, and my experience will teach those who come after me to inquire into the character of the steam-boat before they enter it.

CHAPTER II.
PARIS TO MARSEILLES.

Description of Paris--Departure by the Diligence--The Country--The Vineyards--Hotels and fare--Arrival at Lyons--Description of the City--Departure in the Steam-boat for Arles--Descent of the Rhone--Beauty and Variety of the Scenery--Confusion on disembarking at Beaucaire--A Passenger Drowned--Arrival at Arles--Description of the Town--Embarkation in the Steamer for Marseilles--Entrance into the Mediterranean--Picturesque approach to Marseilles--Arrival in the Harbour--Description of Marseilles--Observations upon the Journey through France by Ladies.

A week's residence in Paris does not give a stranger any title to decide upon the merits or demerits of that far-famed city. The period of the year (September) was not the most favourable for a visit, all the best families having emigrated to their country habitations, and the city consequently exhibited a deserted air, at variance with every preconceived notion of the gaiety of the French capital. The mixture of meanness and magnificence in the buildings, the dirt and bad smells, combine to give an unfavourable impression, which time only, and a better acquaintance with the more agreeable features of the place, can remove.

We had entertained a hope, upon our arrival in Paris, of getting the ***malle poste*** for our journey to Chalons; but it was engaged for at least a month in advance. We were not more fortunate, our party now being reduced to three, in our endeavour to secure the ***coupe***, and were obliged to be contented with places (corners) in the interior. We despatched all our heavy goods--that is, the portmanteaus--by ***mes-***

sagerie, to Marseilles, which was a great saving of trouble. Though the expense of this conveyance is enormous, it has the great advantage of speed, travelling nearly as quickly as the diligence, while by the ***roulage***, which is cheaper, very inconvenient delays may be incurred.

We quitted Paris on the 13th of September, well pleased with the treatment we had received. Though the charges for lodging, washing, &c. were high, there was no attempt at imposition; our landlady would not allow us to pay any thing for the eighth day of our abode, although we thereby entered into another week. We had the pleasure of leaving every body well satisfied with us, and willing to receive another English party.

The diligence started at the appointed hour, namely, six o'clock in the evening. Unaccustomed to travel all night, we were rather anxious about breakfast, as we had merely stopped to change horses, without resting for any refreshment since we quitted Paris. Upon our arrival at Sens, at about seven o'clock in the morning, we were amused by the appearance of a party of persons running, gesticulating, and talking with all their might, who brought hot coffee, milk, bread, and fruit to the carriage-door. At first we were disinclined to avail ourselves of the breakfast thus offered, but learning that we should not get any thing else before twelve o'clock in the day, we overcame our scruples, and partook of the despised fare, which we found very good of its kind.

The country we passed through was rich with vineyards, and, on account of the undulating nature of the land, and the frequency of towns and villages, exceedingly pleasing to the eye. We were continually delighted with some splendid burst of scenery. There was no want of foliage, the absence of the magnificent timber which we find in England being the less remarkable, in consequence of the number of trees which, if not of very luxuriant growth, greatly embellish the landscape, while we saw the vine everywhere, the rich clusters of its grapes reaching to the edge of the road. Though robbed of its grace, and its lavish display of leaf and tendril, by the method of cultivating, each plant being reduced to the size of a small currant-bush, the foliage, clothing every hill with green, gave the country an aspect most grateful to those who are accustomed to English verdure.

We made our first halt at Auxerre, when a ***dejeuner a la fourchette*** was served up to the travellers in the diligence. A bad English dinner is a very bad thing, but a bad French one is infinitely worse. Hitherto, we had fed upon nothing but the most dainty fare of the best hotels and *cafes*, and I, at least, who wished to see as much as I could of France, was not displeased at the necessity of satisfying the cravings of appetite with bread and melon. There were numerous dishes, all very untempting, swimming in grease, and brought in a slovenly manner to the table; a roast fowl formed no exception, for it was sodden, half-raw, and saturated with oil. It was only at the very best hotels in France that we ever found fowls tolerably well roasted; generally speaking, they are never more than half-cooked, and are as unsightly as they are unsavoury. Our fellow-passengers did ample justice to the meal, from which we gladly escaped, in order to devote the brief remainder of our time to a hasty toilet.

From what we could see of it, Auxerre appeared to be a very pretty place, it being at this time perfectly enwreathed with vines. In fact, every step of our journey increased our regret that we should be obliged to hurry through a country which it would have delighted us to view at leisure, each town that we passed through offering some inducement to linger on the road. Active preparations were making for the vintage, the carts which we met or overtook being laden with wine-casks, and much did we desire to witness a process associated in our minds with the gayest scenes of rural festivity.

It would not be a fair criterion to judge of the accommodation afforded at the hotels of the French provinces by those at which the diligence changed horses; in some I observed that we were not shown into the best apartments reserved for public entertainment, but in none did we find any difficulty in procuring water to wash with, nor did we ever see a dish substituted for a basin. From our own observation, it seems evident that the inns in the provinces have been much improved since the peace with England, and it appeared to us, that no reasonable objection could be made to the accommodation supplied. Auxerre certainly furnished the worst specimen we met with on the road; at no other place had we any right to complain of our entertainment, and at some the fare might be called sumptuous.

On the third morning from our departure from Paris, when nearly exhausted, the rising sun gave us a view of the environs of Lyons. We had been afraid to stop at Chalons the day before, having been informed that the Saone was not sufficiently full to ensure the certainty of the steam-boat's arrival at the promised time at Lyons.

This was a great disappointment, but we were rewarded by the rich and beautiful scenery which characterises the route by land. We could not help fancying that we could distinguish the home of Claude Melnotte amid those villages that dotted the splendid panorama; and the pleasure, with which I, at least, contemplated the fine old city, was not a little enhanced by its association with the Lady of Lyons and her peasant lover.

Lyons more than realised all the notions which I had formed concerning it, having an air of antique grandeur which I had vainly expected to find at Rouen. It is well-built throughout, without that striking contrast between the newer buildings and the more ancient edifices, which is so remarkable in the capital of Normandy. The Hotel de Ville, in the large square, is a particularly fine building, and the whole city looks as if it had been for centuries the seat of wealth and commerce.

Friends in England, and the few we met with or made in Paris, had furnished us with the names of the hotels it would be most advisable to put up at; but these lists were, as a matter of course, lost, and we usually made for the nearest to the place where we stopped. The Hotel de Paris, which looks upon the Hotel de Ville, was the one we selected at Lyons; it was large and commodious, but had a dull and melancholy air. As it is usual in French hotels, the building enclosed a court-yard in the centre, with galleries running round the three sides, and reaching to the upper stories. The furniture, handsome of its kind, was somewhat faded, adding to the gloom which is so often the characteristic of a provincial inn.

As soon as possible, we sallied forth, according to our usual wont, to see as much as we could of the town and its environs; both invited a longer stay, but we were anxious to be at Marseilles by the 19th, and therefore agreed to rise at half-past three on the following morning, in order to be ready for the steamer, which started an hour after. We had begun, indeed, to fancy sleep a superfluous indulgence; my female friend (Miss E.), as well as myself, suffering no other inconvenience from three nights spent in a diligence than that occasioned by swelled feet and ancles.

We found a very considerable number of persons in the steam-boat, many of whom were English, and amongst them a gentleman and his wife, who, with four children, were travelling to Nice, where they proposed to spend the winter. The fine weather of the preceding day had deserted us, and it rained in torrents during the first hours of the descent of the Rhone. The wet and cold became so difficult to bear, that I was glad to take up a position under the funnel of the steamer, where, protected a little from the rain, I speedily got dry and warm, enjoying the scenery in despite of the very unfavourable state of the weather. We missed our communicative boatman of the Seine, but met with a very intelligent German, who gave us an account of the remarkable places *en route*, pointing out a spot once exceedingly dangerous to boats ascending or descending, in consequence of a projecting rock, which, by the orders of the Emperor Napoleon, had been blown up.

All the steamers which leave Lyons profess to go as far as Arles; but, in order to ensure conveyance to that place the same evening, it is necessary to ascertain whether they carry freight to Beaucaire, for in that case they always stay the night to unlade, taking the boat on at an early hour the following morning. We found ourselves in this predicament; and perhaps, under all the circumstances to be related, it would be advisable to leave the Lyons boat at Avignon and proceed by land to Marseilles. Many of the passengers pursued this plan.

The weather cleared up in the middle of the day, and we passed Avignon in a rich crimson sunset, which threw its roseate flush upon the ruins of the Papal palace, and the walls and bastions of this far-famed city. Experience had shown us the impossibility of taking more than a cursory view of any place in which we could only sojourn for a single day, and therefore we satisfied ourselves with the glimpses which we caught of Avignon from the river. A half-finished bridge, apparently of ancient date, projects rudely into the middle of the stream; we passed through another more modern, though somewhat difficult to shoot; our voyage the whole day having been made under a succession of bridges, many upon the suspension principle, and extremely light and elegant. The beauty and variety of the scenery which presented itself, as we shot along the banks of the Rhone, were quite sufficient to engage our attention, and to make the hours fly swiftly along; there were few, however, of our fellow-travellers who did not resort to other methods of amusement.

After the weather had cleared, the decks dried, and the sun-beams, warming, without scorching, glanced through fleecy clouds, the greater number of the passengers remained in the cabin below, whence, the windows being small and high, there was literally nothing to be seen. They employed themselves in reading, writing, or working; the French ladies in particular being most industrious in plying the needle. We noticed one family especially, who scarcely shewed themselves upon deck. It consisted of the mother, an elderly lady, of a very prepossessing appearance, with her son and daughter; the former about thirty years old, the latter considerably younger. The dress of the ladies, which was perfectly neat, consisting of printed muslin dresses, black silk shawls, and drawn bonnets, seemed so completely English, that we could scarcely believe that they were not our own countrywomen; they were the most diligent of the workers and readers, and as we never went down into the cabin unless to take some refreshment, or to fetch any thing we wanted, a few brief civilities only passed between us, but these were so cordially offered, that we regretted that want of inclination to enjoy the air and prospect upon deck which detained the party below.

There was a *restaurateur* on board the steamer, who supplied the passengers, at any hour they pleased, with the articles inserted in his *carte*; every thing was very good of its kind, but the boat itself was neither handsomely nor conveniently fitted up, and I should recommend in preference the new iron steamers which have been lately introduced upon the Rhone.

It was about nine o'clock in the evening when we reached Beaucaire; one other boat stopped at this place, but the rest, to our mortification, went on to Arles. We were told that we must be at the river-side at four the next morning, in order to proceed, and we therefore could not reckon upon more than four or five hours' sleep. The night was very dark, and a scene of great confusion took place in the disembarkation. We had agreed to wait quietly until the remainder of the passengers got on shore; and Miss E. and myself, glad to escape from the bustle and confusion of the deck, went down below to collect our baggage, &c. The quay was crowded with porters, all vociferating and struggling to get hold of parcels to carry, while the commissionaires from the hotels were more than ever eager in their recommendations of their respective houses: their noise and gesticulations were so great, and their requests urged with so much boldness, that we might have been led to suppose we had fallen into the hands of banditti, who would plunder us the moment they got us into their clutches.

Miss E. had posted herself at an open window, watching this strange scene, and while thus employed, was startled by hearing a piercing scream, and a plunge into the water; at the same moment, the clamour on shore became excessive. We instantly rushed upon deck, where we found our other friend safe; and upon inquiring what had happened, were told that a box had fallen into the river. Not quite satisfied of the truth of this statement, we asked several other persons, and received the same answer, the master of the steamer assuring us that no more serious accident had occurred.

We soon afterwards went on shore, which was then perfectly quiet, and, preceded by a commissionaire, who had persuaded the gentleman of our party to put himself under his convoy, we walked into the town. At a short distance from the water, we came upon an hotel of very prepossessing appearance, which we concluded to be the one to which we were bound. The windows of the lower and upper floors were all open, the rooms lighted, showing clean, gay-looking paper upon the walls, and furniture of a tempting appearance. Our conductor, however, passed the door, and dived down a lane, upon which we halted, and declared our resolution to go no further. After a little parley, and amongst other representations of the superior accommodations of the unknown hotel, an assurance that the stables were magnificent, we gained our point, and entered the house which had pleased us so much. We were met at the door by two well-dressed, good-looking women, who showed us into some excellent apartments up-stairs, all apparently newly-fitted up, and exceedingly well-furnished.

Ordering supper, we descended to the public room, and as we passed to a table at the farther end, noticed a young man sitting rather disconsolately at a window. We were laughing and talking with each other, when, suddenly starting up, the stranger youth exclaimed, "You are English? how glad I am to hear my own language spoken again!" He told us that he was travelling through France to Malta, and had come by the other steam-boat, in which there were no other English passengers beside himself. He then inquired whether a lady had not been drowned who came by our vessel; we answered no; but upon his assurance that such was the fact, we began to entertain a suspicion that the truth had been concealed from us. It was not, however, until the next morning, that we could learn the particulars. The gentleman who had accompanied us, and who had likewise been deceived by the statements made to him, ascertained that the accident had befallen the elderly French lady, with whose appearance we had been so much pleased. She had got on board a boat moored close to ours, and believing that she had only to step on shore, actually walked into the river. She was only ten minutes under water, and the probabilities are, that if the circumstance had been made known, and prompt assistance afforded, she might have been resuscitated. Amid the number of English passengers on board the steamer, the chances were very much in favour of its carrying a surgeon, accustomed to the best methods to be employed in such cases. No inquiry of the kind was made, and we understood that the body had been conveyed to a church, there to await the arrival of a medical man from the town.

We were, of course, inexpressibly shocked by this fatal catastrophe, the more so because we all felt that we might have been of use had we been told the truth. The grief and distraction of the son and daughter, who had thus lost a parent, very possibly prevented them from taking the best measures in a case of such emergence; whereas strangers, anxious to be of service, and having all their presence of mind at command, might have afforded very important assistance. How little had we thought, during the day spent so pleasantly upon the Rhone, that a fiat had passed which doomed one of the party to an untimely and violent death! Our spirits, which had been of the gayest nature, were damped by this incident, which recurred to our minds again and again, and we were continually recollecting some trifling circumstance which had prepossessed us in favour of the family, thus suddenly overwhelmed by so distressing an event.

A couple of hours brought us to Arles, where we arrived before the town was astir; the steamer to Marseilles did not leave the quay until twelve o'clock, and we were tantalized by the idea of the excellent night's rest we might have had if the steamer had fulfilled its agreement to go on to Arles. The Marseilles boat, though a fine vessel of its class, was better calculated for the conveyance of merchandize than of passengers; there being only one cabin, and no possibility of procuring any refreshment on board. This is the more inconvenient, as there is danger in bad weather of the passage into the harbour of Marseilles being retarded for several hours. We now lamented having slighted an invitation to comfortable quarters in Avignon, which we found on board the Lyons steamer, printed upon a large card.

We were much pleased with what we saw of Arles; it is a clean, well-built town, the streets generally rather narrow, but the houses good. In walking about, we found many of the outer doors open, and neat-looking female servants employed in sweeping the halls and entries. With what I hope may be deemed a pardonable curiosity, we peeped and sometimes stepped into these interiors, and were gratified by the neatness and even elegance which they exhibited. We found the people remarkably civil, and apparently too much accustomed to English travellers to trouble themselves about us. The hotel was not of the best class, and we only saw some very inferior *cafes*, consisting of one small room, with a curtain before the open door, and on the outside a rude representation, on a board, of a coffee-pot, and a cup and saucer. All the shops at Arles had curtains at the doors, a peculiarity which we had not previously observed in the towns of France. We went into a handsome church, where we found a few people, principally beggars, at prayers, and leaving a small donation in the poor-box, beguiled the time by walking and sitting in the **boulevard** of the town.

We were glad to embark at twelve o'clock, and soon afterwards we were again in motion. The Rhone is at this place a fine broad stream; but its banks were less interesting than those which we had passed the previous day. We came at length to a large tract of low land, washed on the other side by the Mediterranean, which we were told was tenanted by troops of wild horses, known by their being invariably white. There were certainly many horses to be seen, and amongst them numerous white ones; but they appeared to be exceedingly tame, and had probably only been turned out for the benefit of grazing on the salt marsh. Possibly there might be some difficulty in catching them in so large a plain, perfectly unenclosed, and they might have bred in these solitudes. There were also some very peaceable-looking donkeys to be seen, and now and then a few cows. We did not perceive any human habitations until we came to the extreme point, where one or two low, dreary-looking tenements had been raised.

The view for the last hour had been magnificent, extending over a splendid country to the lower Alps, and now Marseilles appeared in the distance, spread upon the side of a hill down to the water, and its environs stretching far and wide, villas and country mansions appearing in every direction. Upon entering the Mediterranean, we were struck by the line of demarcation which kept the green waters of the Rhone and the deep dark blue of the sea perfectly distinct from each other, there being no blending of tints. Here we were delighted by the appearance of a shoal of large fish, which were seen springing out of the water; several approached the steamer, gamboling about in the most beautiful manner possible, darting along close to the surface, and then making long leaps with their bodies in the air. One of our fellow-passengers, a German, with whom we had made acquaintance, hastened to fetch a gun; but, much to our joy, it missed fire in several attempts to discharge it at the beautiful creatures which had thus amused us with their sports. How strong must be the destructive propensity, when it leads men to wanton acts of barbarity like this; since, had a hundred fish been killed, there would have been no possibility of getting one on board, and the slaughter must merely have been perpetrated for slaughter's sake! Our remonstrances passed unheeded, and we therefore did not conceal our rejoicing over the disappointment.

The entrance into Marseilles is very picturesque, it being guarded on either side by high rocks, bold, and projecting in various shapes. We found the harbour crowded with vessels of various denominations, and amongst them several steamers, one a French ship of war, and another the English Government steamer, appointed to carry the mails to Malta. The smell arising from the stagnant water in the harbour of Marseilles was at first almost intolerable, and it was not without surprise that we saw several gay gondola-looking boats, with white and coloured awnings, filled with ladies and gentlemen, rowing about apparently for pleasure.

The clock struck five as we got on shore, and, much to our annoyance, we found that our first visit was to be paid to the customhouse. Upon embarking at Arles, a **gens-d'armes** had laid his finger upon our baggage, and demanded our keys; but upon a remonstrance at the absurdity of a re-examination, after it had passed through the whole of France, he allowed it to be put on board inviolate. Here, however, there was no escaping, and, tired as we were, and anxious to get to our hotel, we were obliged to submit to the delay. Fortunately, we were the first arrivals, and the search not being very strict, we were not detained more than ten minutes, or a quarter of an hour, which, under the circumstances, seemed an age. The nearest hotel was of course our place of refuge, and we were fortunate in speedily ending a very good one, the Hotel des Embassadeurs, an immense establishment, exceedingly well-conducted in every respect. Here we enjoyed the prospect of a night's rest, having, during a hundred and ten hours, only had about ten, at two different periods, in bed. Refreshed, however, by a change of dress, we had no inclination to anticipate the period of repose, but hurried our toilet, in order to join the dinner at the **table-d'hote.**

Marseilles struck us as being the handsomest and the cleanest town we had yet seen in France. All the houses are spacious and lofty, built of white stone, and in good condition, while every portion of the city is well paved, either after the English fashion, or with brick, quite even, and inserted in a very tasteful manner. Many of the streets are extremely wide, and some are adorned with handsome fountains. The shops are very elegant, and much more decorated than those of any other place in France; some had paintings upon glass, richly gilded, on either side of the doors, handsome curtains hung down within, and the merchandise displayed was of the best description. These shops were also well lighted, and together with the brilliant illuminations of the neighbouring *cafes*, gave the streets a very gay appearance. We wandered about until rather a late hour; the *cafes*, both inside and outside, were crowded with gentlemen; but in the promenades we saw fewer ladies than we had expected, and came to the conclusion--an erroneous one in all probability--that French women stay very much at home. Assuredly, the beauty of the night was most inviting; but, worn out at last, we were obliged to retire to our hotel.

The next day, we made inquiries concerning the steamers, and learned that the French boat was certainly to start on the following afternoon, the 21st, while the departure of the English vessel was uncertain, depending upon the arrival of the mails. Though disappointed at finding that the French steamer did not touch at Naples, as I had been led to believe, I felt inclined to take my passage in her; but the advantage of being in time to meet the Bombay steamer at Suez was so strongly urged upon me, in consequence of the ticklish state of affairs in Egypt, that, finding plenty of room on board the *Niagara*, we engaged a couple of berths in the ladies' cabins. Mehemet Ali was represented to us as being so obstinately determined to retain possession of the Turkish fleet, and the British Government so urgent with France to support the Porte against him, that, if this intelligence was to be depended upon, no time ought to be lost. It was with reluctance that I gave up my original intention of lingering on the road, and at Malta, but my unwillingness to run any risk of being shut out of Egypt prevailed. After executing this necessary business, we engaged a carriage, and paying a visit to the British consul, drove about the town and its environs, being the more pleased the more we saw of both. There appeared to be a deficiency of trees in the landscape, but a peculiar air of its own compensated for the want of foliage.

The private streets and houses of Marseilles are very regular and well built, nor did we see any portion of the town of a very inferior description. I should have liked much to have remained a few weeks in it, and indeed regretted the rapidity of my journey through France, not being able to imagine any thing more delightful than a leisure survey of the country through which we passed. I had been so strongly determined to make the overland trip to India, that I would have undertaken it quite alone, had I not met with a party to accompany me; some kind friends would not allow me, however, to make the experiment; nor do I recommend ladies, unless they are very well acquainted with the country, to travel through it without the protection of a gentleman, a courier, or a good servant. Miss E. and myself performed the whole distance without a care or a thought beyond the objects on the road; but this we owed entirely to the attention of the gentleman who put us safely on board the Malta steamer, and who managed every thing for us upon the way, so that we were never in one single instance subjected to the slightest annoyance.

CHAPTER III.
MARSEILLES TO ALEXANDRIA.

Venations at the Custom-house--Embarkation on the Malta Steamer--Difficulties of exit from the Harbour--Storm--Disagreeable Motion of the Steam-vessel--Passengers--Arrival at Malta--Description of the City--Vehicles--Dress of the Maltese Women--State of Society--Church of St. John--The Palace--The Cemetery of the Capuchin Convent--Intolerance of the Roman Catholic Priesthood--Shops, Cafes, and Hotels--Manufactures and Products of Malta--Heat of the Island--Embarkation on board an English Government Steamer--Passengers--A young Egyptian--Arrival at Alexandria--Turkish and Egyptian Fleets--Aspect of the City from the Sea--Landing.

At twelve o'clock on the morning of the 21st of September, we were informed that the English Government-mails had not arrived, and that the probabilities were in favour of their not reaching Marseilles until five o'clock; in which event, the steamer could not leave the harbour that night. We, therefore, anticipated another day in our pleasant quarters; but thought it prudent to take our baggage on board. Upon getting down to the quay, we were stopped by a ***gens-d'armes,*** who desired to have our keys, which we of course immediately surrendered. On the previous day, while driving about the town, our progress had been suddenly arrested by one of these officials, with an inquiry whether we had any thing to declare. He was satisfied with our reply in the negative, and allowed us to proceed. A gentleman afterwards asked me whether, in my travels through France, I had not observed that the police was a mere political agent, established for the purpose of strengthening the hands of the government, and not, as in England, intended for the protection of the people? I could only reply, that we had lost nothing in France, and that property there appeared to be as secure as at home. Certainly, the interference of the **gens-d'armes** about the baggage, and the continual demand for our passports, were very vexatious, detracting in a great degree from the pleasure of the journey.

We found the rate of porterage excessively high; the conveyance of our baggage to and fro, as we passed from steam-boats to hotels, proving, in the aggregate, enormous; the whole went upon a truck, which one man drew, with apparent ease, and for a very short distance, we paid nearly double the sum demanded for the hire of a horse and cart in London, from Baker Street, Portman Square, to the Custom House.

Upon getting on board the **Megara**, we found that the mails were in the act of delivery, and that the vessel would start without delay. We had now to take leave of the friend who had seen us so far upon our journey, and to rely wholly upon ourselves, or the chance civilities we might meet with on the road. Our spirits, which had been so gay, were much damped by the loss of a companion so cheerful and ready to afford us every enjoyment within our reach, and we in consequence thought less of the danger to which we were shortly afterwards exposed, the pain of parting being the paramount feeling.

There is always some difficulty in getting out of the harbour of Marseilles, and the natural obstacles are heightened by the want of a superintending power. There is no harbour-master, to regulate the movements of vessels, and to appoint their respective places; consequently, there is generally a great deal of confusion; while serious accidents are not unfrequent.

Before we got under weigh, I saw my old acquaintance, Hussein Khan, the Persian ambassador, go on board the French steamer, which was anchored within a short distance of us. He was received with all the honours due to his rank; which, by the way, was not acknowledged in England; and his suite, whom we had seen lounging at the doors of the **cafes** the evening before, made a gay appearance on the deck.

We got foul of one or two ships as we went out, and just as we left the harbour, the clouds, which had threatened all the morning, burst upon us in a tremendous storm, accompanied by thunder and lightning. The rain came down in torrents, sweeping along the decks, while a heavy squall threatened to drive us upon the rocks, which we had admired so much as the guardians of the port. In this emergency, we were compelled to drop our anchor, and remain quiescent until the fury of the elements had abated. The storm passed away about midnight, and getting the steam up, we were far away from Marseilles and *la belle France* before morning.

The *Megara* belonged to a class of steamers built for the government upon some new-fangled principle, and which have the art of rolling in any sea. Though the waters of the Mediterranean were scarcely ruffled by the breeze, which was in our favour, there was so much motion in the vessel, that it was impossible to employ ourselves in any way except in reading. In other respects, the *Megara* was commodious enough; the stern cabin, with smaller ones opening into it, and each containing two bed-places, was appropriated to the ladies, the whole being neatly fitted up. We found some agreeable fellow-passengers; the only drawback being a family of three children. In consequence of the cabins being thus occupied, we could not preserve the neatness and order which are so essential to comfort, and which need not be dispensed with even in a short voyage.

Our commandant, Mr. Goldsmith, a descendant of the brother of the poet, and who appeared to have inherited the benevolence of his distinguished relative, was indefatigable in his exertions to render us happy. He had procured abundant supplies for the table, which was every day spread with a profusion of good things, while eight or ten different kinds of wine, in addition to ale and porter, were placed at the disposal of the guests. Nothing, indeed, was wanting, except a French cook. No single meal had ever disagreed with us in France; but though partaking sparingly, we felt the inconvenience of the heavy English mode of cookery.

Amongst the attendants at table was one who speedily grew into the good graces of all the passengers. A little fellow, eight years old, but who did not look more than seven, placed himself at the commandant's elbow, who immediately upon seeing him exclaimed, with a benevolent smile, "What, are you here, Jemmy? then we are all right." Jemmy, it seems, was the boatswain's son, and no diminutive page belonging to a spoiled lady of quality, or Lilliputian tiger in the service of a fashionable aspirant, could have been dressed in more accurate costume. Jemmy was every inch a sailor; but, while preserving the true nautical cut, his garments were fashioned with somewhat coxcombical nicety, and he could have made his appearance upon any stage as a specimen of aquatic dandyism. Jemmy would be invaluable on board a yacht. His services at table were rewarded by a plateful of pudding, which he ate standing at the captain's right hand, after having, with great propriety, said grace. The little fellow had been afloat for a year and a half; but during this period his education had not been neglected, and he could read as well as any person in the ship.

Amongst our passengers was a French gentleman, the commandant and owner of an Indiaman, which had sailed from Bordeaux to Bombay under the charge of the first officer. He had previously made twelve voyages to India; but now availed himself of the shorter route, and proposed to join his vessel at Bombay, dispose of the cargo, and, after taking in a new freight, return through Egypt. The only coasts in sight, during our voyage from Marseilles to Malta, were those of Sardinia and Africa, Sicily being too far off to be visible. We were not near enough to Sardinia to see more than a long succession of irregular hills, which looked very beautiful under the lights and shades of a lovely summer sky. The weather was warm, without being sultry, and nothing was wanting excepting a few books. Mr. Goldsmith regretted the absence of a library on board, but expressed his intention of making a collection as speedily as possible.

The excessive and continual motion of the vessel caused me to suffer very severely from seasickness; the exertion of dressing in the morning always brought on a paroxysm, but I determined to struggle against it as much as possible, and was only one day so completely overpowered as to be unable to rise from the sofa. This sickness was the more provoking, since there was no swell to occasion it, the inconvenience entirely arising from Sir Somebody Symonds' (I believe that is the name) method of building. What the ***Megara*** would be in a heavy sea, there is no saying, and I should be very sorry to make the experiment.

We found ourselves at Malta at an early hour of the morning of the 25th, having been only five nights and four days on board. Mr. Goldsmith celebrated our last dinner with a profusion of champaigne, and though glad to get out of the vessel, we felt unfeignedly sorry to take leave of our kind commandant. We were, of course, up by daylight, in order to lose nothing of the view.

Much as I had heard of the gay singularity of the appearance of Malta, I felt surprise as well as delight at the beautiful scene around; nor was I at all prepared for the extent of the city of Valetta. The excessive whiteness of the houses, built of the rock of which the island is composed, contrasted with the vivid green of their verandahs, gives to the whole landscape the air of a painting, in which the artist has employed the most brilliant colours for sea and sky, and habitations of a sort of fairy land. Nor does a nearer approach destroy this illusion; there are no prominently squalid features in Malta, the beggars, who crowd round every stranger, being the only evidence, at a cursory gaze, of its poverty.

Soon after the *Megara* had dropped anchor, a young officer from the *Acheron*, the steamer that had brought the mails from Gibraltar, came on board to inquire whether I was amongst the passengers, and gave me the pleasing intelligence that a lady, a friend of mine, who had left London a few days before me, was now in Malta, and would proceed to India in the vessel appointed to take the mails. She was staying at Durnsford's Hotel, a place to which I had been strongly recommended. Mr. Goldsmith was kind enough to promise to see our heavy baggage on board the *Volcano*, the vessel under sailing orders; and a clergyman and his wife, resident in Malta, who had gone to Marseilles for a change of scene and air, inviting Miss E. and myself to accompany them on shore, we gladly accepted their offer.

We found a *caless* in waiting for us; a very singular description of vehicle, but one common to the island. I had seen representations of these carriages in old engravings, but had not the least idea that they were still in use. They have only two wheels, placed behind, so that the horse has to bear the weight of the vehicle as well as to draw it; and there is something so inexpressibly odd in the whole arrangement, that it put me in mind of the equipages brought on the stage in a Christmas pantomime. Our *caless* held four persons very conveniently, and was really a handsome vehicle, gaily lined with scarlet leather, and having spring seats. We saw others plying for hire, of a very inferior description; some only calculated for two persons, and of a faded and dilapidated appearance. They seem to be dangerous conveyances, especially for the poor horse; we heard of one being upset, on a steep hill, and breaking the neck of the animal that drew it. In driving, we were obliged to take rather a circuitous route to our inn, though the distance, had we walked, would have been very inconsiderable. We were glad of the opportunity of seeing a little of the suburbs, and were almost sorry to arrive at the place of our destination.

As we came along we were delighted with the picturesque appearance of the Maltese women, whose national dress is at once nunlike and coquettish. A black petticoat envelopes the form from the waist, and over that is thrown a singular veil, gathered into a hood, and kept out with a piece of whalebone. This covering, which is called the *faldetta*, is capable of many arrangements, and is generally disposed so as to "keep one eye free to do its worst of witchery." When one of the poorer classes is enabled to clothe herself in a veil and petticoat of silk, she considers that she has gained the *acme* of respectability. The streets of the city of Valetta are extremely narrow, and the houses high; a great advantage in such a climate, as it ensures shade, while, as they generally run at right angles, they obtain all the breeze that is to be had.

The appearance of our hotel was prepossessing. We entered through a wide gateway into a hall opening upon a small court, in the centre of which stood a large vase, very well sculptured, from the stone of the island, and filled with flowers. A wide handsome staircase, also of stone, with richly-carved balustrades, and adorned with statues and vases, conducted us to a gallery, two sides of which were open, and the other two closed, running round the court-yard, and affording entrance to very good apartments. Every thing was perfectly clean; the bedsteads of iron, furnished with mosquito-curtains; and we were supplied immediately with every article that we required.

As the rolling of the *Megara* had prevented the possibility of forming a sentence, we sat down to write letters, and having despatched a few of the introductions to residents, with which my friends in England had supplied me, I was agreeably surprised by some visits which I had scarcely expected, as we found that we should be obliged to embark for Alexandria in the evening.

I did not hear very flattering accounts of the state of society at Malta, which, like that of all other confined places, is split into factions, and where there seems to be a perpetual struggle, by the least fortunate classes, to assert equality with those whose rank is acknowledged; thus every person attached to the government assumes eligibility for the *entre* into the best circles, while the magnates of the place are by no means inclined to admit them to these privileges. It appeared that the endeavours of the Commissioner to produce a greater degree of cordiality between the Maltese inhabitants and the English residents, so far from succeeding, had tended to widen the distance between them, and that the Maltese were by no means grateful for the efforts made for their improvement. However, though the fruits may not at present appear, the seed having been sown, we may entertain a strong hope that they will show themselves in time.

While an undertaking so gigantic as the diffusion of the English language throughout India has been attempted, it seems rather extraordinary that the efforts of the committee should not have been directed to the same result in Malta, and that the progress of education should not have been conducted in the language that promised to prove the most useful to subjects of the British crown; but it appears that the committee decided otherwise, and complaints are making, that the instruction now supplied at the schools is of the most superficial nature, and by no means calculated to produce the desired end.

Every object in Malta bears witness to the ingenuity and industry of its inhabitants. The softness of the stone renders it easily cut, and the Dowager Marchioness of Hastings (who has left imperishable marks of her desire to benefit those who came under her observation), in supplying the best designs, has filled the shops of Malta with a tasteful species of **bijouterie**, which is eagerly sought after by all the visitors. The carved work of Malta is sold very cheap; but the same quality, which renders it so easily cut, occasions it to chip, and, therefore, great care is necessary in packing these fragile articles.

As soon as possible, we sallied forth to inspect the far-famed church of St. John, and found our expectations more than gratified by the interior of this gorgeous edifice. It was not, however, without melancholy feelings, that we reflected on the miserable remnant of those valiant knights, who had made Malta celebrated throughout all history, and who, on the suppression of the order, were suffered to languish out the remainder of their existence in obscurity. Mass was performing at the time of our entrance, and seating ourselves in one of the side chapels until it should be over, we were at its conclusion accosted by a priest, who, finding that we did not speak Italian, sent another person to show the beauties of the church. Some Maltese ladies greeted us very courteously, and though, perhaps, we would rather have wandered about alone, indulging in our own recollections of the past, we could not help being pleased with the attentions which were paid us.

Upon returning to our inn, we met a gentleman with whom we were slightly acquainted, who, upon learning that I had a letter to Sir Henry Bouverie, the governor, recommended me to deliver it in person, the palace being close at hand. Our party met with a very courteous reception, and we were happy in the opportunity thus afforded of seeing the palace, which showed remains of former grandeur far more interesting than any modern improvements could have been. One apartment, in particular, hung round with tapestry, which, though brought from France 135 years ago, retains all the brilliancy of its original colouring, pleased us exceedingly.

There are some good paintings upon the walls; but the armoury is the most attractive feature in the palace. It consists of one splendid apartment, running the whole length of the building, and makes a very imposing appearance; the arms of various periods being well arranged. The collection of ancient weapons was not so great as I had expected; still there were very interesting specimens, and an intelligent corporal, belonging to one of the Queen's regiments, who acted as **Cicerone**, gave us all the information we could require.

Some of our party had the curiosity to visit the cemetery of the Capuchin convent, in which the monks who die, after having undergone a preserving process, are dressed in the habit of the order, and fastened up in niches; when the skeletons, from extreme age, actually fall to pieces, the skulls and bones are formed into funeral trophies for the decoration of the walls; and the whole is described as a most revolting and barbarous spectacle. The last occupant was said to have departed this life as late as 1835, adding, by the comparative newness of his inhumation, to the horrors of the scene.

The influence of the priesthood, though still very great, is represented to be upon the decline; they have lately, however, shown their power, by retarding the progress of the building of the Protestant church, to which the Dowager Queen Adelaide so munificently subscribed. All the workmen employed are obliged to have dispensations from the Pope, and every pretext is eagerly seized upon to delay the erection of the edifice. At present, the Protestant community, with few exceptions, are content to have service performed in an angle of the court-yard of the palace, formerly a cellar and kitchen, but now converted into an episcopal chapel and vestry-room. The members of the society have a small chapel, not adequate to the accommodation of those who desire to attend it, belonging to the Methodist persuasion; but its minister is afraid to encounter the difficulties and delays which would be consequent upon an attempt to enlarge it. There is a public library adjoining the palace, originally formed by the knights, but considered now to be more extensive than valuable.

The period which I spent upon the island was too brief to allow me to make any inquiries respecting its institutions, the novelties of the scene engaging my attention so completely, that I could give no thought to anything else. The shops and *cafes* of La Valetta have a very gay appearance, and the ingenuity of the inhabitants is displayed in several manufactures; the black lace mittens, now so fashionable, being particularly well made. Table-linen, also of superior quality, may be purchased, wrought in elegant patterns, and, if bespoken, with the coat-of-arms or crest worked into the centre or the corners. In the fashioning of the precious metals, the Maltese likewise excel, their filagree-work, both in gold and silver, being very beautiful: the Maltese chains have long enjoyed a reputation in Europe, and other ornaments may be purchased of equal excellence.

To the eye of a stranger, Malta, at this period of the year (the end of September), seems bare and destitute of verdure; yet, from the quantity of every kind of vegetables brought to market, it must be amazingly productive. The growth of cotton, lately introduced into Egypt, has been injurious to the trade and manufactures of Malta, and the attempt to supply its place with silk failed. In the opinion of some persons, the experiment made had not a fair trial. The mulberry trees flourished, and the silk produced was of an excellent quality; but the worms did not thrive, and in consequence the design was abandoned. Inquiry has shown, that the leaves from old trees are essential to the existence of the silk-worm, and that, had the projectors of the scheme been aware of a fact so necessary to be known, they would have awaited the result of a few more years, which seems all that was necessary for the success of the undertaking. How many goodly schemes have been ruined from the want of scientific knowledge upon the part of their projectors, and how frequently it happens that a moment of impatience will destroy the hopes of years!

Fruit is cheap, plentiful, and excellent at Malta, the figs and grapes being of very superior quality, while the island affords materials for the most luxurious table. The golden mullet and the *Becca fica* are abundant; and all the articles brought to market are procurable at low prices. I can scarcely imagine a more agreeable place to spend a winter in, and I promise myself much gratification in the sojourn of a few weeks at this delightful island upon my return to England. I can very strongly recommend Durnsford's Hotel as a place of residence, the accommodation being excellent and the terms moderate. In remaining any time, arrangement may be made for apartments and board, by which means the rate of living is much cheaper, while the style is equally good.

There is an opera at Malta, in which performances of various degrees of mediocrity are given. The gay period to a stranger is that of the carnival; but, at other times, the festivals of the church, celebrated in this isolated place with more of the mummeries of Roman Catholicism than obtain in many other countries professing the same faith, afford amusement to the lovers of the grotesque.

Though the thermometer at Malta seldom rises to 90 deg., yet the heat in the sultry season is very great. Every person, who is in the habit of studying the glass, becomes aware of the difference between the heat that is actually felt and that which is indicated by instruments; and in no place is this discrepancy more sensibly experienced than Malta, in which the state of the winds materially affects the comfort of the inhabitants. A good authority assures us, that "the heat of Malta is most oppressive, so much so, as to justify the term 'implacable,' which is often applied to it. The sun, in summer, remains so long above the horizon, and the stone walls absorb such an enormous quantity of heat, that they never have sufficient time to get cool; and during the short nights, this heat radiates from them so copiously, as to render the nights, in fact, as hot as the days, and much more oppressive to the feelings of those who are accustomed to associate the idea of coolness with darkness. I have seen the thermometer, in a very sheltered part of my house, steadily maintain, during the night, the same height to which it had arisen in the day, while I marked it with feelings of incalculably increased oppression, and this for three successive weeks in August and September, 1822."

At Malta, we were recommended, in consequence of the unsettled state of affairs between Mehemet Ali and the European powers, to proceed forthwith to Egypt, and though strongly tempted to prolong my stay in the island, I thought it advisable to make the best of my way to the Red Sea, and defer the pleasure, which a more protracted residence promised, until my return in the ensuing year. Lieut. Goldsmith, our kind commandant of the **Megara**, called upon us, according to promise, to conduct us on board the new steamer, the **Volcano**, the vessel appointed to carry the mails on to Alexandria. This ship was in quarantine, and it was consequently necessary to take some precautions in going on board. We proceeded, in the first instance, to a police station, where we took a second boat in tow, and a *guadiano*, an official appointed to see that no persons transgress the rules and regulations of the port instituted for the preservation of health.

Upon getting alongside of the **Volcano**, our baggage was placed in this boat; Miss E. and myself were then handed in, and cast adrift, to my great astonishment; for not having had any previous intimation of the method to be pursued, I was not at all prepared to hold on, as I believe it is called, without assistance. Miss E., however, who was more observant, hooked her parasol into one of the ropes, which she subsequently caught. We were now to be taught a new lesson--the extreme non-chalance with which the officers of a Government steamer treat the passengers who have the misfortune to choose these boats instead of making the voyage on board merchant vessels. Some minutes elapsed before any notice was taken of us, or any assistance afforded in getting up our baggage; our own people being obliged to look on and do nothing, since, had they touched the ship, they would have been obliged to perform eighteen days of quarantine.

Upon reaching the deck, we requested that our baggage might be taken down into the ladies' cabin, in order that we might get our small dormitories put to rights before the rest of the passengers came on board; but, though it could have made no earthly difference to the people employed, we met with a refusal, and the whole was deposited in the grand saloon, already encumbered with luggage, every quarter of an hour adding to the heap and the confusion, and the difficulty of each person recognizing the identical carpet-bag or portmanteau that he might claim as his property.[3]

Among our new fellow-passengers there was a young English gentleman, who intended to travel into Syria, and who, though looking scarcely twenty, had already spent some years in foreign countries. He was very modest and unassuming, and both agreeable and intelligent; and, having had a good deal of conversation together, I was sorry to lose sight of him at Alexandria.

We had also one of Mehemet Ali's *proteges* on board, a young Egyptian, who had been educated at the Pasha's expense in England, where he had resided for the

---

3   The author followed up these remarks with others, still more severe, upon the treatment which she and her fellow-travellers experienced on board this vessel; but as these remarks seem to have caused pain, and as Miss Roberts, without retracting one particle of her statements, regretted that she had published them, it has been deemed right to omit them in this work.

last ten years, latterly in the neighbourhood of a dock-yard, in order to study the art of ship-building. This young man was a favourite with those persons on board who could make allowances for the circumstances in which he had been placed, and who did not expect acquirements which it was almost impossible for him to attain. His natural abilities were very good, and he had cultivated them to the utmost of his power. Strongly attached to European customs, manners, and institutions, he will lose no opportunity of improving the condition of his countrymen, or of inducing them to discard those prejudices which retard the progress of civilization. He was naturally very anxious concerning his future destiny, for the Pasha's favour is not always to be depended upon, while the salary of many of the appointments which he does bestow is by no means adequate to the support of men whom his liberality has enabled to live in great respectability and comfort in England. Our new acquaintance also felt that, in returning to his friends and relatives, he should shock all their prejudices by his entire abandonment of those customs and opinions by which they were still guided; he grieved especially at the distress which he should cause his mother, and determined not to enter into her presence until he had assumed the national dress, and could appear, outwardly at least, like an Egyptian.

The weather, during our short voyage, was remarkably favourable, although it got rather too warm, especially at night, for comfort. There are, however, great alleviations to heat in the Mediterranean steamers. The ladies can have a wind-sail in their cabin, which, together with the air from the stern windows, renders the temperature at all times very delightful. They enjoy another advantage in having a light burning all night, a comfort which cannot be too highly appreciated, since darkness on board ship increases every other annoyance.

We left Malta on the evening of the 25th, and arrived at Alexandria early in the morning of the 30th. Every eye was strained to catch the first view of the Egyptian coast, and especially of the Pharos, which in ancient time directed the mariners to its shores; but the great object of attraction at this period consisted of the united fleets, Turkish and Egyptian, which rode at anchor in the port. Our steamer threaded its way amid these fine-looking vessels, some of which we passed so closely, as to be able to look into the cabin-windows. To my unprofessional eye, these ships looked quite as efficient as any warlike armament of the same nature that I had yet seen. They all appeared to be well kept, and in good order, while the sailors were clean, neatly dressed, and actively engaged, some in boats, and others performing various duties. Though steamers are now very common sights, we in turn attracted attention, all eyes being directed to our deck.

Our Egyptian fellow-passenger was especially interested and agitated at his approach to his native shore, and the evidences which he saw before him of the power and political influence of the Pasha. From a gentleman who came on board, we learned that an apprehension had been entertained at Alexandria of the arrival of a hostile fleet from Europe, in which event a collision would in all probability have taken place. Mehemet Ali, it was said, was so foolishly elated by his successes, and by the attitude he had assumed, as to be perfectly unaware of his true position, and of the lesson which he would receive, should he persist in defying the remonstrances of his European allies. It was also said, that nothing but the favour shown by the French cabinet to the Pasha had hitherto prevented the commencement of hostilities, since the British Government, taking the view of its representative at Constantinople, felt strongly inclined to proceed to extremities. I merely, of course, state the rumour that prevailed; whether they carried the slightest authority or not, I do not pretend to determine.

Alexandria, from the sea, presents a very imposing appearance; long lines of handsome buildings, apparently of white stone, relieved by green Venetian blinds, afford evidence of increasing prosperity, and a wish to imitate the style of European cities. There is nothing, however, in the landing-place worthy of the approach to a place of importance; a confused crowd of camels, donkeys, and their drivers, congregated amidst heaps of rubbish, awaited us upon reaching the shore. We had been told that we should be almost torn to pieces by this rabble, in their eagerness to induce us to engage the services of themselves or their animals. Accustomed as we had been to the attacks of French waiters, we were astonished by the indifference of the people, who very contentedly permitted us to walk to the place of our destination.

The lady-passengers, who arrived in the steamer, agreed to prosecute the remainder of the journey in company; our party, therefore, consisted of four, with two servants, and a baby; the latter a beautiful little creature, of seven months old, the pet and delight of us all. This darling never cried, excepting when she was hungry, and she would eat any thing, and go to any body. One of the servants who attended upon her was a Mohammedan native of India, an excellent person, much attached to his little charge; and we were altogether a very agreeable party, quite ready to enjoy all the pleasures, and to encounter all the difficulties, which might come in our way.

Having formed my expectations of Alexandria from books of travels, which describe it as one of the most wretched places imaginable, I was agreeably disappointed by the reality. My own experience of Mohammedan cities had taught me to anticipate much more of squalor and dilapidation than I saw; though I confess, that both were sufficiently developed to strike an European eye. We wended our way through avenues ancle-deep in sand, and flanked on either side with various descriptions of native houses, some mere sheds, and others of more lofty and solid construction. We encountered in our progress several native parties belonging to the respectable classes; and one lady, very handsomely dressed, threw aside her outer covering, a dark silk robe, somewhat resembling a domino, and removing her veil, allowed us to see her dress and ornaments, which were very handsome. She was a fine-looking woman, with a very good-natured expression of countenance.

CHAPTER IV.
ALEXANDRIA TO BOULAK.

Description of Alexandria--Hotels--Houses--Streets--Frank
Shops--Cafes--Equipages--Arrangements for the Journey to
Suez--Pompey's Pillar--Turkish and Arab Burial-grounds--Preparations
for the Journey to Cairo--Embarkation on the Canal--Bad accommodation
in the Boat--Banks of the Canal--Varieties of Costume in
Egypt--Collision during the night--Atfee--Its wretched appearance--The
Pasha--Exchange of Boats--Disappointment at the Nile--Scarcity of
Trees--Manners of the Boatmen--Aspect of the Villages--The Marquess
of Waterford--The Mughreebee Magician--First sight of the
Pyramids--Arrival at Boulak, the Port of Cairo.

There are several excellent hotels at Alexandria for the accommodation of European travellers. We were recommended to Rey's, in which we found every comfort we could desire. The house is large and handsome, and well situated, being at the end of a wide street, or rather ***place***, in which the more wealthy of the Frank inhabitants reside, and where there are several houses belonging to the consuls of various nations. These latter are usually detached mansions, of a very handsome description, and one especially, facing the top, will be magnificent when finished.

All the houses in this quarter are very solidly constructed, lofty, and with flat roofs. The ground-floor seems to be appropriated to merchandize, or as domestic offices, the habitable apartments being above. The windows are supplied with outside Venetian blinds, usually painted green, which, together with the pure white of the walls, gives them a fresh and new appearance, which I had not expected to see. In fact, nothing could exceed the surprise with which I viewed a street that would have excited admiration in many of our European capitals. It will in a short time be embellished by a fountain, which was erecting at the period of my visit: could the residents get trees to grow, nothing more would be wanting to render it one of the most superb avenues of the kind extant; but, a few inches below the surface, the earth at Alexandria is so completely impregnated with briny particles, as to render the progress of vegetation very difficult at all times, and in some places impossible.

This portion of the city is quite modern; near it there is a more singular and more ancient series of buildings, called the **Okella**; a word, I believe, derived from *castle*. This consists of one large quadrangle, or square, entered by gateways at different sides. A terrace, approached by flights of steps, extends all round, forming a broad colonnade, supported upon arches. The houses belonging to the Franks open upon this terrace; they are large and commodious, but the look-out does not equal that from the newer quarter; the quadrangle below exhibiting any thing rather than neatness or order. Goods and utensils of various kinds, donkeys, camels, and horses, give it the appearance of the court of a native serai, though at the same time it may be said to be quite as well kept as many places of a similar description upon the continent of Europe. The Frank shopkeepers have their establishments in a narrower avenue at the end of the wide street before-mentioned. Here are several ***cafes***, apparently for the accommodation of persons to whom the hotels might be too expensive; some of these are handsomely fitted up in their way: one, especially, being panelled with shewy French paper, in imitation of the Gobelins tapestry. I was not sufficiently near to discern the subject, but when lighted, the colours and figures produced a very gay effect. I observed a considerable number of druggists' shops; they were generally entirely open in front, so that the whole economy of the interior was revealed to view. The arrangements were very neat; the various articles for sale being disposed upon shelves all round. We did not make any purchases either here or in the Turkish bazaar, which, both morning and evening, was crowded with people. Several very good houses in the European style were pointed out to us as belonging to Turkish gentlemen, high in office and in the receipt of large incomes.

We had ordered dinner at seven o'clock, for the purpose of taking advantage of the cool part of the day to walk about. We confined our peregrinations to the Frank quarter and its immediate neighbourhood, and were amused by the singular figures of other European pedestrians whom we met with, but whose peculiar country it was difficult to discover by their dress. Several gentlemen made their appearance on horseback, but we did not see any females of the superior class. Two English carriages, filled with Turkish grandees, dashed along with the recklessness which usually distinguishes native driving; and other magnates of the land, mounted upon splendid chargers, came forth in all the pride of Oriental pomp. Having sufficiently fatigued ourselves with walking ancle-deep in dust and sand, we returned to our hotel, where we found an excellent dinner, which, among other good things, comprehended a dish of Beccaficos.

As I had not intended to reach Alexandria so soon, neither Miss E. nor myself had given notice of our approach; consequently, there was nothing in readiness. We had, notwithstanding, hoped to have found a boat prepared, a friend in London having promised to mention the possibility of our being in Egypt with the mails that left Marseilles on the 21st; but this precaution had been neglected, and the gentleman, who would have provided us with the best vessel procurable, was too busy with duties which the arrival of the steamer entailed upon him to do more than express his regret that he could not devote his whole attention to our comfort. In this emergency, we applied to Mr. Waghorn, who, in the expectation that I might wish to remain at Alexandria, had most kindly prepared an apartment for my reception at his own house. The aspect of affairs, however, did not admit of my running any risks, and I therefore determined to proceed to Suez without delay. Under these circumstances, he did the best that the nature of the case permitted; assured me that I should have his own boat, which, though small, was perfectly clean, when we got to the Nile, and provided me with all that I required for the passage. Mrs. Waghorn also recommended a servant, whose appearance we liked, and whom we instantly engaged for the trip to Suez.

I had brought letters to the consul-general, and to several residents in Alexandria, who immediately paid me visits at our hotel. Colonel Campbell was most particularly kind and attentive, offering one of the government janissaries as an escort to Cairo; an offer which we most readily accepted, and which proved of infinite service to us. We had no trouble whatever about our baggage; we left it on board, under the care of the trusty black servant. One of the officers of the ship, who had distinguished himself during the voyage by his polite attention to the passengers, had come on shore with us; he sent to the vessel for our goods and chattels, took our keys and the janissary with him to the custom-house, and we had speedily the pleasure of seeing them come upon a camel to the door of the hotel, the fees charged, and the hire of the animal, being very trifling. There was a large apartment on one side of the gateway, in which those boxes which we did not desire to open were deposited, the door being secured by a good lock; in fact, nothing could be better than the whole arrangements of the hotel. It was agreed that as little time as possible should be lost in getting to Suez, and we therefore determined to prosecute our journey as early in the afternoon of the next day as we could get every thing ready. Donkeys were to be in waiting at daylight, to convey the party to Pompey's Pillar, and we retired to rest, overcome by the fatigue and excitement we had undergone. It was sufficiently warm to render it pleasant to have some of the windows open; and once or twice in the night we were awakened by the furious barking of the houseless and ownerless dogs, which are to be found in great numbers throughout Egypt. In the day-time the prevailing sound at Alexandria is the braying of donkeys, diversified by the grunts and moans of the almost equally numerous camels.

Engravings have made every inquiring person well acquainted with the celebrated monument which goes by the name of "Pompey's Pillar," and the feelings with which we gazed upon it are much more easily imagined than described. It has the advantage of standing upon a rather considerable elevation, a ridge of sand, and below it are strewed vast numbers of more humble memorials of the dead. The Turkish and the Arab burial-grounds spread themselves at the feet of the Pillar: each grave is distinguished by a mound of earth and a stone. The piety of surviving relatives has, in some places, forced the stubborn sand to yield proofs of their affectionate remembrance of the deceased; occasionally, we see some single green plant struggling to shadow the last resting-place of one who slept below; and if any thing were wanting to add to the melancholy of the scene, it would have been the stunted and withering leaves thus mournfully enshrouding the silent dead. There is something so unnatural in the conjunction of a scanty vegetation with a soil cursed with hopeless aridity, that the gardens and few green spots, occurring in the neighbourhood of Alexandria, detract from, instead of embellishing, the scene. Though pleasant and beautiful as retreats to those who can command an entrance, these circumscribed patches of verdure offend rather than please the eye, when viewed from a distance.

The antiquities of Egypt have been too deeply studied by the erudite of all Christian countries, for an unlearned traveller to entertain a hope of being able to throw any additional light upon them. Modern tourists must, therefore, be content with the feelings which they excite, and to look, to the present state of things for subjects of any promise of interest to the readers of their journals.

After breakfast, we received a visit from the Egyptian gentleman who had been our fellow-passenger. He brought with him a friend, who, like himself, had been educated in England, and who had obtained a good appointment, together with the rank of a field officer, from the Pasha. The manners of the gentleman were good; modest, but not shy. He spoke excellent English, and conversed very happily upon all the subjects broached. Our friend was still in doubt and anxiety respecting his own destination. Mehemet Ali had left Alexandria for one of his country residences, on the plea of requiring change of air; but, in reality, it was said, to avoid the remonstrances of those who advocated a policy foreign to his wishes. The new arrival could not present himself to the minister until he should be equipped in an Egyptian dress. The friend who accompanied him gave us the pleasing intelligence, that a large handsome boat, with ladies' cabin detached, and capable of carrying forty passengers, had been built by the merchants of Alexandria, and when completed--and it only wanted painting and fitting up--would convey travellers up the canal to Atfee, a distance which, towed by horses, it would perform in twelve hours. Small iron steamers were expected from England, to ply upon the Nile, and with these accommodations, nothing would be more easy and pleasant than a journey which sometimes takes many days to accomplish, and which is frequently attended with inconvenience and difficulty.

We found that Mrs. Waghorn had provided Miss E. and myself with beds, consisting each of a good mattress stuffed with cotton, a pillow of the same, and a quilted coverlet, also stuffed with cotton. She lent us a very handsome canteen; for the party being obliged to separate, in consequence of the small accommodation afforded in the boats, we could not avail ourselves of that provided by the other ladies with whom we were to travel, until we should all meet again upon the desert. As there may be a danger of not meeting with a canteen, exactly suited to the wants of the traveller, for sale at Alexandria, it is advisable to procure one previously to leaving Europe; those fitted up with tin saucepans are necessary, for it is not easy to carry cooking apparatus in any other form. We did not encumber ourselves with either chair or table, but would afterwards have been glad of a couple of camp-stools. Our supplies consisted of tea, coffee, wine, wax-candles (employing a good glass lanthorn for a candlestick), fowls, bread, fruit, milk, eggs, and butter; a pair of fowls and a piece of beef being ready-roasted for the first meal. We also carried with us some bottles of filtered water. The baggage of the party was conveyed upon three camels and a donkey, and we formed a curious-looking cavalcade as we left the hotel.

In the first place, the native Indian servant bestrode a donkey, carrying at the same time our beautiful baby in his arms, who wore a pink silk bonnet, and had a parasol over her head. All the assistance he required from others was to urge on his beast, and by the application of sundry whacks and thumps, he soon got a-head. The ladies, in coloured muslin dresses, and black silk shawls, rode in a cluster, attended by the janissary, and two Arab servants also on donkey-back; a gentleman, who volunteered his escort, and the owners of the donkeys, who walked by our sides. As I had never rode any animal, excepting an elephant, until I landed at Alexandria, I did not feel perfectly at home on the back of a donkey, and therefore desired Mohammed, our new servant, to give directions to my attendant to take especial care of me. These injunctions he obeyed to the letter, keeping close at my side, and at every rough piece of road putting one hand on the donkey and the other in front of my waist. I could not help shrinking from such close contact with a class of persons not remarkable for cleanliness, either of garment or of skin; but the poor fellow meant well, and as I had really some occasion for his services, and his appearance was respectable, I thought it no time to be fastidious, and could not help laughing at the ridiculous figure I made.

We passed some fine buildings and baths; the latter very tempting in their external appearance, and, according to general repute, excellent of their kind. When we came to the gate of the wall of Alexandria, we encountered a funeral procession returning from the cemetery close to Pompey's Pillar. They were a large party, accompanied by many women, who, notwithstanding their grief, stopped to gratify their curiosity, by a minute inspection of our strange persons, and still stranger garb. We were all huddled together in the gateway, which, the walls being thick, took a few minutes to pass through, and thus had an opportunity of a very close examination of each other; the veils of the women, however, prevented us from scanning their countenances very distinctly; and as we passed on, we encountered a herd of buffaloes, animals quite new to Miss E., who had never seen one even as a zoological specimen. We passed the base of Pompey's Pillar, and through the burying-grounds; and in another quarter of an hour came to the banks of the canal, and got on board the boat, which had been engaged to take us to Atfee.

In the whole course of my travels, I had never seen any thing so forlorn and uncomfortable as this boat. The accommodation destined for us consisted of two cabins, or rather cribs, opening into each other, and so low in the roof as not to permit a full-grown person to stand upright in either. Some attempt had been formerly made at painting and carving, but dirt was now the predominant feature, while the holes and crannies on every side promised free egress to the vermin, apparently long tenants of the place. Although certain of remaining the night upon the canal, we would not suffer our beds to be unpacked; but, seating ourselves upon our boxes, took up a position near the door, in order to see as much as possible of the prospect.

The banks of the canal are very luxuriant; but, lying low, are infested with insects of various kinds; musquitoes came on board in clouds, and the flies were, if possible, more tormenting; it is, therefore, very desirable to get out of this channel as speedily as possible. We saw the vessel, a fine, large, handsome boat, which had been mentioned to us as building for the purpose of conveying passengers to Atfee; consequently, should the political questions now agitating be amicably settled, and Egypt still continue to be a high road for travellers to India, the inconveniences of which I now complain will soon cease to exist.

We passed some handsome houses, built after the European fashion, one of which we were told belonged to the Pasha's daughter, the wife of the dufturdar; it was surrounded by gardens, but had nothing very imposing in its appearance. We came also upon an encampment of the Pasha's troops, which consisted of numerous small round tents, huddled together, without the order displayed by an European army. The men themselves, though report speaks well of their discipline, had not the soldierlike look which I had seen and admired in the native troops of India. The impossibility of keeping their white garments clean, in such a country as Egypt, is very disadvantageous to their appearance, and it is unfortunate that something better adapted to withstand the effects of dust should not have been chosen. The janissary who accompanied us, and who was clothed in red, had a much more military air. He was a fine-looking fellow, tall, and well-made; and his dress, which was very becoming, was formed of fine materials. Our servant Mohammed had also a pleasing countenance, full of vivacity and good humour, which we found the general characteristics of the people of Egypt, especially those immediately above the lower class, and who enjoyed any degree of comfort.

There are several varieties of costume worn in Egypt, some consisting of long gowns or vests worn over the long trowser. The military dress, which was that worn by the janissary and our servant, is both graceful and becoming. It is rather difficult to describe the nether garment, which is wide to the knee, and very full and flowing behind; added to this, the janissary wore a light pantaloon, descending to the ancle; but Mohammed, excepting when he encased them in European stockings, had his legs bare: the waistcoat and jacket fit tight to the shape, and are of a tasteful cut, and together with a sash and the crimson cap with a dark blue tassel, almost universal, form a picturesque and handsome dress. That worn by our servant was made of fine blue stuff, embroidered, or rather braided, at the edges; and this kind of ornament is so general, that even some of the poorest fellahs, who possess but one coarse canvas shirt, will have that garnished with braiding in some scroll-pattern.

There was not much to be seen on the banks of the Mahmoudie: here and there, a priest at his devotions at the water-side, or a few miserable cottages, diversified the scene. We encountered, however, numerous boats; and so great was the carelessness of the navigators, that we had considerable difficulty in preventing a collision, which, but for the good look-out kept by the janissary, must have happened more than once. Whenever the breeze permitted, we hoisted a sail; at other times, the boatmen dragged the boat along; and in this manner we continued our voyage all night. We regretted much the absence of moonlight, since, the moment the day closed, all our amusement was at an end. Cock-roaches, as large as the top of a wine-glass, made their appearance; we heard the rats squeaking around, and found the musquitoes more desperate in their attacks than ever. The flies with one accord went to sleep, settling in such immense numbers on the ceiling immediately over my head, that I felt tempted to look for a lucifer-match, and put them all to death. The expectation, however, of leaving the boat early the next morning, deterred me from this wholesale slaughter; but I had no mercy on the musquitoes, as, attracted by the light, they settled on the glasses of the lanthorn.

It was a long and dismal night, the only accident that occurred being a concussion, which sent Miss E. and myself flying from our portmanteaus. We had run foul of another boat, or rather all the shouting of the Arab lungs on board our vessel had failed to arouse the sleepers in the craft coming down. At length, the day dawned, and we tried, by copious ablution and a change of dress, to refresh ourselves after our sleepless night.

Finding that we wanted milk for breakfast, we put a little boy, one of the crew, on shore, in order to procure some at a village; meanwhile, a breeze sprung up, and we went on at so quick a rate, that we thought we must have left him behind. Presently, however, we saw the poor fellow running as fast as possible, but still careful of his pannikin; and after a time we got him on board. In accomplishing this, the boy was completely ducked; but whether he was otherwise hurt, or this catastrophe occurring when out of breath or fatigued with over-exertion, I do not know; but he began to cry in a more piteous manner than could be justified by the cause alleged, namely, the wetting of his only garment, an old piece of sacking. I directed Mohammed to reward his services with a piastre, a small silver coin of the value of 2-1/2d.; and never, perhaps, did so trifling a sum of money produce so great an effect. In one moment, the cries were hushed, the tears dried, and in the contemplation of his newly-acquired riches, he lost the recollection of all his troubles.

It was nearly twelve o'clock in the day before we reached Atfee; and with all my previous experience of the wretched places inhabited by human beings, I was surprised by the desolation of the village at the head of the canal. The houses, if such they might be called, were huddled upon the side of a cliff; their mud walls, covered on the top with a few reeds or a little straw, looking like the cliff itself. A few irregular holes served for doors and windows; but more uncouth, miserable hovels could not have been seen amongst the wildest savages. Some of these places I perceived had a small court-yard attached, the hut being at the end, and only distinguishable by a poor attempt at a roof, the greater part of which had fallen in.

We were here obliged to leave our boat; landing on the opposite side to this village, and walking a short distance, we found ourselves upon the banks of the Nile. The place was in great confusion, in consequence of the actual presence of the Pasha, who, for himself and suite, we were told, had engaged every boat excepting the one belonging to Mr. Waghorn, in which the mails, entrusted to him, had been put. As it was impossible that four ladies, for our friends had now joined us, with their European female servant and the baby, could be accommodated in this small vessel, we despatched our janissary, with a letter in the Turkish language to the governor of Atfee, with which we had been provided at Alexandria, and we were immediately politely informed that the best boat attainable should be at our disposal.

The Pasha had taken up his quarters at a very mean-looking house, and he soon afterwards made his appearance in front of it. Those who had not become acquainted with his person by portraits, or other descriptions, were disappointed at seeing a common-looking man, short in stature, and very plainly clad, having formed a very different idea of the sovereign of Egypt. Not having any proper introductions, and knowing that the Pasha makes a great favour of granting an audience to European ladies, we made no attempt to address him; thus sacrificing our curiosity to our sense of decorum. There was of course a great crowd round the Pasha, and we embarked for the purpose of surveying it to greater advantage.

Our boat was moored in front of a narrow strip of ground between the river and a large dilapidated mansion, having, however, glass windows in it, which bore the ostentatious title of **Hotel du Mahmoudie.** This circumscribed space was crowded with camels and their drivers; great men and their retainers passing to and fro; market people endeavouring to sell their various commodities, together with a multitudinous collection of men, dogs, and donkeys. I observed that all the people surveyed the baby as she was carried through them, in her native servant's arms, with peculiar benignity. She was certainly a beautiful specimen of an English infant, and in her pretty white frock, lace cap, and drawn pink silk bonnet, would have attracted attention anywhere; such an apparition the people now assembled at Atfee had probably never seen before, and they were evidently delighted to look at her. She was equally pleased, crowing and spreading out her little arms to all who approached her.

The smallness of the boat rendered it necessary that I should open one of my portmanteaus, and take out a supply of clothes before it was sent away; while thus occupied, I found myself overlooked by two or three respectably-clad women, who were in a boat, with several men, alongside. I did not, of course, understand what they said, but by their gestures guessed that they were asking for some of the strange things which they saw. I had nothing that I could well spare, or that I thought would be useful to them, excepting a paper of needles, which I put into one of their hands, through the window of the cabin. The envelope being flourished over with gold, they at first thought that there was nothing more to be seen, but being directed by signs to open it, they were in ecstasy at the sight of the needles, which they proceeded forthwith to divide.

We now pushed off, and found that, in the narrow limits to which we were confined, we must only retain our carpet-bags and dressing-cases. The small cabin which occupies the stern was surrounded on three sides with lockers, which formed seats, but which were too narrow to hold our beds; moveable planks, of different dimensions, to suit the shape of the boat, fitted in, making the whole flush when requisite, and forming a space amply wide enough for our mattresses, but in which we could not stand upright. To our great joy, we found the whole extremely clean, and in perfect repair, so that we could easily submit to the minor evils that presented themselves.

We had found Mohammed very active, attentive, and ready in the departments in which we had hitherto employed him, but we were now about to put his culinary abilities to the test. He spoke very tolerable English, but surprised us a little by inquiring whether we should like an Irish stew for dinner. A fowl was killed and picked in a trice, and Mohammed had all his own way, excepting with regard to the onions, which were, in his opinion, woefully restricted. A fowl stewed with butter and potatoes, and garnished with boiled eggs, is no bad thing, especially when followed by a dessert of fresh dates, grapes, and pomegranates. A clerk of Mr. Waghorn's, an European, who had the charge of the mails, went up in the boat with us; but as we could not possibly afford him any accommodation in our cabin, his situation at the prow must have been very uncomfortable. He was attended by a servant; there were ten or twelve boatmen, which, together with Mohammed and the janissary, completely crowded the deck, so that it was impossible for them all to lie down at full length.

I have not said a word about the far-famed river, which I had so long and so anxiously desired to see; the late inundations had filled it to the brim, consequently it could not have been viewed at a more favourable period; but I was dreadfully disappointed. In a flat country, like Lower Egypt, I had not expected any thing beyond luxuriance of vegetation; but my imagination had been excited by ideas of groves of palms. I found the date trees so thinly scattered, as to be quite insignificant as a feature in the scene, and except when we came to a village, there were no other.

The wind being strong, we got on at first at a rapid rate, and as we carried a press of sail, the boat lay over completely, as to put the gunwale (as I believe it is called) in the water. We looked eagerly out, pleased when we saw some illustration of old customs with which the Bible had made us acquainted, or when the janissary, who was an intelligent person, pointed to a Bedouin on the banks. Miss E. flattered herself that she had caught sight of a crocodile, and as she described the huge jaws of some creature gaping out of the water, I thought that she was right, and envied her good fortune: however, afterwards, being assured that crocodiles never make their appearance below Cairo, I was convinced that, unaccustomed to see animals belonging to the Bovine group in a foreign element, she had taken the head of a buffalo emerging from the river, for one of the classic monsters of the flood. When weary of looking out, without seeing any thing but sky and water, and a few palm trees, I amused myself with reading Wordsworth, and thus the day passed away.

When evening came, we seated ourselves in front of the cabin, outside, to enjoy the sunset, and after our loss of rest on the preceding night, slept very comfortably. The next morning at noon, we had accomplished half the distance to Cairo, having some time passed every boat we saw upon the river. Arriving at a village, Mr. Waghorn's agent determined upon going on shore, and carrying the mails on the backs of donkeys, in order to ensure their arrival at Suez time enough to meet the steamer. He had been assured that we had passed the boat containing the Government mails in the night, but had not been able to ascertain the fact himself. I think it necessary to mention this, as a proof of the indefatigable endeavours made by Mr. Waghorn to ensure the speediest method of transit.

As the people had worked very hard, we directed Mohammed to purchase some meat for them in the bazaar, in order that they might indulge in a good meal; we also took the opportunity of purchasing a supply of eggs, fowls, and fruit, lest we should fall short before we reached Cairo. The fowls were so small, that, having our appetites sharpened by the fresh air of the river, we could easily manage one between us for breakfast, and another at dinner. We did not make trial of the unfiltered waters of the Nile, not drinking it until it had deposited its mud. Though previously informed that no beverage could be more delightful than that afforded by this queen of rivers in its unsophisticated state, I did not feel at all tempted to indulge; but am quite ready to do justice to its excellence when purified from the grosser element.

We were much pleased with the alacrity and good humour of our boatmen, and the untiring manner in which they performed their laborious duties. When a favouring breeze allowed them to rest, they seldom indulged in sleep, but, sitting round in a ring upon the narrow deck, either told stories, or were amused by the dancing of one of the group, who, without changing his place, contrived to shift his feet very vigorously to the music of his own voice, and that of two sticks struck together to keep the time. They frequently used their oars in parts of the river where they could not find a towing-path, and when rowing, invariably accompanied their labours with a song, which, though rude, was not unpleasant. The breeze, which had hitherto favoured us, dying away, the poor fellows were obliged to work harder than ever, dragging the boat up against the stream: upon these occasions, however, we enjoyed a very agreeable degree of quietude, and were, moreover, enabled to take a more accurate survey of the river's banks. Living objects were not numerous, excepting in the immediate vicinity of the villages. I was delighted when I caught sight of an ibis, but was surprised at the comparatively small number of birds; having been accustomed to the immense flocks which congregate on the banks of Indian rivers.

Our arrival at a village alone relieved the monotony of the landscape. Some of these places were prettily situated under groves of dates and wild fig trees, and they occasionally boasted houses of a decent description; the majority were, however, most wretched, and we were often surprized to see persons respectably dressed, and mounted upon good-looking donkeys, emerge from streets and lanes leading to the most squalid and poverty-stricken dwellings imaginable. The arrival of a boat caused all the beggars to hasten down to the river-side; these chiefly consisted of very old or blind persons. We had provided ourselves with paras, a small copper coin, for the purpose of giving alms to the miserable beings who solicited our charity, and the poor creatures always went away well satisfied with the trifling gift bestowed upon them.

Every morning, the janissary and the Arab captain of the boat came to the door of the cabin to pay their respects; with the latter we could not hold much communication, as he did not speak a word of English; we were, nevertheless, excellent friends. He was very good-humoured, and we were always laughing, so that a bond of union was established between us. He had once or twice come into such close contact with some of our crockery-ware, as to put me in a fright, and the comic look, with which he showed that he was aware of the mischief he had nearly done, amused me excessively. He was evidently a wag, and from the moment in which he discovered the congeniality of our feelings, when any droll incident occurred, he was sure to look at us and laugh.

The janissary spoke very tolerable English, and after sunset, when we seated ourselves outside the cabin-door, he came forward and entered into conversation. He told us that a quarrel having taken place between the boatmen of a small vessel and the people of a village, the former came on board in great numbers in the night, and murdered six of the boatmen; and that on the affair being represented to the Pasha, he sent three hundred soldiers to the village, and razed it to the ground. He said that he had been in the service of several English gentlemen, and had once an opportunity of going to England with a captain in the navy, but that his mother was alive at that time, and when he mentioned his wishes to her, she cried, and therefore he could not go. The captain had told him that he would always repent not having taken his offer; but though he wished to see England, he was glad he had not grieved his mother. He had been at Malta, but had taken a dislike to the Maltese, in consequence of a wrong he had received, as a stranger, upon his landing.

Amongst the noblemen and gentlemen whom he had served, he mentioned the Marquess of Waterford. We asked him what sort of a person he was, and he immediately replied, "A young devil." Mohammed, who had been in various services with English travellers, expressed a great desire to go to England; he said, that if he could once get there, he would "never return to this dirty country." Both he and the janissary apparently had formed magnificent ideas of the wealth of Great Britain, from the lavish manner in which the English are accustomed to part with their money while travelling.

We inquired of Mohammed concerning the magician, whose exploits Mr. Lane and other authors have recorded. At first, he did not understand what we meant;

but, upon further explanation, told us that he thought the whole an imposture. He said, that when a boy, about the age of the Arab captain's son, who was on board, he was in the service of a lady who wished to witness the exhibition, and who selected him as the medium of communication, because she said that she knew he would tell her the truth. The ceremonies, therefore, commenced; but though anxiously looking into the magic mirror, he declared that he saw nothing: afterwards, he continued, "A boy was called out of the bazaar, who saw all that the man told him." But while Mohammed expressed his entire disbelief in the power of this celebrated person, he was not devoid of the superstition of his creed and country, for he told us that he knew of another who really did wonderful things. He then asked us what we had called the Mughreebee whom we had described to him: we replied, a magician; and he and the janissary repeated the word over many times, in order to make themselves thoroughly acquainted with it. In all cases, they were delighted with the acquisition of a new word, and were very thankful to me when I corrected their pronunciation. Thus, when the janissary showed me what he called **kundergo**, growing in the fields, and explained that it made a blue dye, and I told him that we called it ***indigo***, he never rested until he had learned the word, which he repeated to Mohammed and Mohammed to him. I never met with two more intelligent men in their rank of life, or persons who would do greater credit to their teachers; and brief as has been my intercourse with the Egyptians, I feel persuaded, that a good method of imparting knowledge is all that is wanting to raise them in the scale of nations.

During our progress up the river, I had been schooling myself, and endeavouring to keep down my expectations, lest I should be disappointed at the sight of the Pyramids. We were told that we should see them at the distance of five-and-thirty miles; and when informed that they were in view, my heart beat audibly as I threw open the cabin door, and beheld them gleaming in the sun, pure and bright as the silvery clouds above them. Far from being disappointed, the vastness of their dimensions struck me at once, as they rose in lonely majesty on the bare plain, with nothing to detract from their grandeur, or to afford, by its littleness, a point of comparison. We were never tired of gazing upon these noble monuments of an age shrouded in impenetrable mystery. They were afterwards seen at less advantage, in consequence of the intervention of some rising ground; but from all points they created the strongest degree of interest.

We had a magnificent thunder-storm just as it was growing dark, and the red lightning lit up the pyramids, which came out, as it were, from the black masses of clouds behind them, while the broad waters of the Nile assumed a dark and troubled aspect. The scene was sublime, but of short duration; for the tempest speedily rolled off down the river; when, accompanied by a squall and heavy rain, it caught several boats, which were obliged to put into the shore. We did not experience the slightest inconvenience; and though the latter part of the voyage had been protracted from want of wind, arrived at the port of Boulak at half-past nine on the second evening of our embarkation.

CHAPTER V.
CAIRO.

Arrival at Boulak--Description of the place--Moolid, or Religious Fair--Surprise of the People--The Hotel at Cairo--Description of the City--The Citadel--View from thence--The City--The Shops--The Streets--The interior of the Pasha's Palace--Pictures--Furniture--Military Band--Affray between a Man and Woman--Indifference of the Police to Street Broils--Natives beaten by Englishmen--Visit to an English Antiquary--By-ways of the City--Interior of the Houses--Nubian Slave-market--Gypsies--Preparations for Departure to Suez--Mode of driving in the Streets of Cairo--Leave the City--The Changes in travelling in Egypt--Attractions of Cairo.

It was half-past nine o'clock, on the evening of the 4th of October, 1839, that we arrived at the port of Boulak. We expected to find some person in waiting to give us the pass-word, and thus enable us to get into Cairo, the gates of the city being closed at nine o'clock. Depending upon the attendance of the hotel-keeper at Cairo, who had been apprised of our approach, we had not put the janissary on shore, as we ought to have done, at the British Consul's country-house, who would have furnished us with a talisman to pass the gates. We sent Mohammed and the janissary on shore, to see what could be done. Including the voyage up the canal, Miss E. and myself had passed (we could not say slept) three nights on board a boat, the first without an attempt at repose, the two latter lying down in our dressing-gowns upon thin mattresses, stretched upon hard boards; we, therefore, could not very easily relinquish the endeavour to procure a bed during the time which would intervene between the period (an hour before day-light) in which the gates of the city would be open.

I had a letter to the British Consul, which I gave Mohammed, telling him to try the effect of bribery upon the guardians of the city. During his absence, the Arab captain, feeling that we were left under his protection, came and seated himself beside us, outside the cabin-door. We conversed together without understanding each other's language; he had nothing to offer us except snuff, of which we each took a pinch, giving him in return, as he refused wine, a pomegranate, to which I added a five-franc piece from the remains of my French money. If any thing had been wanting to establish a good understanding between us, this would have accomplished it. The rais, or captain, took my hand in his, and pressed his own to his lips, in token of gratitude; and when upon the return of Mohammed he perceived that I was rather nervous at the idea of crossing the plank from the boat to the shore, he plunged at once into the water to assist me over it. The janissary brought word that there was a moolid, or religious fair, held at the opposite end of the city, and that if we would make a circuit of three miles round the walls, we might enter Cairo that night, as the gate was left open for the convenience of the people in the neighbourhood. Mohammed had aroused a donkey-man of his acquaintance, who was in attendance, with a youth his son, and two donkeys. To the boy was entrusted the care of the lanthorn, without which no person is allowed to traverse the streets after nightfall, and mounting, we set forward.

The streets of Boulak are narrow, but the houses appear to be lofty and substantially built. We were challenged by the soldiers at the gates, but allowed to pass without farther inquiry. The ride round the walls at night was dreary enough, over broken ground, occupied by bandogs barking at us as we passed. We met occasionally groups of people coming from the fair, who gave us the welcome intelligence that the gates were still open, and, pushing on, we came at length to the entrance, an archway of some magnitude. Upon turning an angle of this wall, we suddenly emerged upon a very singular scene. The tomb of the saint, in whose honour the moolid was held, was surrounded by devotees, engaged in the performance of some religious rite. Around, and in front, throughout the neighbouring streets, gleamed a strong illumination, produced by an assemblage of lamps and lanthorns of various kinds. Some of the shops boasted handsome cut-glass chandeliers, or Argand lamps, evidently of European manufacture; others were content with a circular frame, perforated with holes, in which all sorts of glass vessels, wine-glasses, tumblers, mustard-pots, &c., were placed, filled with oil, and having several wicks.

The articles displayed for sale at the fair were, as far as we could judge from the hasty glances we cast as we passed along, good of their kind, and of some value; the confectioners' shops made a gay appearance with their variously-coloured sweetmeats, piled up in tempting heaps, and we saw enough of embroidery and gold to form a very favourable idea of the taste and splendour of the native dress.

We were, of course, objects of great surprise and curiosity; the sudden appearance of two European ladies, the only women present, at eleven o'clock at night, riding on donkeys through the fair, could not fail to create a sensation. Our boy with the lanthorn walked first, followed by the janissary, who, flourishing his silver stick, made room for us through the crowd. Had we not been accompanied by this respectable official, we should scarcely have dared to venture in such a place, and at such a period. Mohammed and the donkey-man attended at the side of Miss E. and myself, and though some of the people could not help laughing at the oddity of our appearance, we met with no sort of insult or hinderance, but made our way through without the slightest difficulty, much more easily, in fact, than two Arabs in their native costume, even if attended by a policeman, would have traversed a fair in England.

The scene was altogether very singular, and we thought ourselves fortunate in having had an opportunity of witnessing a native fair under such novel circumstances. We could scarcely believe that we were in a Mohammedan city, noted for its intolerance, and could not help feeling grateful to the reigning power which had produced so striking a change in the manners and conduct of the people. Upon leaving the fair, we turned into dark streets, dimly illumined by the light of the lanthorn we carried; occasionally, but very seldom, we met some grave personage, preceded also by a lanthorn, who looked with great astonishment at our party as we passed. At length we came to the door of our hotel, and having knocked loudly, we were admitted into the court-yard, when, dismounting, we proceeded up a flight of stone steps to a verandah, which led into some very good-sized apartments. The principal one, a large dining-room, was furnished at the upper end in the Egyptian fashion, with divans all round; it was, however, also well supplied with European chairs and tables, and in a few minutes cold turkey and ham, and other good things, appeared upon the board.

Being the first arrivals from the steamer, we had to answer numerous questions before we could retire to bed. Upon asking to be conducted to our chamber, we were shown up another flight of stone stairs, leading to a second and much larger verandah, which was screened off in departments serving as ante-chambers to the bed-rooms. There was sufficient space on the terraces of this floor, for the descent of a few steps led to another platform, to afford a walk of some extent, but of this we were not aware until the morning. We found a very comfortable two-bedded room, supplied with glass windows, and everything belonging to it in excellent repair, and apparently free from vermin; most thankfully did we lie down to enjoy the repose which our late exertions had rendered so needful.

Our trusty Mohammed had engaged donkeys for us the next day, and promised to take us to every place worth seeing in the city. We were strongly tempted to visit the Pyramids, but were deterred by the danger of losing the steamer at Suez, and by the difficulties of the undertaking. We were told that the Nile was not sufficiently flooded to admit of our approach in a boat, and that we should be up to the donkey's knees in mud if we attempted to go upon the backs of those animals. We, therefore, reluctantly relinquished the idea, and contented ourselves with what we could see of Cairo.

Our first visit was directed to the Citadel, a place which, I do not scruple to say, was to me quite as interesting as any of the monuments of ancient art that Egypt contains. The remains of ages long past, and whose history is involved in unfathomable obscurity, excite our wonder and admiration, and fill us with an almost painful curiosity to draw aside the veil which time has thrown around them, and to learn secrets that all the learning of man has hitherto been unable to unfold. The citadel of Cairo, on the contrary, has been the theatre of comparatively recent events; it is filled with recollections of the hero whose exploits, narrated by the most eloquent pens, have charmed us in our childhood, and still continue to excite interest in our breasts--the Sultan Saladin. Here are the remains of a palace which he once inhabited, and here is a well which bears his name. Who could sit under the broken pillars of that roofless palace, or drink the water from the deep recesses of that well, without allowing their thoughts to wander back to the days of the Crusades, those chivalric times, in which love, and war, and religion, swayed the hearts and the actions of men; when all that was honoured and coveted was to be found in a soldier of the cross, and when half-frantic enthusiasts, pursuing the vainest of hopes, the recovery of the Holy Land, brought away with them what they did not go to seek, the arts, and learning, and science of the East! The janissary, who was with us, pointed out the direction in which Damietta now stands, and I was instantly filled with a desire to see Damietta, of which I had heard and read so much.

The most exciting romance of Oriental history is to be found amid the deserts that surround Egypt; and even if the most spirit-stirring tale of all, the ***Talisman***, had not been written, the scenes in which our own lion-hearted Richard figured, and which witnessed the exploits of the Templars and the knights of St. John of Jerusalem, could not fail to create the highest degree of pleasurable feeling in minds capable of enjoying such brilliant reveries of the past. The Citadel of Cairo is also fraught with the recollections of an event which startled all Europe within the memory of many of the present generation--the massacre of the Mamelukes. We were shown the broken cleft in the wall from which the only one of the devoted men who escaped urged his gallant horse; it was, indeed, a fearful leap, and we gazed upon, the spot and thought of the carnage of that dreadful hour with an involuntary shudder.

The Citadel of Cairo has less the air of a regular fortification than any place of arms I ever recollect to have entered; it is, however, I believe, exceedingly strong by nature, the situation being very commanding. I regretted that I could not look upon these things with a professional eye, and that I had no military authority at hand to refer to. Near to the ruins of Saladin's palace, the Pasha is now constructing a mosque, which, when finished, will be one of the most splendid temples of the kind in all the Moslem land. It is to be lined and faced with marble, very elegantly carved, but it will take three years to complete it, and should any circumstances occur to delay the work during the lifetime of the present ruler of Egypt, the chances seem much in favour of its never being completed at all. Mounting on the embrasure of one of the guns, I feasted my eyes upon one of the finest and most interesting views I had ever beheld. The city, with its minarets, towers, kiosks, and stately palm-trees, lay at my feet, displaying, by its extent, the solidity, loftiness, and magnificence of its buildings, its title to the proud name of "Grand Cairo." Beyond, in one wide flood of silver, flowed the Nile, extending far as the eye could reach along a plain verdant with its fertilizing waters. To the left, the tombs of the caliphs spread themselves over a desert waste, looking, indeed, like a city of the dead. These monuments, though not equalling in size and grandeur the tombs which we find in India, are very striking; they are for the most part surmounted by cupolas, raised upon lofty pillars, with the spaces open between. Upon one of these buildings we were shown a vessel in the form of a boat, which upon a certain festival is filled with grain and water, for the service of the birds.

The Pyramids, which rise beyond the City of Tombs, are not seen to advantage from this point, an intervening ridge of sand cutting off the bases, and presenting the pinnacles only to view; but the whole of the landscape, under the clear bright atmosphere of an Egyptian sky, is of so exquisite a nature, that the eye can never tire of it, and had I been detained as a prisoner in the Pasha's dominions, I might have become reconciled to my fate, had I been confined in a situation which commanded this splendid prospect.

About the middle of the day we again sallied forth, the streets of Cairo being so narrow that the sun is completely shut out, and shade thus afforded at noon. The air was not unpleasantly warm, and we suffered no inconvenience, excepting from the crowd. Mounted upon donkeys, we pushed our way through a dense throng, thrusting aside loaded camels, which scarcely allowed us room to pass, and coming into the closest contact with all sorts of people. The perusal of Mr. Lane's book had given me a very vivid idea of the interior of the city, though I was scarcely prepared to mingle thus intimately with its busy multitude.

We had some shopping to execute, or rather we had to pay for some purchases made by Mohammed for us in the morning, and to return that portion of the goods sent for inspection that we did not intend to keep. We liked the appearance of the shops, which, in all cases of the more respectable kind, were well stocked, whole streets being devoted to the sale of one particular branch of merchandize. A long avenue was occupied by saddlers and the sellers of horse-furniture; another displayed nothing but woollen cloths; a third was devoted to weapons of every description, &c. &c. The wax-chandlers reminded me very much of those in England, being decorated in a similar manner, while the display of goods everywhere was much greater than I had ever seen in Eastern cities, in which for the most part merchandize of the best description is hidden in warehouses, and not to be found without deep research.

The greater number of the streets are covered in with matting in rather a dilapidated state, and having many holes and crevices for the admission of air; this gives to the whole a ragged appearance, and we were told that the Pasha had determined not to allow in future awnings of these frail and unsightly materials. The Frank quarter, which is much better contrived, is the model for subsequent erections. This avenue has a roof of wood sufficiently high to allow of a free circulation of air, and having apertures, at regular distances near the top, to admit the light. The streets in this part of Cairo are wider than usual, and the shops appear to be large and convenient.

All sorts of European manufactures are to be found here, for the most part at reasonable prices. The gentlemen who proposed to cross the desert purchased Leghorn hats of very good quality, and admirably adapted, from their size, lightness, and durability, for Indian wear. Wearied, at length, with the confusion and bustle of the streets, we took again the road to the Citadel, being exceedingly desirous to feast our eyes with the sunset view.

After gazing long and earnestly upon a scene which, once beheld, can never be forgotten, we gladly accepted the offer of Mohammed to show us into the interior of the Pasha's palace, a large irregular building, having no great pretensions to architectural beauty, and mingling rather oddly the European with the Oriental style. Ascending a broad flight of steps, we passed through a large kind of guard-room to the state-apartments. These were of rather a singular description, but handsome and well adapted to the climate. A third portion, consisting of the front and part of the two sides of each room, was entirely composed of windows, opening a few feet from the ground, and having a divan running round, furnished in the usual manner with pillows at the back. The windows of some of these apartments opened upon gardens, laid out in the English taste and full of English flowers; others commanded the finest prospects of the city and the open space below. Round these rooms, at the top, forming a sort of cornice, were pictures in compartments or panels, one series consisting of views of the Pasha's palaces and gardens, another of the vessels of war which belong to him, and more especially his favourite steam-boat, of which there are many delineations. There is nothing that more strongly exhibits the freedom with which Mehemet Ali has thrown off the prejudices of the Moslem religion, than his permitting, contrary to its established principles, the representation of objects natural and artificial, which, both in painting and sculpture, is strictly forbidden. Much cannot be said for the execution of these pictures, which seem to have been the work of a native artist; but they become exceedingly interesting as proofs of the decline of a religion so completely opposed to the spread of knowledge, and to all improvement in the moral condition of its followers.

The furniture in the Pasha's palace, though in a great measure limited to carpets and cushions, is very handsome. The divans are covered with rich brocade, figured satin, damask, or cut velvet. The attendants drew aside, with great pride, the curtains which concealed the looking-glasses, evidently fancying that we had never beheld mirrors of such magnitude in our lives. I observed that the chandeliers in some of the apartments did not match each other, but the whole was very creditable to the taste and spirit of the owner. Below them was a handsome apartment entirely lined with marble, and apparently designed as a retreat for the hot weather, the floor being divided into two parts--the one ascended by a step, in which the family might repose upon cushions; the other scooped into basins, with a fountain to play in the centre: the water either had not as yet been laid on, or the season did not render it necessary. Near to this apartment was the Pasha's bed-chamber, a fine room, also lined with marble, and containing a fire-place, which in the warm weather revolved upon a pivot, and was concealed in a recess made on purpose in the wall. The bathing-rooms, close at hand, were of the most beautiful description, the principal apartment and the antechamber having roofs which might serve as models for all erections of the kind. These were fretted in small compartments, light being admitted by a thick piece of ground-glass in the centre of each, thus securing the utmost privacy, together with one of the most beautiful methods of lighting possible.

While we were still sitting in the Pasha's palace, the military band of the garrison began to play upon the parade-ground immediately below. Mohammed, who seemed to be quite at home, conducted us to an apartment which overlooked this space, opened one of the windows, and requested us to seat ourselves upon the cushions, where we remained for some time, listening to the well-known French airs played in the court-yard of the palace of a Turkish prince! The band was not a very large one, but the performers had been well-taught, and the wind-instruments produced in such a situation a very animating effect. They marched up and down the parade-ground, occasionally relieved by the drums and fifes also playing French music. The performers were clothed in white, like the men belonging to the ranks, and had the same soiled appearance, it being impossible to keep white garments pure in the dust of Egyptian cities.

The sun was now completely down, and we returned to our hotel, where, to our great joy, we found our two female friends, who had not been able to reach Boulak until many hours after our landing. We had ordered dinner at seven o'clock, in the hope that our fellow-passengers in the steamer would come up, and according to our calculations, several dropped in. The possibility of getting to the Pyramids was again discussed; the greater number of the gentlemen determined at least to try, but we thought it best to avoid all danger of missing the **Berenice**, and the ladies, adhering to their original intention, determined to cross the desert together. We passed a most agreeable evening, telling over our voyage up the Nile, and upon retiring to my chamber, I regretted that it would be the last I should for some time spend in Cairo.

Nothing can be more quiet than the nights in a city where all the inhabitants retire after dark to their own homes, the streets being perambulated by few persons, and those of the soberest description; but with the sun, a scene of bustle and noise ensues, which effectually prevents repose. The windows of my apartment looked out upon a narrow street, in which the ground-floors were, as it is usual, composed of shops, while several persons, having vegetables or grain to sell, were seated upon the ground. The hum of human voices, the grunting of the camels, and the braying of donkeys, kept up an incessant din, and therefore some minutes elapsed before my attention was attracted by a wordy war which took place beneath my window. Hastily arraying myself in my dressing-gown, and looking out, I saw a man and woman engaged in some vehement discussion, but whether caused by a dispute or not, I could not at first decide. They both belonged to the lower class, and the woman was meanly dressed in a blue garment, with a hood of the same over her head, her face being concealed by one of those hideous narrow black veils, fastened across under the eyes, which always reminded me of the proboscis of an elephant. Her hands were clasped upon the arms of the man just above the elbow, who held her in the same manner, and several people were endeavouring to part them, as they struggled much in the same manner which prevails in a melodrame, when the hero and heroine are about to be separated by main force. I thought it, therefore, probable that they were a loving couple, about to be torn asunder by the myrmidons of the law. Presently, however, I was set right upon this point, for the man, seizing a kind of whip, which is generally carried in Cairo, and flogging off his friends, dashed the poor creature on the ground, and inflicted several severe strokes upon her prostrate body, not one of the by-standers attempting to prevent him. The woman, screaming fearfully, jumped up, and seizing him again, as if determined to gain her point, whatever it might be, poured forth a volley of words, and again the man threw her upon the ground and beat her most cruelly, the spectators remaining, as before, quite passive, and allowing him to wreak his full vengeance upon her.

Had I been dressed, or could I have made my way readily into the street, I should have certainly gone down to interpose, for never did I witness any scene so horrible, or one I so earnestly desired to put an end to. At length, though the pertinacity of the woman was astonishing, when exhausted by blows, she lay fainting on the ground, the man went his way. The spectators, and there were many, who looked on without any attempt to rescue this poor creature from her savage assailant, now raised her from the earth. The whole of this time, the veil she wore was never for a moment displaced, and but for the brutal nature of the scene, it would have been eminently ridiculous in the eyes of a stranger. After crying and moaning for some time, in the arms of her supporters, the woman, whom I now found to be a vender of vegetables in the street, told her sad tale to all the passers-by of her acquaintance, with many tears and much gesticulation, but at length seated herself quietly down by her baskets, though every bone in her body must have ached from the severe beating she had received. This appeared to me to be a scene for the interference of the police, who, however, do not appear to trouble themselves about the protection of people who may be assaulted in the street.

I afterwards saw a drunken Englishman, an officer of the Indian army, I am sorry to say, beat several natives of Cairo, with whom he happened to come in contact in the crowd, in the most brutal and unprovoked manner, and yet no notice was taken, and no complaint made. It was certainly something very unexpected to me to see a Frank Christian maltreating the Moslem inhabitants of a Moslem city in which he was a stranger, and I regretted exceedingly that the perpetrator of acts, which brought disgrace upon his character and country, should have been an Englishman, or should have escaped punishment. No sooner have we been permitted to traverse a country in which formerly it was dangerous to appear openly as a Christian, than we abuse the privilege thus granted by outrages on its most peaceable inhabitants. I regret to be obliged to add, that it is but too commonly the habit, of Englishmen to beat the boat-men, donkey-men, and others of the poorer class, whom they may engage in their service. They justify this cowardly practice--cowardly, because the poor creatures can gain no redress--by declaring that there is no possibility of getting them to stir excepting by means of the whip; but, in most cases, all that I witnessed, they were not at the trouble of trying fairer methods: at once enforcing their commands by blows. The comments made by the janissary and our own servant upon those who were guilty of such wanton brutality showed the feeling which it elicited; and when upon one occasion Miss E. and myself interposed, declaring that we would not allow any person in our service to be beaten, they told us not to be alarmed, for that the rais (captain of the boat), who was an Arab, would not put up with ill-treatment, but had threatened to go on shore at the next village with all his men.

An English gentleman, long resident in Cairo, had done me the honour to call upon me on the day after my arrival, and had invited me to come to his house, to see some mummies and other curiosities he had collected. Accompanied by two of my female friends, and escorted by a gentleman who was well acquainted with the topography of the city, we set out on foot, traversing blind alleys and dark lanes, and thus obtaining a better idea of the intricacies of the place than we could possibly have gained by any other means. Sometimes we passed under covered ways perfectly dark, which I trod, not without fear of arousing some noxious animal; then we came to narrow avenues, between the backs of high stone houses, occasionally emerging into small quadrangles, having a single tree in one corner. We passed a house inhabited by one of the superior description of Frank residents, and we knew that it must be tenanted by a European by the handsome curtains and other furniture displayed through its open windows. Turning into a street, for the very narrow lanes led chiefly along the backs of houses, we looked into the lower apartments, the doors of which were usually unclosed, and here we saw the men at their ordinary occupations, and were made acquainted with their domestic arrangements. At length we arrived at a court, which displayed a door and a flight of steps at the corner. Upon knocking, we were admitted by an Egyptian servant, who showed us up stairs into a room, where we found the master of the house seated upon one of the low stools which serve as the support of the dinner-trays in Egypt, the only other furniture that the room contained being a table, and the customary divan, which extended all round. Coffee was brought in, served in small China cups; but all the coffee made in Egypt was too like the Nile mud for me to taste, and warm and fatigued with a walk through places from which the fresh air was excluded, I felt myself unequal to make the trial now.

Our friend's collection of antiquities appeared to be very valuable; but I had been at the opening of a mummy-case before, and though interested by the different articles which his researches had brought to light, was more so in the examination of his house. It was very oddly arranged, according to the ideas formed in Europe, many of the rooms looking like lanthorns, in consequence of their having windows on the stairs and passages, as well as to the street. This was probably caused by a desire to secure a free circulation of air, but it at the same time destroyed every idea of privacy, and therefore looked exceedingly uncomfortable. There were glass-windows to several of the apartments, but the house exhibited considerable quantities of that wooden trellice-work, represented in Mr. Lane's book. Nothing, indeed, can be more accurate than his descriptions; the English inhabitants of Cairo say that, reading it upon the spot, they cannot detect a single error; the designs are equally faithful, and those who study the work carefully may acquire the most correct notion of the city and its inhabitants.

The apartments at the top of the house opened, as usual, upon a rather extensive terrace or court, but the surrounding wall was too high to admit of any prospect; both here, and in a similar place at our hotel, persons walking about could neither see their neighbours nor be seen by them. We, therefore, gained nothing by climbing so high, and I was disappointed at not obtaining any view of the city. I tried in each place to make acquaintance with an Egyptian cat, but I found the animal too shy. I noticed several, which seemed to be domestic pets; they were fine-looking creatures of the kind, and I fancied larger than the common English cat, but the difference, if existing at all, was very slight. I returned home, so much fatigued with my walk, as to be unable to go out again, especially as we were to start at four o'clock for the desert.

Two of the ladies of the party, not having completed their purchases at the bazaars, went out upon a shopping excursion, and passing near the Nubian slave-market, were induced to enter. Christians are not admitted to the place in which Circassian women are sold, and can only obtain entrance by assuming the Turkish dress and character. My friends were highly interested in one woman, who sat apart from the rest, apparently plunged into the deepest melancholy; the others manifested little sorrow at their condition, which was not, perhaps, in reality, changed for the worse: all eagerly scrambled for some pieces of money which the visitors threw amongst them, and the sight was altogether too painful for Christian ladies to desire to contemplate long.

They were much more amused by some gipsies, who were anxious to show their skill in the occult science. Upon the morning after our arrival, Miss E., who was always the first upon the alert, accepted the escort of a gentleman, who conducted her to a neighbouring shop; while making some purchases, a gipsy came and seated herself opposite, and by way of showing her skill, remarked that the lady was a stranger to Cairo, and had a companion, also of her own sex, who pretended to be a friend, but who would prove treacherous.

As we had ridden through the fair together on the preceding evening, it did not require any great effort of art to discover that two Frank ladies had arrived at Cairo; but in speaking of treachery, the gipsy evidently wished to pique the curiosity of my friend, and tempt her to make further inquiry. Much to my regret, she did not take any notice of the fortune-teller, whose words had been repeated by the gentleman who had accompanied her, and who was well acquainted with the language in which they were spoken. I should like to have had a specimen of the talents of a modern scion of this race, in the country in which the learned have decided that the tribe, now spread over the greater part of the world, originated.

The arrival of the **Berenice** at Suez had been reported the evening before, and the mails had been brought to Cairo in the coarse of the night. All was, therefore, bustle and confusion in our hotel; gentlemen hourly arriving from the Nile, where they had been delayed by squalls and contrary winds, or snatching a hasty meal before they posted off to the Pyramids. Our camels and donkeys had been laden and despatched to the outskirts of the city, to which we were to be conveyed in a carriage.

I had observed in the court-yard of the hotel an English-built equipage, of the britschka fashion, with a dark-coloured hood, for, whatever might have been its original tint, it had assumed the common hue of Egypt; and I found that two spirited horses were to be harnessed to the vehicle, which was dragged out into the street for our accommodation. A gentleman volunteered his services as coachman, promising that he would drive carefully, and we accordingly got in, a party of four, taking the baby along with us. Although the horses kicked and plunged a little, I did not fancy that we could be in any danger, as it was impossible for them to run away with us through streets so narrow as scarcely to be passable, neither could we have very easily been upset. I, therefore, hoped to have enjoyed the drive amazingly, as it promised to afford me a better opportunity than I had hitherto possessed of seeing Cairo, seated at my ease, instead of pushing and jostling through the crowd either on foot or upon a donkey. The gentleman, however, bent upon showing off, would not listen to our entreaties that the grooms should lead the horses, but dashed along, regardless of the danger to the foot-passengers, or the damage that the donkeys might sustain.

So long as we proceeded slowly, the drive was very agreeable, since it enabled me to observe the effect produced by our party upon the spectators. Many sat with the utmost gravity in their shops, scarcely deigning to cast their eyes upon what must certainly have been a novel sight; others manifested much more curiosity, and seemed to be infinitely amused, while heads put out of the upper windows showed that we attracted some attention. My enjoyment was destined to be very brief, for in a short time our coachman, heedless of the mischief that might ensue, drove rapidly forward, upsetting and damaging every thing that came in his way. In vain did we scream and implore; he declared that it was the fault of the people, who would not remove themselves out of danger; but as we had no ***avant-courrier*** to clear the road before us, and our carriage came very suddenly upon many persons, I do not see how they could have managed to escape. At length, we drove over an unfortunate donkey, which was pulled down by a piece of iron sticking from the carriage, and thus becoming entangled in the load he bore. I fear that the animal was injured, for the poor boy who drove him cried bitterly, and though we (that is, the ladies of the party) would gladly have remunerated him for the damage he might have sustained, neither time nor opportunity was permitted for this act of justice. On we drove, every moment expecting to be flung out against the walls, as the carriage turned round the corners of streets placed at right angles to each other. At length, we succeeded in our wish to have the grooms at the horses' heads, and without further accident, though rendered as nervous as possible, passed through the gate of the city. We drove forward now without any obstacle through the Necropolis, or City of Tombs, before-mentioned, and I regretted much that we had not left Cairo at an earlier hour, which would have permitted us to examine the interiors.

The desert comes up to the very walls of Cairo, and these tombs rise from a plain of bare sand. I observed some gardens and cultivated places stretching out into the wilderness, no intermediate state occurring between the garden and the arid waste in which vegetation suddenly ceased. We might have performed the whole journey across the desert in the carriage which had brought us thus far, but as one of the ladies was a little nervous, and moreover thought the road too rough, I readily agreed to choose another mode of conveyance; in fact, I wished particularly to proceed leisurely to Suez, and in the manner in which travellers had hitherto been conveyed.

The mighty changes which are now effecting in Egypt, should nothing occur to check their progress, will soon render the track to India so completely beaten, and so deeply worn by wheels, that I felt anxious to take advantage of the opportunity now offered to traverse the desert in a more primitive way. I disliked the idea of hurrying through a scene replete with so many interesting recollections. I had commenced reading the ***Arabian Nights' Entertainment*** at the age of five years; since which period, I had read them over and over again at every opportunity, finishing with the last published number of the translation by Mr. Lane. This study had given me a strong taste for every thing relating to the East, and Arabia especially. I trust that I am not less familiar with the writings of the Old and New Testament, and consequently it may easily be imagined that I should not find three days in the desert tedious, and that I felt anxious to enjoy to the uttermost the reveries which it could not fail to suggest.

In parting with our friend and the carriage, he declared that he would indemnify himself for the constraint we had placed upon him, by driving over two or three people at least. Fortunately, his desire of showing off was displayed too soon; we heard, and rejoiced at the tidings, that he upset the carriage before he got to the gate of Cairo. Two or three lives are lost, it is said, whenever the Pasha, who drives furiously, traverses the city in a European equipage. That he should not trouble himself about so mean a thing as the life or limb of a subject, may not be wonderful; but that he should permit Frank strangers to endanger both, seems unaccountable.

No Anglo-Indian resident in either of the three presidencies thinks of driving a wheel-carriage through streets never intended for such conveyances. In visiting Benares, Patna, or any other of the celebrated native cities of India, elephants, horses, palanquins, or some other vehicle adapted for the occasion, are chosen. It, therefore, appears to be the more extraordinary that English people, who are certainly living upon sufferance in Egypt, should thus recklessly expose the inhabitants to danger, to which they are not subjected by any of their own people under the rank of princes. Nothing can be more agreeable or safe than a drive across the desert, and probably the time is speedily approaching in which the rich inhabitants of Cairo will indulge, as they do at Alexandria, in the luxury of English carriages, and for this purpose, the streets and open spaces best adapted for driving will be improved and widened.

I cannot take leave of Cairo without paying the tribute due to the manner in which the streets are kept. In passing along the narrow lanes and avenues before-mentioned, not one of the senses was shocked; dust, of course, there is every where, but nothing worse to be seen at least; and the sight and smell were not offended, as at Paris or even in London, when passing through the by-ways of either. Altogether, if I may venture to pronounce an opinion, after so short a residence, I should say that, if our peaceful relations with Egypt should continue to be kept up, in no place will travellers be better received or entertained than in Cairo.

CHAPTER VI.
THE DESERT.

Equipage for crossing the Desert--Donkey-chairs--Sense of calmness and tranquillity on entering the Desert--Nothing dismal in its aspect--The Travellers' Bungalow--Inconvenient construction of these buildings--Kafila of the Governor of Jiddah and his Lady--Their Equipage--Bedouins--Impositions practised on Travellers--Desert Travelling not disagreeable--Report of the sailing of the Steamer--Frequency of false reports--Ease with which an infant of the party bore the journey--A wheeled carriage crossing the Desert--Parties of Passengers from Suez encountered--One of Mr. Hill's tilted Caravans--Difficulty of procuring water at the Travellers' Bungalow--A night in the Desert--Magnificent sunrise--First sight of the Red Sea and the Town of Suez--Miserable appearance of the latter--Engagement of a Passage to Bombay.

We found the equipages in which we were to cross the desert waiting for us at the City of Tombs. They consisted of donkey-chairs, one being provided for each of the females of the party, while my friend Miss E. had also an extra donkey, with a saddle, to ride upon occasionally. Nothing could be more comfortable than these vehicles; a common armchair was fastened into a sort of wooden tray, which projected in front about a foot, thereby enabling the passenger to carry a small basket or other package; the chairs were then slung by the arms to long bamboos, one upon either side, and these, by means of ropes or straps placed across, were fastened upon the backs of donkeys, one in front, the other, behind. Five long and narrow vehicles of this kind, running across the desert, made a sufficiently droll and singular appearance, and we did nothing but admire each other as we went along. The movement was delightfully easy, and the donkeys, though not travelling at a quick pace, got on very well. Our cavalcade consisted besides of two stout donkeys, which carried the beds and carpet-bags of the whole party, thus enabling us to send the camels a-head: the three men-servants were also mounted upon donkeys, and there were three or four spare ones, in case any of the others should knock up upon the road. In this particular it is proper to say that we were cheated, for had such an accident occurred, the extra-animals were so weak and inefficient, that they could not have supplied the places of any of those in use. There were eight or ten donkey-men, and a boy; the latter generally contrived to ride, but the others walked by the side of the equipages.

In first striking into the desert, we all enjoyed a most delightful feeling of repose; every thing around appeared to be so calm and tranquil, that, especially after encountering the noises and multitudes of a large and crowded city, it was soothing to the mind thus to emerge from the haunts of men and wander through the vast solitudes that spread their wastes before us. To me there was nothing dismal in the aspect of the desert, nor was the view so boundless as I had expected.

In these wide plains, the fall of a few inches is sufficient to diversify the prospect; there is always some gentle acclivity to be surmounted, which cheats the sense with the expectation of finding a novel scene beyond: the sand-hills in the distance also range themselves in wild and fantastic forms, many appearing like promontories jutting out into some noble harbour, to which the traveller seems to be approaching. Nor were there wanting living objects to animate the scene; our own little kafila was sufficiently large and cheerful to banish every idea of dreariness, and we encountered others much more picturesque.

Soon after losing sight of the tombs, we came upon a party who had bivouac'd for the night; the camels, unladen, were, with their burthens, placed in a circle, and the people busily employed in preparing their evening meal. Other evidences there were, however, to show that the toils of the desert were but too frequently fatal to the wretched beasts of burthen employed in traversing these barren wastes; the whitened bones of camels and donkeys occurred so frequently, as to serve to indicate the road.

Our first stage was the shortest of the whole, and we came to the rest-house, or travellers' bungalow, just as night closed in, and long before I entertained any idea that we should have been able to reach it, travelling as we did at an easy walk. The bungalow was not yet completed, which we found rather an advantage, since it seems to be exceedingly questionable whether the buildings erected for the accommodation of travellers on the track to Suez will be habitable even for a few hours in the course of another year. The funds of the Steam-committee have been lamentably mismanaged in this instance. However, there being no windows, we were enabled to enjoy the fresh air, and the room we occupied, not having been long whitewashed, was perfectly clean.

Nothing can have been worse planned than the construction of these houses. The only entrance is in front, down a narrow passage, open at the top, and having apartments on either side, the two in front being sleeping-rooms for travellers, with a kitchen and other offices beyond, and at the back of all a stable, which occupies the whole width of the building. The consequence is, that all the animals, biped and quadruped, inhabiting the stable, must pass the traveller's door, who is regaled with the smell proceeding from the said stable, cook-rooms, &c.; all the insects they collect, and all the feathers from the fowls slaughtered upon the spot; the plan being, when parties arrive, to drive the unhappy creatures into the house, kill and pluck them immediately.

The persons in care of these bungalows are usually a mongrel sort of Franks, who have no idea of cleanliness, and are regardless of the most unsavoury odours. The furniture of the rooms consisted of a deal table and a moveable divan of wicker-work, while another, formed of the same solid materials as the house, spread in the Egyptian fashion along one side. Upon this Miss E. and myself laid our beds; our two other lady friends, with the infant and female attendant, occupying the opposite apartment. We concluded the evening with tea and supper, for which we were amply provided, having cold fowls, cold ham, hard-boiled eggs, and bread and fruit in abundance. Wrapped up in our dressing-gowns, we passed a very comfortable night, and in the morning were able to procure the luxury of warm water for washing with.

Having discovered that the people of the hotel at Cairo had forgotten to put up some of the articles which we had ordered, and being afraid that our supplies might fail, we had sent Mohammed back for them. He did not rejoin us until eight o'clock the following morning, just as we had begun to grow uneasy about him; it appeared that, although apparently well acquainted with the desert, having crossed it many times, he had missed the track, and lost his way, and after wandering about all night, was glad to meet with a man, whom he engaged as a guide. The poor fellow was much exhausted, but had not omitted to bring us a bottle of fresh milk for our breakfast. We desired him to get some tea for himself, and he soon recovered; his spirits never forsaking him.

In consequence of these delays, it was rather late, past nine o'clock, before we set forward. I had provided myself with a pair of crape spectacles and a double veil, but I speedily discarded both; the crape fretted my eye-lashes, and would have produced a greater degree of irritation than the sand. A much better kind are those of wire, which tie round the head with a ribbon, and take in the whole eye. Though the sun was rather warm, its heat was tempered by a fresh cold air, which blew across the desert, though not strongly enough to lift the sand; we, therefore, travelled with much less inconvenience than is sustained upon a turnpike-road in England in dusty weather. I could not endure to mar the prospect by looking at it through a veil, and found my parasol quite sufficient protection against the rays of the sun.

The kafila, which we had passed the preceding evening, overtook us soon after we started. It consisted of a long train of camels, and belonged to the native governor of Jiddah, who was proceeding to that place with, his wife and family, a native vessel being in waiting at Suez to take him down the Red Sea. We saw several females wrapped closely from head to foot in long blue garments, mounted upon these camels. The governor's wife travelled in a sort of cage, which I recognised immediately, from the description in Anastatius. This vehicle is formed of two rude kinds of sophas, or what in English country phrase would be called settles, canopied overhead, and with a resting place for the feet. They are sometimes separated, and slung on either side of a camel; at other times joined together, and placed on the top, with a curtain or cloth lining, to protect the inmates from the sun, and secure the privacy so necessary for a Mohammedan lady. The height of the camels with their lading, and this cage on the summit of all, give an extraordinary and almost supernatural appearance to the animal as he plods along, his head nodding, and his whole body moving in a strange ungainly manner.

Occasionally we saw a small party of Bedouins, easily distinguished by the fierce countenances glaring from beneath the large rolls of cloth twisted over their turbans, and round their throats, leaving nothing besides flashing eyes, a strongly developed nose, and a bushy beard, to be seen. One or two, superior to the rest, were handsomely dressed, armed to the teeth, and rode camels well-groomed and richly caparisoned; wild-looking warriors, whom it would not have been agreeable to meet were the country in a less tranquil state.

To the present ruler of Egypt we certainly owe the security now enjoyed in passing the desert; a party of ladies, having only three servants and a few donkey-drivers, required no other protection, though our beds, dressing-cases, and carpet-bags, to say nothing of the camels laden with trunks and portmanteaus a-head, must have been rather tempting to robbers by profession. The Pasha is the only person who has hitherto been able to oblige the Sheikhs to respect the property of those travellers not strong enough to protect themselves from outrage. It is said that occasionally these Bedouins, when desirous of obtaining water, make no scruple of helping themselves to the supplies at the bungalows; the will, therefore, is not wanting to commit more serious depredations. Consequently, in maintaining a good understanding with Egypt, we must likewise endeavour to render its sovereign strong enough to keep the neighbouring tribes in awe.

Having made a slight refection on the road, of hard-boiled eggs, bread, grapes, and apples, we came up at mid-day to a rest-house, where it was determined we should remain for an hour or two, to water the donkeys, and afford them needful repose, while we enjoyed a more substantial luncheon. Our companions were so well satisfied with the management of Mohammed, who conducted the whole line of march, that they sent their Egyptian servant forward to order our dinner at the resting-place for the night. We found, however, that advantage had been taken of Mohammed's absence the preceding evening, and of the hurry of the morning's departure, to send back some of the animals we had engaged and paid for, and to substitute others so weak as to be perfectly useless. We were likewise cheated with regard to the water; we were told that the camel bearing the skins, for which we had paid at Cairo, had been taken by mistake by two gentlemen travelling in advance, and as we could not allow the poor animals to suffer, we of course purchased water for them. This was no doubt an imposition, but one for which, under the circumstances, we had no remedy.

Upon reaching the bungalow, we again came up with the kafila that we had seen twice before; the wife of the governor of Jiddah, with her women, vacated the apartment into which we were shown, when we arrived; but her husband sent a message, requesting that we would permit her to occupy another, which was empty. We were but too happy to comply, and should have been glad to have obtained a personal interview; but having no interpreter excepting Mohammed, who would not have been admitted to the conference, we did not like to make the attempt. From the glance which we obtained of the lady, she seemed to be very diminutive; nothing beyond height and size could be distinguishable under the blue envelope she wore, in common with her women: some of the latter occasionally unveiled their faces, which were certainly not very attractive; but others, probably those who were younger and handsomer, kept their features closely shrouded.

Again betaking ourselves to our conveyances, we launched forth into the desert, enjoying it as much the second day as we had done the first. I entertained a hope of seeing some of the beautiful gazelles, for which Arabia is famous; but not one appeared. A pair of birds occasionally skimmed over the desert, at a short distance from its surface; but those were the only specimens of wild animals we encountered. The skeletons of camels occurred as frequently as before; many nearly entire, others with their bones scattered abroad, but whether borne by the winds, or by some savage beast, we could not learn. Neither could we discover whether the deaths of these poor animals had been recent or not; for so short a time only is required in Eastern countries for the insects to anatomize any animal that may fall in their way, that even supposing that jackalls and hyaenas should not be attracted to the spot, the ants would make quick work even of so large a creature as a camel.

There were hills in the back ground, which might probably shelter vultures, kites, and the family of quadrupeds that feed upon offal, and much did I desire to mount a high trotting camel, and take a scamper amongst these hills--obliged to content myself with jogging soberly on with my party, I was fain to find amusement in the contemplation of a cavalcade, the like of which will probably not be often seen again. Our five vehicles sometimes trotted abreast, affording us an opportunity of conversing with each other; but more frequently they would spread themselves all over the plain, the guides allowing their beasts to take their own way, provided they moved straight forward. Occasionally, a spare donkey, or one carrying the baggage, would stray off in an oblique direction, and then the drivers were compelled to make a wide detour to bring them in again. Once or twice, the ropes slipped, and my chair came to the ground; fortunately, it had not to fall far; or a donkey would stumble and fall, but no serious accident occurred; and though one of the party, being behind, and unable to procure assistance in righting the carriage, was obliged to walk a mile or two, we were all speedily in proper trim again. Towards evening, the easy motion of the chair, and the inclination I felt to close my eyes, after staring about all day, caused me to fall asleep; and again, much sooner than I had expected, I found myself at the place of our destination.

Either owing to a want of funds, or to some misunderstanding, the bungalow at this place, which is considered to be nearly midway across the desert, had only been raised a few inches from the ground; there were tents, however, for the accommodation of travellers, which we infinitely preferred. The one we occupied was of sufficient size to admit the whole party--that is, the four ladies, the baby, and its female attendant. There were divans on either side, to spread the beds upon, and the openings at each end made the whole delightfully cool.

We found Ali, the servant sent on in the morning, very busy superintending the cookery for dinner, which was performed in the open air. The share of bread and apples given to me upon the road I now bestowed upon my donkeys, not having reflected at the time that the drivers would be glad of it; so the next day, when the usual distributions were made, I gave the grapes, &c. to the donkey-men, who stuffed them into their usual repository, the bosoms of their blue shirts, and seemed very well pleased to get them.

The adjoining tent was occupied by two gentlemen, passengers of the ***Berenice***; their servant, a European, brought to some of our people the alarming intelligence that the steamers would leave Suez in the course of a few hours, and that our utmost speed would scarcely permit us to arrive in time. Distrusting this information, we sent to inquire into its truth, and learned that no danger of the kind was to be apprehended, as the steamer required repair, the engines being out of order, and the coal having ignited twice on the voyage up the Red Sea.

Whatever may be the cause, whether from sheer misconception or an intention to mislead, it is almost impossible to rely upon any intelligence given concerning the sailing of vessels and other events, about which it would appear very possible to obtain authentic information. From the time of our landing at Alexandria, we had been tormented by reports which, if true, rendered it more than probable that we should be too late for the steamer appointed to convey the Government mails to Bombay. Not one of these reports turned out to be correct, and those who acted upon them sustained much discomfort in hurrying across the desert.

We were, as usual, rather late the following morning; our dear little play-thing, the baby, bore the journey wonderfully; but it seemed very requisite that she should have good and unbroken sleep at night, and we found so little inconvenience in travelling in the day-time, that we could make no objection to an arrangement which contributed so much to her health and comfort. It was delightful to see this lovely little creature actually appearing to enjoy the scene as much as ourselves; sometimes seated in the lap of her nurse, who travelled in a chair, at others at the bottom of one of our chairs; then in the arms of her male attendant, who rode a donkey, or in those of the donkey-men, trudging on foot; she went to every body, crowing and laughing all the time; and I mention her often, not only for the delight she afforded us, but also to show how very easily infants at her tender age--she was not more than seven months old--could be transported across the desert.

After breakfast, and just as we were about to start upon our day's journey, we saw what must certainly be called a strange sight--a wheeled carriage approaching our small encampment. It came along like the wind, and proved to be a phaeton, double-bodied, that is, with a driving-seat in front, with a European charioteer guiding a pair of horses as the wheelers, while the leaders were camels, with an Arab riding postillion. An English and a Parsee gentleman were inside, and the carriage was scarcely in sight, before it had stopped in the midst of us. The party had only been a few hours coming across. We hastily exchanged intelligence; were told that the ***Berenice*** had lost all its speed, being reduced, in consequence of alterations made in the dock-yard in Bombay, from twelve knots an hour to eight, and that the engines had never worked well during the voyage up.

During this day's journey, we met several parties, passengers of the steamer, coming from Suez. One lady passed us in a donkey-chair, with her daughter riding a donkey by the side; another group, consisting of two ladies and several gentlemen, were all mounted upon camels, and having large umbrellas over their heads, made an exceedingly odd appearance, the peculiar gait of the camel causing them to rise and fall in a very singular manner. At a distance, their round moving summits looked like the umbrageous tops of trees, and we might fancy as they approached, the lower portion being hidden by ridges of sand, that "Birnam Wood was coming to Dunsinane."

The monotony usually complained of in desert travelling cannot be very strongly felt between Cairo and Suez, for though there is little else but sand to be seen, yet it is so much broken and undulated, that there is always some diversity of objects. The sand-hills now gave place to rock, and it appeared as if many ranges of hills stretched out both to the right and left of the plains we traversed; their crags and peaks, piled one upon the other, and showing various colours, rich browns and purples, as they stood in shade or sunshine. Greenish tints assured us that vegetation was not quite so seamy upon these hills as in the desert they skirted, which only showed at intervals a few coarse plants, scarcely deserving the name. It has been said, that there is only one tree between Cairo and Suez; but we certainly saw several, though none of any size; that which is called, *par excellence*, "the tree," affording a very poor idea of timber.

We made a short rest, in the middle of the day, at a travellers' bungalow; and just as we were leaving it, one of Mr. Hill's caravans arrived--a tilted cart upon springs, and drawn by a pair of horses; it contained a family, passengers by the **Berenice,** consisting of a gentleman and his wife, two children and a servant. We conversed with them for a few minutes, and learned that they had not found the road very rough, and that where it was heavy they added a camel as a leader.

At this place we found some difficulty in purchasing, water for the donkeys; competition in the desert is not, as in other places, beneficial to the traveller. By some understanding with the Steam Committee, Mr. Hill has put his people into the bungalows; and they, it appears, have orders not to sell water to persons who travel under Mr. Waghorn's agency. If the original purpose of these houses was to afford general accommodation, the shelter which cannot be refused is rendered nugatory by withholding the supplies necessary for the subsistence of men and cattle. We procured water at last; but every thing attainable at these places is dear and bad.

We arrived, at rather an early hour, at our halting place for the night; and as we considered it to be desirable to get into Suez as speedily as possible, we agreed to start by three o'clock on the following morning. Just as we had finished our evening meal, three gentlemen of our acquaintance, who had scrambled across the desert from the Pyramids, came up, weary and wayworn, and as hungry as possible. We put the best that we had before them, and then retired to the opposite apartment. But in this place I found it impossible to stay; there was no free circulation of air throughout the room, and it had all the benefit of the smell from the stable and other abominations.

Leaving, therefore, my companions asleep, and wrapping myself up in my shawl, I stole out into the passage, where there were several Arabs lying about, and not without difficulty contrived to step between them, and to unfasten the door which opened upon the desert. There was no moon, but the stars gave sufficient light to render the scene distinctly visible. A lamp gleamed from the window of the apartment which I had quitted, and the camels, donkeys, and people belonging to the united parties, formed themselves into very picturesque groups upon the sand, constituting altogether a picture which could not fail to excite many agreeable sensations. The whitened bones of animals perishing from fatigue and thirst, while attempting to cross the arid expanse, associated in our minds with privation, toil, and danger, told too truly that these notions were not purely ideal; but here was a scene of rest and repose which the desert had never before presented; and mean and inconvenient as the building I contemplated might be, its very existence in such a place seemed almost a marvel, and the imagination, kindling at the sight, could scarcely set bounds to its expectations for the future. In the present frame of my mind, however, I was rather disturbed by the indications of change already commenced, and still to increase. I had long desired to spend a night alone upon the desert, and without wandering to a dangerous distance, I placed a ridge of sand between my solitary station and the objects which brought the busy world to view, and indulged in thoughts of scenes and circumstances which happened long ago.

According to the best authorities, we were in the track of the Israelites, and in meditations suggested by this interesting portion of Bible history, the time passed so rapidly, that I was surprised when I found the people astir and preparing for our departure. My garments were rather damp with the night-dews, for, having left some of my friends sleeping upon my fur cloak, I had gone out more lightly attired than perhaps was prudent. I was not, therefore, sorry to find myself warmly wrapped up, and in my chair, in which I should have slept very comfortably, had

Hot the man who guided the donkeys taken it into his head to quarrel with one of his comrades, and to bawl out his grievances close to my ear. My wakefulness was, however, amply repaid by the most glorious sunrise I ever witnessed. The sky had been for some time obscured by clouds, which had gathered themselves in a bank upon the Eastern horizon. The sun's rays started up at once, like an imperial crown, above this bank, and as they darted their glittering spears, for such they seemed, along the heavens, the clouds, dispersing, formed into a mighty arch, their edges becoming golden; while below all was one flush of crimson light. Neither at sea nor on land had I ever witnessed any thing so magnificent as this, and those who desire to see the god of day rise in the fulness of his majesty must make a pilgrimage to the desert.

We made no stay at the rest-house, which we reached about nine o'clock in the morning; and here, for the last time, we saw the governor of Jiddah and his party, winding along at some distance, and giving life and character to the desert. The fantastic appearance of the hills increased as we advanced; the slightest stretch of fancy was alone necessary to transform many into fortresses and towers, and at length a bright glitter at a distance revealed the Red Sea. The sun gleaming upon its waters shewed them like a mirror, and soon afterwards the appearance of some low buildings indicated the town of Suez.

I happened to be in advance of the party, under the conduct of one of the gentlemen who had joined us on the preceding evening; I therefore directed Mohammed to go forward, to announce our approach; and either the sight of the Red Sea, or their eagerness to reach a well-known spring of water, induced my donkeys to gallop along the road with me; a fortunate circumstance, as the day was beginning to be very sultry, and I felt that I should enjoy the shelter and repose of a habitation. As we went along, indications of the new power, which had already effected the easy transit of the desert, were visible in small patches of coal, scattered upon the sand; presently we saw a dark nondescript object, that did not look at all like the abode of men, civilized or uncivilized; and yet, from the group hovering about an aperture, seemed to be tenanted by human beings. This proved to be an old boiler, formerly belonging to a steam-vessel, and appearing, indeed, as if some black and shapeless hulk had been cast on shore. The well, which had attracted my donkeys, was very picturesque; the water flowed into a large stone trough, or rather basin, beneath the walls of a castellated edifice, pierced with many small windows, and apparently in a very dilapidated state. Those melancholy ***memento moris,*** which had tracked our whole progress through the desert, were to be seen in the immediate vicinity of this well. The skeletons of five or six camels lay in a group within a few yards of the haven which they had doubtless toiled anxiously, though so vainly, to reach. I never could look upon the bones of these poor animals without a painful feeling, and in the hope that European skill and science may yet bring forward those hidden waters which would disarm the desert of its terrors. It is said that the experiment of boring has been tried, and failed, between Suez and Cairo, but that it succeeded in the great desert; some other method, perhaps, may be found, if the project of bringing water from the hills, by means of aqueducts, should be too expensive. We heard this plan talked of at the bungalow, but I fear that, in the present state of Egypt, it is very chimerical.

This was now our fourth day upon the desert, and we had not sustained the smallest inconvenience; the heat, even at noon, being very bearable, and the sand not in the least degree troublesome. Doubtless, at a less favourable period of the year, both would prove difficult to bear. The wind, we were told, frequently raised the sand in clouds; and though the danger of being buried beneath the tombs thus made, we had reason to believe, was greatly exaggerated, yet the plague of sand is certainly an evil to be dreaded, and travellers will do well to avoid the season in which it prevails. The speed of my donkeys increasing, rather than diminishing, after we left the well, for they seemed to know that Suez would terminate their journey, I crossed the intervening three miles very quickly, and was soon at the walls of the town.

Distance lends no enchantment to the view of Suez. It is difficult to fancy that the few miserable buildings, appearing upon the margin of the sea, actually constitute a town; and the heart sinks at the approach to a place so barren and desolate. My donkeys carried me through a gap in the wall, which answered all the purposes of a gateway, and we passed along broken ground and among wretched habitations, more fit for the abode of savage beasts than men. Even the superior description of houses bore so forlorn and dilapidated an appearance, that I actually trembled as I approached them, fearing that my guide would stop, and tell me that, my journey was at an end.

Before I had time to make any observations upon the place to which I was conducted, I found myself at the foot of a flight of steps, and reaching a landing place, saw another above, and Mohammed descending to meet me. I followed him to the top, and crossing a large apartment, which served as dining and drawing room, entered a passage which led to a light and certainly airy bed-chamber; for half the front wall, and a portion of one of the sides, were entirely formed of wooden trellice, which admitted, with the utmost freedom, all the winds of heaven, the sun, and also the dust. There was a mat upon the floor, and the apartment was whitewashed to the rafters, which were in good condition; and upon Mohammed's declaration that it was free from rats, I felt an assurance of a share of comfort which I had dared not expect before. There were two neat beds, with musquito-curtains, two tables, and washing apparatus, but no looking-glass; an omission which I could supply, though we had dispensed with such a piece of luxury altogether in the desert. Well supplied with hot and cold water, I had enjoyed the refreshment of plenteous ablutions, and nearly completed my toilet, before the arrival of the friends I had so completely distanced. I made an attempt to sit down to my desk, but was unable to write a line, and throwing myself on my bed full dressed, I fell asleep in a moment, and enjoyed the deepest repose for an hour, or perhaps longer.

I was awakened by my friend, Miss E., who informed me that the purser of the ***Berenice*** was in the drawing-room, and that I must go to him and pay my passage-money. I was not, however, provided with the means of doing this in ready cash, and as the rate of exchange for the thirty pounds in sovereigns which I possessed could not be decided here, at the suggestion of one of my fellow-passengers, I drew a bill upon a banker in Bombay for the amount, eighty pounds, the sum demanded for half a cabin, which, fortunately, I could divide with the friend who had accompanied me from England. This transaction so completely roused me, that I found myself equal to the continuation of the journal which I had commenced at Cairo. I despatched also the letter with which I had been kindly furnished to the British Consul, and was immediately favoured by a visit from him. As we expressed some anxiety about our accommodation on board the steamer, he politely offered to take us to the vessel in his own boat; but to this arrangement the purser objected, stating that the ship was in confusion, and that one of the best cabins had been reserved for us. With this assurance we were accordingly content.

We arrived at Suez on Wednesday, the 9th of October, and were told to hold ourselves in readiness to embark on Friday at noon. We were not sorry for this respite, especially as we found our hotel, which was kept by a person in the employment of Mr. Waghorn, more comfortable than could have been hoped for from its exterior. The greatest annoyance we sustained was from the dust, which was brought in by a very strong wind through the lattices. I endeavoured to remedy this evil, in some degree, by directing the servants of the house to nail a sheet across the upper portion of the perforated wood-work. The windows of our chamber commanded as good a view of Suez as the place afforded; one at the side overlooked an irregular open space, which stretched between the house and the sea. At some distance opposite, there were one or two mansions of much better appearance than the rest, and having an air of comfort imparted to them by outside shutters, of new and neat construction. These we understood to be the abodes of officers in the Pasha's service. Mehemet Ali is said to be extremely unwilling to allow English people to build houses for themselves at Suez; while he freely grants permission to their residence at Alexandria and Cairo, he seems averse to their settling upon the shores of the Red Sea. Mr. Waghorn and Mr. Hill are, therefore, compelled to be content to fit up the only residences at their disposal in the best manner that circumstances will admit. I had no opportunity of forming any opinion respecting Mr. Hill's establishment, but am able to speak very well of the accommodation afforded by the hotel at which we sojourned.

Judging from the exterior, for the desert itself does not appear to be less productive than Suez, there must have been some difficulty in getting supplies, notwithstanding we found no want of good things at our breakfast and dinner-table, plenty of eggs and milk, fowl and fish being supplied; every article doing credit to the skill of the cook. Nor was the cleanliness that prevailed, in despite of all the obstacles opposed to it, less worthy of praise: the servants were civil and attentive, and the prices charged extremely moderate. All the guests of the hotel of course formed one family, assembling daily at meals, after the continental fashion. The dining-room was spacious, and divided into two portions; the one ascended by a step was surrounded by divans, after the Egyptian fashion, and here were books to be found containing useful and entertaining knowledge. A few stray numbers of the **Asiatic Journal**, half a dozen volumes of standard novels, files of the **Bombay Times**, and works illustrative of ancient and modern Egypt, served to beguile the time of those who had nothing else to do. Meanwhile, travellers came dropping in, and the caravanserai was soon crowded.

CHAPTER VII.
SUEZ TO ADEN.

Travellers assembling at Suez--Remarks on the Pasha's Government--Embarkation on the Steamer--Miserable accommodation in the Berenice, and awkwardness of the attendants--Government Ships not adapted to carry Passengers--Cause of the miserable state of the Red Sea Steamers--Shores of the Red Sea--Arrival at Mocha--Its appearance from the Sea--Arrival at Aden--Its wild and rocky appearance on landing--Cape Aden--The Town--Singular appearance of the Houses--The Garrison expecting an attack by the Arabs--Discontent of the Servants of Europeans at Aden--Complaints by Anglo-Indians against Servants--Causes--Little to interest Europeans in Aden.

Amongst the travellers who came dropping in at the hotel, was the Portuguese governor of Goa and his suite, consisting of four gentlemen, the private and public secretaries, an aide-de-camp, and the fourth holding some other appointment. They came by the French steamer, which had left Marseilles on the day of our departure. The governor, a fine old soldier, and a perfect gentleman, proved a great acquisition to our party; and knowing the state of Goa, and the disappointment he would in all probability sustain upon arriving at the seat of his government in the present low condition to which it is reduced, we could not help feeling much interested in his welfare. This gentleman, who inherited the title of baron, and was moreover an old general officer, had mixed in the very best society, and was evidently well acquainted with courts and camps; he spoke several languages, and in the course of his travels had visited England. His retinue were quiet gentlemanly men, and the young aide-de-camp, in particular, made himself very agreeable.

There were two other travellers of some note at Suez, who had put up at Hill's Hotel; one, an American gentleman, who had come across the desert for the purpose of looking at the Red Sea. I saw him mounted upon a donkey, and gazing as he stood upon the shore at the bright but narrow channel, so interesting to all who have read the history of the Israelites, with reverential feelings. I felt a strong inclination to accost him; but refrained, being unwilling to disturb his reveries with what he might have thought an impertinent interruption. It was evidently a last look, for he was veiled for the journey, and at length, tearing himself away, he turned his donkey's head, and struck into the desert. The other traveller was a young Scotsman, who proposed to go as far as Aden in the **Berenice**, on his way to Abyssinia, trusting that a residence of some months in Egypt would enable him to pass for a Turk. He had no very precise object in view, but intended to make an attempt to explore the sources of the Nile.

There was nothing in Suez that could make a longer stay desirable, and we quitted it without regret. My journey through Egypt had been much too rapid for me to presume to give any decided opinion concerning the strongly agitated question respecting the merits of the Pasha's government. It is very evident that he has not learned the most instructive lesson of political economy, nor has yet understood that the way to render himself powerful is to make his subjects rich; nevertheless, though his exactions and monopolies may be felt at present as very serious evils, yet, in establishing manufactories, and in embodying a national force, there can be no doubt that he has sown the seeds of much that is good; and should his government, after his death, fall into the hands of people equally free from religious prejudices, we may reasonably hope that they will entertain more enlarged and liberal views, and thus render measures, now difficult to bear, of incalculable advantage to the future prosperity of the country.

The British Consul politely offered to conduct myself and my female friends on board the steamer; he accordingly called for us, and I bade, as I hoped, a last adieu to Suez, it being my wish and intention to return home by way of Cosseir. Previous to our embarkation, a series of regulations had been placed in our hands for the engagement of passages in the Honourable Company's armed steamers, with instructions to passengers, &c.

Upon repairing to our cabin, Miss E. and myself were surprised and disappointed at the miserable accommodation it afforded. The three cabins allotted to the use of the ladies had been appropriated, in two instances, to married couples, and we were obliged to put up with one of smaller size, which had the additional inconvenience of opening into the public saloon. There were no Venetian blinds to the door, consequently, the only means of obtaining a free circulation of air was to have it open. A locker with a hinged shelf, which opened like a shutter, and thus afforded space for one mattress to be placed upon it, ran along one side of the cabin, under the port-hole, but the floor was the only visible means of accommodation for the second person crammed by Government regulation into this den. There was not a place in which a wash-hand basin could be put, so awkwardly were the doors arranged, to one of which there was no fastening whatsoever. Altogether, the case seemed hopeless, and as cock-roaches were walking about the vessel by dozens, the prospect of sleeping on the ground was anything but agreeable, especially with the feeling that we were paying at the rate of four pounds a day for our accommodation.

We were, however, compelled to postpone our arrangements, by a summons to dinner; and in the evening, when repairing again to the cabin, I found my mattress placed upon two portmanteaus and a box. Of course, no attention was paid to the inequalities of the surface, and I endeavoured, by folding my fur cloak and a thick dressing-gown under my sheet, to render this miserable apology for a bed tenable. Hitherto, our berth-places in the Government-steamers had been very comfortable; though small, they answered the purpose of sleeping and of washing, while the larger cabin into which they opened, and which was set apart for the ladies, enabled us all to complete our toilets without inconvenience. A sail had been hung before the door by way of curtain, but the heat was still difficult to bear, and we found that we had adventured upon the Red Sea at least a month too soon. The next morning, the captain, hearing that I had, as might have been expected, passed a wretched night, kindly sent his cot for my future accommodation; after the second night, however, the servants thinking it too much trouble to attend to it properly, the ropes gave way, and it came down. The cabin being much too small to allow it to remain hanging all day, I at first trusted to the servants to put it up at night; but, after this accident, and finding them to be incorrigibly stupid, lazy, and disobliging,

I contented myself with placing the cot upon two portmanteaus, and thus forming a bed-place. Subsequently, one of the passengers having kindly adjusted the ropes, Miss E. and myself contrived to sling it; a fatiguing operation, which added much to the discomforts of the voyage. The idea of going upon the quarter-deck, or writing a letter, which might perhaps be handed up to Government, to make a formal complaint to the captain, was not to be thought of, and seeing the impossibility of getting any thing properly done by the tribe of uncouth barbarians dignified by the name of servants, the only plan was to render myself quite independent of them, and much did we miss the activity, good humour, and readiness to oblige manifested by our Egyptian attendant, Mohammed. Where a wish to please is evinced, though wholly unattended by efficiency in the duties undertaken by a servant, I can very easily excuse awkwardness, forgetfulness, or any other fault; but the wretched half-castes, who take service on board the Government steamers, have not even common civility to recommend them; there was not a passenger in the vessel who did not complain of the insults to which all were more or less subjected.

Where the blame lay, it is difficult to state exactly; no one could be more kind and obliging than the captain, and it was this disposition upon his part which rendered us all unwilling to worry him with complaints. The charge of a steamer in the Red Sea seems quite enough to occupy the commandant's time and attention, without having the comforts of seven or eight-and-twenty passengers to look after; but these duties might have been performed by a clever and active steward. Whether there was a personage on board of that designation, I never could learn; I asked several times to speak with him, but he never in a single instance attended the summons.

We had no reason to complain of want of liberality on the part of the captain, for the table was plentifully supplied, though the cooks, being unfortunately most worthy of the patronage of that potentate who is said to send them to our kitchens, generally contrived to render the greater portion uneatable. The advantage of rising from table with an appetite is one which I have usually tried on board ship, having only in few instances, during my numerous voyages, been fortunate enough to find food upon which I dared to venture.

The more I have seen of government ships, the more certain I feel that they are not adapted to carry passengers. The authorities appear to think that people ought to be too thankful to pay an enormous price for the worst species of accommodation. The commandants have not been accustomed to attend to the minutiae which can alone secure the comfort of those who sail with them, while the officers, generally speaking, endeavour to show their contempt of the service in which they are sent, against their inclination, by neglect and even rudeness towards the passengers.

While on board the ***Berenice***, the following paragraph in a Bombay newspaper struck my eye, and as it is a corroboration of the statements which I deem it to be a duty to make, I insert it in this place. "The voyager (from Agra) must not think his troubles at an end on reaching Bombay, or that the steam-packets are equal to the passenger Indiaman in accommodation. In fact, I cannot conceive how a lady manages; we have, however, five. There are only seven very small cabins, into each of which two people are crammed; no room to swing cats. Eight other deluded individuals, of whom I am one, are given to understand that a cabin-passage is included in permission to sleep on the benches and table of the cuddy. For this you pay Rs. 200 extra. The vessel is dirty beyond measure, from the soot, and with the difficulty of copious ablution and private accommodation, is almost worse, to a lover of Indian habits, than the journey to Bombay from Agra upon camels. No civility is to be got from the officers. If they are not directly uncivil, the passengers are luckier than we have been. They declare themselves disgusted with passenger ships, but do not take the proper way of showing their superiority to the duty."

The only officer of the ***Berenice*** who dined at the captain's table was the surgeon of the vessel, and in justice to him it must be said, that he left no means untried to promote the comfort of the passengers. It is likewise necessary to state, that we were never put upon an allowance of water, although, in consequence of late alterations made in the dockyard, the vessel had been reduced to about half the quantity she had been accustomed to carry in iron tanks constructed for the purpose. Notwithstanding this reduction, we could always procure a sufficiency, either of hot or cold water, for ablutions, rendered doubly necessary in consequence of the atmosphere of coal-dust which we breathed. Not that it was possible to continue clean for a single hour; nevertheless, there was some comfort in making the attempt.

There were eight cabins in the ***Berenice***, besides the three appropriated to ladies; these were ranged four on either side of the saloon, reaching up two-thirds of the length. The apartment, therefore, took the form of a T, and the upper end or cross was furnished with horse-hair sofas; upon these, and upon the table, those passengers slept who were not provided with cabins. Many preferred the deck, but being washed out of it by the necessary cleaning process, which took place at day-break, were obliged to make their toilettes in the saloon. This also formed the dressing-place for dinner, and the basins of dirty water, hair-brushes, &c. were scarcely removed from the side-tables before the party were summoned to their repast. The preparations for this meal were a work of time, always beginning at half-past one; an hour was employed in placing the dishes upon the table, in order that every thing might have time to cool.

The reason assigned for not putting Venetian blinds to the cabin-doors was this: it would injure the appearance of the cabin--an appearance certainly not much improved by the dirty sail which hung against our portal. The saloon itself, without this addition, was dingy enough, being panelled with dark oak, relieved by a narrow gilt cornice, and the royal arms carved and gilded over an arm-chair at the rudder-case, the ornaments of a clock which never kept time. All the servants, who could not find accommodation elsewhere, slept under the table; thus adding to the abominations of this frightful place. And yet we were congratulated upon our good fortune, in being accommodated in the ***Berenice***, being told that the ***Zenobia***, which passed us on our way, had been employed in carrying pigs between Waterford and Bristol, and that the ***Hugh Lindsay*** was in even worse condition; the ***Berenice*** being, in short, the crack ship.

Every day added to the heat and the dirt, and in the evening, when going upon deck to inhale the odours of the hen-coops, the smell was insufferable. When to this annoyance coal-dust, half an inch deep, is added, my preference of my own cabin will not be a subject of surprise. With what degree of truth, I cannot pretend to say, all the disagreeable circumstances sustained on board the ***Berenice*** were attributed to the alterations made in the docks. Previously to these changes, we were told, the furnaces were supplied with coal by a method which obviated the necessity of having it upon deck, whence the dust was now carried all over the ship upon the feet of the persons who were continually passing to and fro.

Occasionally, we suffered some inconvenience from the motion of the vessel, but, generally speaking, nothing more disagreeable occurred than the tremulous action of the engines, an action which completely incapacitated me from any employment except that of reading. The only seats or tables we could command in our cabin consisted of our boxes, so that being turned out of the saloon at half-past one, by the servants who laid the cloth for dinner, it was not very easy to make an attempt at writing, or even needle-work. Doubtless the passengers from Bombay could contrive to have more comforts about them. It was impossible, however, that those who had already made a long overland journey should be provided with the means of furnishing their cabins, and this consideration should weigh with the Government when taking money for the accommodation of passengers. Cabins ought certainly to be supplied with bed-places and a washing-table, and not to be left perfectly dismantled by those occupants who arrive at Suez, and who, having previously fitted them up, have a right to all they contain.

The miserable state of the Red Sea steamers, of course, often furnished a theme for conversation, and we were repeatedly told that their condition was entirely owing to the jealousy of the people of Calcutta, who could not endure the idea of the importance to which Bombay was rising, in consequence of its speedy communication with England. Without knowing exactly where the fault may lie, it must be said that there is great room for improvement. In all probability, the increased number of persons who will proceed to India by way of the Red Sea, now that the passage is open, will compel the merchants, or other speculators, to provide better vessels for the trip. At present, the price demanded is enormously disproportioned to the accommodation given, while the chance of falling in with a disagreeable person in the commandant should be always taken into consideration by those who meditate the overland journey. The consolation, in so fine a vessel as the **Berenice**, consists in the degree of certainty with which the duration of the voyage may be calculated, eighteen or twenty days being the usual period employed. In smaller steamers, and those of a less favourable construction, accidents and delays are very frequent; sometimes the coal is burning half the voyage, and thus rendered nearly useless to the remaining portion, the vessel depending entirely upon the sails.

During the hot weather and the monsoons, the navigation of the Red Sea is attended with much inconvenience, from the sultriness of the atmosphere and the high winds; it is only, therefore, at one season of the year that travellers can, with any hope of comfort, avail themselves of the route; it must, consequently, be questionable whether the influx of voyagers will be sufficiently great to cover the expense of the vessels required. A large steamer is now building at Bombay, for the purpose of conveying the mails, and another is expected out from England with the same object.

The shores of the Red Sea are bold and rocky, exhibiting ranges of picturesque hills, sometimes seceding from, at others approaching, the beach. A few days brought us to Mocha. The captain had kindly promised to take me on shore with him; but, unfortunately, the heat and the fatigue which I had sustained had occasioned a slight attack of fever, and as we did not arrive before the town until nearly twelve o'clock, I was afraid to encounter the rays of the sun during the day. We could obtain a good view of the city from the vessel; it appeared to be large and well built, that is, comparatively speaking; but its unsheltered walls, absolutely baked in the sun, and the arid waste on which it stood, gave to it a wild and desolate appearance.

We were told that already, since the British occupation of Aden, the trade of Mocha had fallen off. It seldom happens that a steamer passes down the Red Sea without bringing emigrants from Mocha, anxious to establish themselves in the new settlement; and if Aden were made a free port, there can be little doubt that it would monopolize the whole commerce of the neighbourhood. The persons desirous to colonize the place say, very justly, that they cannot afford to pay duties, having to quit their own houses at a loss, and to construct others, Aden being at present destitute of accommodation for strangers. If, however, encouragement should be given them, they will flock thither in great numbers; and, under proper management, there is every reason to hope that Aden will recover all its former importance and wealth, and become one of the most useful dependencies of the British crown.

We were to take in coals and water at Aden, and arriving there in the afternoon of Saturday, the 19th of October, every body determined to go on shore, if possible, on the ensuing morning. By the kindness of some friends, we had palanquins in waiting at day-break, which were to convey us a distance of five miles to the place now occupied as cantonments. Our road conducted us for a mile or two along the sea-shore, with high crags piled on one side, a rugged path, and rocks rising out of the water to a considerable distance. We then ascended a height, which led to an aperture in the hills, called the Pass. Here we found a gate and a guard of sepoys. The scenery was wild, and though nearly destitute of vegetation--a few coarse plants occurring here and there scarcely deserving the name--very beautiful.

It would, perhaps, be too much to designate the bare and lofty cliffs, which piled themselves upwards in confused masses, with the name of mountains; they nevertheless conveyed ideas of sublimity which I had not associated with other landscapes of a similar nature. The Pass, narrow and enclosed on either side by winding rocks, brought us at length down a rather steep declivity to a sort of basin, surrounded upon three sides with lofty hills, and on the fourth by the sea.

Cape Aden forms a high and rocky promontory, the most elevated portion being 1,776 feet above the level of the sea. This lofty headland, when viewed at a distance, appears like an island, in consequence of its being connected with the interior by low ground, which, in the vicinity of Khora Muckse, is quite a swamp. Its summits assume the aspect of turretted peaks, having ruined forts and watch-towers on the highest elevations. The hills are naked and barren, and the valley little better; the whole, however, presenting a grand, picturesque, and imposing appearance. The town of Aden lies on the east side of the Cape, in the amphitheatre before mentioned. A sketch of its history will be given, gathered upon the spot, in a subsequent paper, the place being sufficiently interesting to demand a lengthened notice; meanwhile a passing remark is called for on its present appearance.

At first sight of Aden, it is difficult to suppose it to be the residence of human beings, and more especially of European families. The town, if such it may be called, consists of a few scattered houses of stone, apparently loosely put together, with pigeon-holes for windows, and roofs which, being flat, and apparently surrounded by a low parapet, afford no idea of their being habitable. It is difficult to find a comparison for these dwellings, which appeared to be composed of nothing more than four walls, and yet, to judge from the apertures, contained two or more stories. The greater number were enclosed in a sort of yard or compound, the fences being formed of long yellow reeds; the less substantial dwellings were entirely made of these reeds, so that they looked like immense crates or cages for domestic fowls.

My palanquin at length stopped at a flight of steps hewn out of the rock; and I found myself at the entrance of a habitation, half-bungalow, half-tent; and certainly, as the permanent abode of civilized beings, the strangest residence I had ever seen. The uprights and frame-work were made of reeds and bamboos, lined with thin mats, which had at one time been double; but the harbour thus afforded for rats being found inconvenient, the outer casing had been removed. Two good-sized apartments, with verandahs all round, and dressing and bathing-rooms attached, were formed in this way; they were well carpeted and well furnished, but destitute both of glass windows and wooden doors; what are called in India *jaumps*, and chicks of split bamboo, being the substitutes.

Government not yet having fixed upon the site for the station intended to be established at Aden, none of the European inhabitants have begun to build their houses, which, it is said, are to be very solidly constructed of stone; at present, they are scattered, in Gipsy fashion, upon the rocks overlooking the sea, and at the time of the year in which I visited them they enjoyed a delightfully cool breeze. What they would be in the hot weather, it is difficult to say. The supplies, for the most part, come from a considerable distance, but appear to be abundant; and when at length a good understanding shall have taken place between the British Government and the neighbouring sheikhs, the markets will be furnished with every thing that the countries in the vicinity produce.

The garrison were prepared, at the period of our arrival, for the outbreak which has since occurred. It is melancholy to contemplate the sacrifice of life which will in all probability take place before the Arabs will be reconciled to the loss of a territory which has for a long time been of no use to them, but which, under its present masters, bids fair to introduce mines of wealth into an impoverished country. The Pasha of Egypt had long cast a covetous eye upon Aden, and its occupation by the British took place at the precise period requisite to check the ambitious designs of a man thirsting for conquest, and to allay the fears of the Imaum of Muscat, who, naturally enough, dreaded encroachments upon his territory.

Aden had hitherto agreed very well with its European residents. The sepoys, servants, and camp-followers, however, had suffered much both from mental and bodily ailments. They were deprived of their usual sources of amusement, and of their accustomed food, and languished under that home-sickness, which the natives of India feel in a very acute degree. The greater number of servants were discontented, and anxious to return to their native country. This natural desire upon their part was highly resented by their masters, who, instead of taking the most obvious means of remedying the evil, and employing the natives of the place, who appeared to be tractable and teachable enough, abused and threatened to beat the unfortunate people, convicted of what self-love styles "ingratitude."

In a very clever work, I have seen the whole sum of the miseries of human life comprised in one word, "servants;" and until we can procure human beings with all the perfections of our fallen nature, and none of our faults, to minister to our wants and wishes, the complaint, so sickening and so general, and frequently so unjust, will be reiterated. Anglo-Indians, however, seem to be more tormented by these domestic plagues than any other set of people. The instant a stranger lands upon Asiatic ground, we hear of nothing else. It is considered to be polite conversation in the drawing-room, aid delicate-looking women will listen with the greatest complacence to the most brutal threats uttered by their male associates against the wretched people whom hard fate has placed about their persons. By some mischance, these very individuals are equally ill-served at home, the greater number who return to England being either rendered miserable there, or driven back to India in consequence of the impossibility of managing their servants. As far as my own experience goes, with the exception of the people in the **Berenice**, who were not in the slightest degree under the control of the passengers, or, it may be said, attached to them in any way, I have always found it easy, both at home and abroad, to obtain good servants, at least quite as good as people, conscious of the infirmities of humanity in their own persons, have a right to expect. My simple rule has been, never to keep a person who did not suit me, and to treat those who did with kindness and indulgence. The system has always answered, and I am probably on that account the less inclined to sympathize with persons who are eternally complaining.

There may be some excuse at Aden for the conversation turning upon domestic matters of this kind, and perhaps I do the station injustice in supposing that they form a common topic. With the exception of those persons who take pleasure in the anticipation of the improvement of the surrounding tribes, there is very little to interest European residents in this arid spot. Should, however, the hopes which many enlightened individuals entertain be realized, or the prospect of their fulfilment continue unclouded, those who now endure a dreary exile in a barren country, and surrounded by a hostile people, will or ought to derive much consolation from the thought, that their employment upon a disagreeable duty may prove of the utmost benefit to thousands of their fellow-creatures. It is pleasant to look forward to the civilization of Abyssinia, and other more remote places, by means of commercial intercourse with Aden.

CHAPTER VIII.
ADEN.

Commanding situation of Aden--Its importance in former times--But few remains of its grandeur--Its facilities as a retreat for the piratical hordes of the Desert--The loss of its trade followed by reduction of the population--Speculations as to the probability of ultimately resisting the Arabs--Exaggerated notions entertained by the Shiekhs of the wealth of the British--Aden a free Port would be the Queen of the adjacent Seas--Its advantages over Mocha--The Inhabitants of Aden--The Jews--The Banians--The Soomalees--The Arabs--Hopes of the prosperity of Aden--Goods in request there--Exports--Re-embarkation on the Steamer--Want of attention--Makallah--Description of the place--Its products--The Gazelle--Traveller in Abyssinia--Adventurous English Travellers--Attractions of the Arab life--Arrival at Bombay.

Wretched and miserable as the appearance of Aden must be deemed at the present moment, its commanding situation rendered it of great importance in former times. During the reign of Constantine, it was an opulent city, forming one of the great emporia for the commerce of the East. The sole remains of the grandeur it once boasted consists of about ninety dilapidated stone houses, the greater number of dwellings which seem to shelter its scanty population being nothing more than huts rudely constructed of reeds. These wretched tenements, huddled together without the slightest attempt at regularity, occupy the crater of an extinct volcano. Unrelieved by trees, and assimilating in colour with the arid soil and barren hills rising around, they scarcely convey an idea of the purpose for which they are designed.

A stranger, entering Aden, finds it difficult to believe that he is in the midst of an inhabited place, the houses appearing to be fewer in number, and more insignificant, than a closer inspection proves them to be. No splendid fragment, imposing in its ruin, records the glory and opulence of the populous city, as it existed in the days of Solyman the Magnificent, the era from whence it dates its decline. The possession of Aden was eagerly contended for by the two great powers, the Turks and the Portuguese, struggling for mastery in the East, and when they were no longer able to maintain their rivalry, it reverted into the hands of its ancient masters, the Arabs. The security afforded by its natural defences, aided by the fortifications, the work of former times, rendered it a suitable retreat for the piratical hordes of the desert. The lawless sons of Ishmael could, from this stronghold, rush out upon the adjacent waters, and make themselves masters of the wealth of those adventurers who dared to encounter the dangers of the Red Sea.

With the loss of every thing approaching to good government, Aden lost its trade. The system of monopoly, which enriches the sovereign at the expense of the subject, speedily ends in ruin. The superior classes of the inhabitants were either driven away, in consequence of the tyranny which they endured, or, reduced to a state of destitution, perished miserably upon the soil, until at length the traces of former magnificence became few and faint, the once flourishing city falling into one wide waste of desolation. The remains of a splendid aqueduct, which was at the first survey mistaken for a Roman road; a solitary watch-tower, and a series of broken walls, alone attest the ancient glories of the place.

Previous to the occupation of the British, the population of Aden scarcely exceeded six hundred souls; it is now, independently of the garrison, more nearly approaching to a thousand, and of these the principal number are Jews, who, together with about fifty Banians, have contrived to amass a little of what, by comparison, may be called wealth. The trade of Aden, for a long time before we obtained our present possession, was very trifling, the imports consisting of a few English cotton cloths, together with lead, iron, and tin, which were brought by Buglas on their way to Mocha; rice, dates, and small numbers of cattle, likewise, coming from neighbouring places; while the exports were limited to a little coffee, millet, and a few drugs.

At the period of my visit to Aden, the garrison were in almost momentary expectation of an attack from the Arabs, who had gathered to the amount of five thousand in the neighbourhood, and kept the new occupants continually upon the alert. Of course, in such a state of affairs, great differences of opinion existed respecting the ultimate fate of this interesting place. Many acute persons consider the project of colonizing a barren spot, surrounded by hostile tribes, by a handful of soldiers from India, chimerical, especially in the teeth of predictions which have for so long a period been fulfilled to the letter. It is stated that the Imaum of Muscat asked, in astonishment, whether we were mad enough to contemplate the subjugation of the Arabs, the sons of his father Ishmael; since we could not be so ignorant of our own Scriptures as not to know that their hands were to be eternally against every man, and every man's hand against theirs. But, although the Arabs should continue hostile, while we are masters of the sea, and can strengthen Aden so completely upon the land-side, as to render it, what many people believe it can be made, a second Gibraltar, we have a wide field for commercial speculation in the opposite coast of Africa.

Aden is, at present, a very expensive possession, and the long period which has elapsed since our occupation, without preparations having been commenced for a permanent residence, has occasioned an apprehension that it may be ultimately abandoned. Many persons are, however, sanguine in the hope that, as soon as scientific men have decided upon the best site for a cantonment, buildings will be erected for the reception of the garrison. These, it is confidently expected, will be upon a grand scale, and of solid construction. The greater portion of the materials must be brought from distant places, and already some of the European inhabitants are conveying from Bombay those portable houses which are commonly set up during the cold season on the Esplanade, and which will afford a great improvement upon the dwellings of bamboos, reeds, and mats, which at present form the abodes of the officers of this establishment. It has been satisfactorily ascertained, that the clearing out and repairing the old tanks and wells will be sufficient to secure an ample supply of water for a very extensive population, the report of those gentlemen employed in analyzing its quality being highly favourable.

A little allowance must, of course, be made for the sanguine nature of the expectations formed by persons whose imaginations are dazzled by the splendid visions of the future arising before them; still, enough appears to have been demonstrated to justify a strong hope that there are no serious difficulties in the way of our permanent occupation of a place which we have succeeded in rescuing from Arab tyranny. It will be long, perhaps, before the neighbouring sheikhs will consent to an amicable arrangement with the British authorities of Aden, for they at present entertain the most exaggerated notions of the wealth of its new possessors.

The English, with their usual thoughtless improvidence, threw about their money so carelessly, that, soon after their arrival, every article of household consumption doubled and trebled in price, the remuneration for labour rising in proportion. This improvident expenditure has had the effect of making the people discontented. Imagining our resources to be inexhaustible, they do not know how much to ask for their commodities or their services, and it will require great firmness and discretion, on the part of the persons in authority, to settle the fair price for both. The erection of new houses, which are called for by nearly every fresh arrival, even in their present light construction, serves very materially to enrich the inhabitants of Aden, the natural consequence being an increase of the industrious portion of the population, while it may be confidently expected that the commencement of superior works will attract a superior class of persons to the place.

The present Resident is a strenuous advocate for the abolition of all duties, at least for a time; and should the representations made by him, and other persons well acquainted with the character and resources of the surrounding countries, succeed in inducing the Government of India to render Aden a free port, it would soon become the queen of the adjacent seas. The town of Senna is only at the distance of seven or eight days' journey for camels and merchandize. The coffee districts are actually nearer to it than to Mocha, and the road equally safe and convenient; other large towns in Yemen are within an easy journey, and the rich and populous places in the province of Hydramut are open for its trade.

The mountains to the north of Aden produce gums, frankincense, and coffee, which would soon find their way to so promising a market. Its harbour being immediately to the north of Barbar, vessels during the north-eastern monsoon would reach it with the produce of Africa in twenty-four hours, returning with British and Indian produce in the same time. All the exports of Hanall, and other large interior towns on the opposite coast, consisting of coffee, gums, myrrh, hides, elephants' teeth, gold dust, ostrich feathers, &c, would be conveyed to Aden, to be exchanged for piece goods, chintzes, cutlery, and rice; all of which would find a ready market.

The manufactures of India and of Great Britain would thus be very extensively introduced, there being good reason to believe that they would be largely purchased in the provinces of Yemen and Hydramut.

Amongst the great advantages which Aden possesses over Mocha, is the situation of its harbour, which may be entered by a ship or boat at any period of the year, and quitted with the same facility: whereas its rival port is so difficult of access in the months of March, April, and May, that boats are sometimes six, seven, or eight days getting to the straits, a distance of forty miles only. These are considerations worthy of the attention of merchants, the length of the voyage not being the sole source of annoyance, since vessels taking cargoes at Aden save the great wear and tear occasioned in their return down the Red Sea.

Perhaps, considering the difficulty of conciliating the semi-barbarous tribes in the neighbourhood, the trade and population of Aden have increased as much as we could reasonably hope; but when peace shall at length be established, it will doubtless attract merchants and Banians from Surat, as well as all other adjacent places. If at this moment our expectations have not been completely answered, we have at least the satisfaction of knowing that, besides having saved the Red Sea from the encroachments of the Pasha of Egypt, we have anticipated a rival power, which has already derived greater advantage from our supineness, with regard to our Eastern possessions, than is desirable.

The Americans, during 1833-4-5, had a small squadron looking all about for a spot which they could turn to good account. Socotra, from its convenient position between Africa and Arabia, proved a point of attraction, and had not Capt. Haines, of the Indian Navy, promptly taken possession, in the name of Great Britain, they would in all probability have succeeded in effecting a settlement. With their usual attention to the interests of their commerce, the Americans have a resident permanently stationed at Zanzibar, and have made advantageous arrangements with the Imaum of Muscat, whereby the trade with the United States has greatly increased; American ships are constantly arriving, with piece-goods, glass-ware, &c, and returning with profitable cargoes, the produce of Africa.

The inhabitants of Aden appear to be a peaceable race, generally well affected to the government, from which they cannot fail to derive advantage. The Jews, as I have before mentioned, are the most important, both in consequence of their number and of their superior wealth; they belong to the tribe of Judah, and are very industrious, being the manufacturers of the place.

It is by the Jews and their families, the females assisting, that a coarse kind of cloth, employed for their own garments, and also sold to strangers, is spun and woven. This cloth is in much esteem amongst the Arabs: when prepared for them, it is dyed blue, sometimes ornamented with red borders, indigo being employed, together with extracts from other plants. The women generally wear a single loose garment, covering the head with a handkerchief when they leave the house; they do not, however, conceal their faces. Previous to the occupation of Aden, the Jewesses were remarkable for the propriety of their manners, but as they are esteemed handsome, and moreover attract by their good temper and intelligence, it is to be feared that they will meet with many temptations to depart from the decorum they have hitherto maintained. Like their sex and peculiar race, they are fond of ornaments, adorning themselves with large silver ear-rings, bracelets, necklaces, and armlets. Hitherto, whatever wealth they possessed, they were obliged to conceal, the Arabs proving very severe and oppressive masters; their prospects are now brightening, and they have already shown a disposition to profit by the new order of things, having opened shops in the bazaar, and commenced trading in a way they never ventured upon before.

Nor is it in spinning and weaving alone that the Jews of Aden excel; artizans in silver and copper are to be found amongst them, together with stone-cutters, and other handicrafts-men. They have a school for the education of their male youth, the females not having yet enjoyed this advantage, in consequence of the intolerance of the Arabs, who view with prejudiced eyes every attempt to emancipate women from the condition to which they have been so long reduced.

The means of instruction possessed by the Jews of Aden are not very extensive, a few printed Bibles and MS. extracts forming the whole of their literature. It has been thought that missionaries would here find a fair field for their exertions; but, unfortunately, the most promising places in the East are, by some mistake, either of ignorance or ambition, left wholly destitute of Christian teachers. While the pledges of Government are compromised in India, and its stability threatened, by the daring attempts to make converts at the presidencies, and other considerable places, where success is attended with great noise and clamour, many portions of the Company's territories, in which much quiet good might be effected, are left entirely without religious aid.

The Banians, though small in number, rank next to the Jews in importance, and are, perhaps, more wealthy; they are not, however, so completely identified with the soil, for they do not bring their families with them when emigrating to Aden from the places of their birth. The greater number come from Cutch, arriving at an early period of life, and with the craft that usually distinguishes them, studying the character of the Arabs, and making the most of it. They are not esteemed such good subjects to the new government as the Jews, their expectations of benefit from a change of masters, in consequence of their having proved the chief gainers heretofore, being less sanguine.

The Soomalees are natives of Barbora, and are in number about two hundred. They employ themselves in making baskets, mats, and fans, from the leaves of a species of palm-tree; they are not so active and industrious as the Jews, but the younger portion, if brought up in European families, might, with the advantage of good tuition, become useful as servants and labourers. They are Mohamedans, but not very strict, either in their religious or moral principles, violating oaths sworn upon the **Koran**, and cheating and thieving whenever they can. The love of money, however, is a strong stimulus to improvement, and where it exists, or can be created, the case is far more hopeful than when the wants and desires are both limited. The Soomalee women are reckoned handsome, though in that respect they cannot compare with the Jewesses, their complexions being much darker and their hair coarse; they have tall, well-proportioned figures, and are as attentive to their dress and appearance as their poverty will admit. The Arabs are the least prepossessing of all the inhabitants of Aden, and it will be long before any confidence can be placed in them. They religiously conceal their women, and are a bigoted, prejudiced race, disaffected of course to the new government, and shy of intercourse with the British occupants.

That the hopes entertained of the prosperity of Aden have not been more speedily realized, may be attributed to the prevalent belief that its new masters could not maintain their ground against the hostile Arabs of the neighbourhood. It is the opinion of a competent judge, that, "as soon as the inhabitants of distant countries feel convinced that our occupation of Aden is intended to be a **permanent**, and not a temporary measure, they will establish agencies there under our flag, in preference to any other, and open an extensive traffic." The same authority states that "it is the opinion of the Banians and Arabs, that Aden ***will regain*** her former commercial renown."

With respect to the goods at present in requisition, or likely to meet a sale, at Aden, we learn from the report above quoted, that "of the manufactures of Europe, coloured handkerchiefs and hardware are only in demand, though longcloths are procurable and are sometimes purchased by the Arabs; but these articles are priced so high, as to prevent any great consumption of them. From what I observed of the Arab disposition and taste, I certainly believe that coloured cotton goods of ***fast*** colours, and of patterns similar to those elsewhere specified, if offered at rates somewhat reasonable, would in a very short period meet with an extensive sale, and be rapidly introduced into common use amongst the Arabs of the interior. The novelty of the experiment would at first induce the Arabs to become purchasers, when, finding the articles ***good***, it is but reasonable to anticipate an extensive demand. The colours should be particularly attended to, for the certainty of obtaining goods of ***fast colours*** would alone ensure the articles in question a speedy sale. The handkerchiefs that have already been introduced into Aden are of the worst sort relative to colour, generally becoming after two or three washings white, or nearly so; thus it cannot be wondered at if these goods meet with but a poor demand."

The ravages committed by the army of the Pasha of Egypt, in the fertile districts of the neighbourhood of Aden, have been prejudicial to the interests of the new settlement, and perhaps so long as the hope of plunder can be entertained by the petty princes, who rule the adjacent districts, they will be unwilling to wait for the slower advantages derivable from commerce. The apparently reckless expenditure of the British residents, and the princely pay given to the soldiers of the garrison, have offered so dazzling a prospect of gain, that they (the native chiefs) will have some difficulty in abandoning the hope of making themselves masters, at a single blow, of all the treasure brought to their shores. It is said that some Turks, deserters from Mehemet Ali, who took refuge in Aden, upon being made acquainted with the amount of pay given to the British troops, and the regularity with which it was issued, exclaimed, "God is great, and the English are immortal!"

During the proper seasons, Aden is well supplied with fruit; its trade in honey and wax might become very important, the adjacent countries yielding abundance of both, and of so fine a quality, as to compete with the produce of the hives of the Mediterranean. Drugs are procurable in equal abundance, together with perfumes and spices. The European inhabitants are, of course, compelled to send to Bombay for those luxuries which habit has rendered necessary; the constant communication with the presidency renders them easily procurable, while the intercourse with India and England, by means of the steamers, relieves the monotony which would otherwise be severely felt.

I could have spent two or three days with great pleasure at Aden, inquiring into its early history, present condition, and future prospects, and regretted much when a summons reached me to depart. We entertained a hope that the steamer would come round and take us off at the northern point; however, we were obliged to return the way we came. There are, and have been since its occupation, several English ladies living at Aden, but whether they have not shown themselves sufficiently often to render their appearance familiar, or the curiosity of the people is not easily satisfied, I cannot say; but I found myself an object of great attention to the women and children.

The sun having declined, the whole of the population of Aden seemed to be abroad, and many well-dressed and good-looking women were seated on the rude steps and broken walls of the stone houses before-mentioned. As they saw me smiling upon them, they drew nearer, salaamed, and laughed in return, and appeared to examine my dress as closely as the open doors of the palanquin would permit. Some of the very little children turned away in horror from a white face, but the greater number seemed much pleased with the notice taken of them. While waiting a few minutes for my party, my bearers wanted to drive them away, but this I would not permit, and we carried on a very amicable intercourse by signs, both being apparently mutually delighted with each other. Their vivacity and good-humour made a favourable impression upon my mind, and I should like to have an opportunity of becoming better acquainted with them, feeling strongly tempted to proceed to Aden on my return to England in a sailing vessel, and await there the arrival of a steamer to convey me up the Red Sea to Cosseir or to Suez.

I was offered a present of a milch-goat at Aden, but not being able to consult with the captain of the ***Berenice*** concerning its introduction on board, I did not like to allow the poor creature to run any risk of neglect. Its productiveness would soon have diminished on board a steamer, and it was so useful in a place like Aden, that I could not feel justified in taking it away for my own gratification. I obtained, however, a bottle of milk, and when I got on board, having dined early, and being moreover exhausted with my journey, as I was only recovering from an attack of fever, I wished to have some tea. This was too great an indulgence to be granted by the petty authorities who ruled over the passengers. Unfortunately, upon leaving Suez, I had given away all my tea to my servant, Mohammed, who was fond of it, nothing doubting that I should be able to procure as much as I pleased on board the steamer. The refusal was the more provoking, as there was plenty of boiling water ready, and I had humbly limited my request to a spoonful of tea. Under the circumstances, I was obliged to content myself with milk and water: had the captain or the surgeon of the vessel been at hand, I should doubtless have been supplied with every thing I wanted, but in their absence, it was impossible to procure a single article. Upon one occasion, while tea was serving, a passenger in the saloon asked for a cup, and was told to go upon deck for it.

I also procured a supply of soda water at Aden. I had suffered much from the want of this refreshing beverage during my fever, the supply taken on board having been exhausted on the voyage up. The passengers down the Red Sea have the disadvantage of sailing with exhausted stores. It seems hardly fair to them, especially in cases of illness, that the whole of any particular article should be given to the people who embark at Bombay, they having a right to expect that, as they pay the same price, a portion should be reserved for their use.

On the second day after our departure from Aden--that is, the 22nd of October--we arrived at Makallah. It was mid-day before the vessel ceased to ply her engines, and though invited to go on shore, as we could not penetrate beyond the walls of the town, we thought it useless to exchange our cabins for a hot room in the mansion of its ruler. The town of Makallah, which forms the principal commercial depot of the south-west of Arabia, is built upon a rocky platform of some length, but of very inconsiderable width, backed by a perfect wall of cliffs, and bounded in front by the sea. It seems tolerably well built for an Arabian town, many of the houses being of a very respectable appearance, two or more stories in height, and ornamented with small turrets and cupolas: the nakib, or governor's residence, is large, with a high square tower, which gives it the air of a citadel.

There is not a tree or shrub to be seen, the absence of vegetation investing the place with a character of its own, and one that harmonizes with the bold and bare rocks which bound the coast on either side. We were told that, between two ranges of hills close to the entrance of the town, a beautiful green valley occurred, watered by delicious springs, and shaded by date-trees. Had we arrived at an early period of the morning, we might have spent the day on this delightful place, proceeding to it on the backs of camels or donkeys, or even on foot; but it being impossible to get thither while the sun was in full power, we were obliged to content ourselves with a description of its beauties.

Although a very good understanding exists between our Government and that of Makallah, which has for some time been a depot of coal for the use of the steamers, it is not advisable for visitors to proceed very far from the town without protection. A midshipman belonging to the Indian navy having gone on shore for the purpose of visiting the valley before-mentioned, and straying away to some distance, attracted by the beauty of the scenery, was suddenly surrounded by a party of Bedouins, who robbed him of all he possessed, cutting off the buttons from his clothes, under the idea that they were of gold--an impression which obtains all over the coast, and which inspired the people who made the last assault upon Aden with the hope of a rich booty.

The population of Makallah is estimated at about 4,600 people, of various tribes and countries, the chief portion being either of the Beni Hassan and Yafai tribes, together with Banians, Kurachies, and emigrants from nearly all parts of the adjacent coasts. It carries on rather a considerable trade in gums, hides, and drugs, which, with coffee, form the exports, receiving in return iron, lead, manufactured cloths, earthenware, and rice, from Bombay, and all the productions of the neighbouring countries, slaves included, in which the traffic is said to be very great.

The gentlemen who went on shore purchased very pretty and convenient baskets, wrought in various colours, and also quantities of sweetmeats, which are much in esteem in India; these are composed of honey and flour, delicately made, the honey being converted into a soft kind of paste, with a coating of the flour on the outside. These sweetmeats were nicely packed in straw baskets, of a different manufacture from those before-mentioned, and were very superior to the common sort which is brought from the coast in small coarse earthenware basins, exceedingly unattractive in their appearance.

The interior of the country is said to be very beautiful, abundantly watered by refreshing springs, and shaded by groves of date-trees. Amongst its animal productions, the most beautiful is the gazelle, which, properly speaking, is only to be found in Arabia; a delicate and lovely creature, with the soft black eye which has been from time immemorial the theme of poets. The gazelle is easily tamed, becoming in a short time very familiar, and being much more gentle, as well as more graceful, than the common antelope. Its movements are the most airy and elegant imaginable. It is fond of describing a circle in a succession of bounds, jumping off the ground on four legs, and touching it lightly as it wheels round and round. At other times, it pirouettes upon the two fore feet, springing round at the same time like an opera-dancer; in fact, it would appear as if Taglioni, and all our most celebrated *artistes*, had taken lessons from the gazelle, so much do their *chefs-d'oeuvre* resemble its graceful motions. When domesticated, the gazelle loves to feed upon roses, delighting apparently in the scent as well as the taste. It is the fashion in the East to add perfume to the violet, and I found these gazelles would eat with much zest roses that had been plentifully sprinkled with their extract, the *goolabee paanee*, so greatly in request. The gazelle is also very fond of crisply-toasted bread, a taste which must be acquired in domestication. It is a courageous animal, and will come readily to the assault, butting fiercely when attacked. In taking a gazelle away from Arabia, it should be carefully guarded against cold and damp, and if not provided with water-proof covering to its feet, would soon die if exposed to the wet decks of a ship.

We had lost at Aden our fellow-passenger, whom I have mentioned as having assumed the Turkish dress for the purpose of penetrating into the interior of Abyssinia. He depended, in a great measure, for comfort and safety, upon two native priests, whom he had brought with him from Cairo, and who, in return for his liberality, had promised all the protection and assistance in their power. He left us with the good wishes of all the party, and not without some fears in the breasts of those who contemplated the hazards which he ran. Young and good-looking, he had, with pardonable, but perhaps dangerous, vanity, studied the becoming in his costume, which was composed of the very finest materials. His long outer garment, of a delicate woollen texture, was lined throughout with silk, and the crimson cap, which he wore upon his head, was converted into a turban by a piece of gold muslin wound round it. He expected nothing less than to be plundered and stripped of this fine apparel, and it will be well for him should he escape with life. The adventure and the romance of the undertaking possessed great charms, and he talked, after spending some years in a wild and wandering career, of sitting down quietly in his paternal halls, introducing as many of the Egyptian customs as would be tolerated in a Christian country.

A short residence in Cairo proves very captivating to many Englishmen; they like the independent sort of life which they lead; their perfect freedom from all the thralls imposed by society at home, and, when tired of dreaming away existence after the indolent fashion of the East, plunge into the surrounding deserts, and enjoy all the excitement attendant upon danger. Numerous anecdotes were related to me of the hardships sustained by young English travellers, who, led by the spirit of adventure, had trusted themselves to the Bedouins, and, though escaping with life, had suffered very severely from hunger, thirst, and fatigue. I have no reason to doubt the veracity of one of these enterprising tourists, who assured me that he had passed through the holy city of Mecca. According to his account, he had made friends with an Arab boy, who offered to afford him a glimpse of the city, provided he would consent to pass rapidly through it, at an early hour in the morning. Accordingly, disguised in Mohamedan garb, and mounted upon a camel, they entered and quitted it at opposite ends, without exciting curiosity or remark. Of course, he could see nothing but the exterior of the houses and mosques, only obtaining a partial view of these; but, considering the difficulty and peril of the undertaking, the pleasure of being able to say that he had succeeded in an achievement which few would be daring enough to attempt, was worth running some risks.

Notwithstanding the intolerant spirit generally manifested by the Arabs, those English strangers who embrace their way of life for a time frequently attach them very strongly to their persons, obtaining concessions from them which could scarcely be expected from a people so bigoted in their religious opinions, and entertaining so contemptible an opinion of those who are followers of other creeds. In spite of the faults of his character--for he is frequently deceitful, treacherous, cruel, and covetous--the Arab of the desert is usually much respected by the dwellers in towns. His independent spirit is admired by those who could not exist without the comforts and conveniences of life, which he disdains. It is no uncommon sight, either at Cairo or Alexandria, to see a handsome young Bedouin, splendidly attired, lodging in the open street by the side of his camel, for nothing will persuade him to sleep in a house; he carries the habits of the desert into the city, and in the midst of congregated thousands, dwells apart.

We, who merely crossed the desert from Cairo to Suez, could form little idea of the pleasures which a longer sojourn and more extended researches would afford--the poetry of the life which the Arab leads. Nothing, I was told, could exceed the enjoyments of the night, when, after a day of burning heat, the cool breezes came down from elevated valleys, occurring between the ranges of hills which I had observed with so much interest. This balmy air brings with it perfumes wafted from sweet-scented flowers, which spring spontaneously in the green spots known to the gazelle, who repairs to them to drink. Although the dews are heavy, the Arab requires no more protection than that afforded by his blanket, and he lies down under the most glorious canopy, the broad vault of heaven with its countless spangles, no artificial object intervening throughout the large circle of that wide horizon. Here, his ablutions, prayers, and evening-meal concluded, he either sinks into profound repose, or listens to the tales of his companions, of daring deeds and battles long ago, or the equally interesting though less exciting narratives of passing events; some love-story between persons of hostile tribes, or the affection of a betrothed girl for a stranger, and its melancholy consequences.

Notwithstanding the slight estimation in which the sex is held by the fierce and jealous Arab--jealous more from self-love than from any regard to the object that creates this feeling--there is still much of the romantic to be found in his domestic history. English travellers, who have acquired a competent knowledge of the language, may collect materials for poems as tragical and touching as those which Lord Byron loved to weave. I could relate several in this place, picked up by my fellow-travellers, but as they may at some period or other desire to give them to the public themselves, it would be scarcely fair to anticipate their intention.

We now began to look out with some anxiety for the arrival of the steamer at Bombay, speculating upon the chances of finding friends able to receive us. As we drew nearer and nearer, the recollection of the good hotels which had opened their hospitable doors for us in the most unpromising places, caused us to lament over the absence of similar establishments at the scene of our destination. Bombay has been aptly denominated the landing-place of India; numbers of persons who have no acquaintance upon the island pass through it on their way to Bengal, or to the provinces, and if arriving by the Red Sea, are totally unprovided with the means of making themselves comfortable in the tents that may be hired upon their landing.

A tent, to a stranger in India, appears to be the most forlorn residence imaginable, and many cannot be reconciled to it, even after long custom. To those, however, who do not succeed in obtaining invitations to private houses, a tent is the only resource. It seems scarcely possible that the number of persons, who are obliged to live under canvas on the Esplanade, would not prefer apartments at a respectable hotel, if one should be erected for the purpose; yet it is said that such an establishment would not answer. Bombay can never obtain the pre-eminence over Calcutta, which it is so anxious to accomplish, until it will provide the accommodation for visitors which the City of Palaces has afforded during several years past. However agreeable the overland journey may be, it cannot be performed without considerable fatigue.

The voyage down the Red Sea, in warm weather especially, occasions a strong desire for rest; even those persons, therefore, who are so fortunate as to be carried off to friends' houses, immediately upon their arrival, would much prefer the comfort and seclusion of a hotel, for the first day or two at least. The idea of going amongst strangers, travel-soiled and travel-worn, is anything but agreeable, more particularly with the consciousness that a week's baths will scarcely suffice to remove the coal-dust collected in the steamers of the Red Sea: for my own part, I contemplated with almost equal alarm the prospect of presenting myself immediately upon the termination of my voyage, or of being left, on the charge of eight rupees *per diem*, to the tender mercies of the vessel.

We entered the harbour of Bombay in the evening of the 29th of October, too late to contemplate the beauty of its scenery, there being unfortunately no moon. As soon as we dropped anchor, a scene of bustle and excitement took place. The boxes containing the mails were all brought upon deck, the vessel was surrounded with boats, and the first news that greeted our ears--news that was communicated with great glee--was the damage done by fire to the *Atalanta* steamer. This open manifestation, by the officers of the Indian navy, of dislike to a service to which they belong, is, to say the least of it, ill-judged. A rapid increase in the number of armed steam-vessels may be calculated upon, while the destruction of half of those at present employed would scarcely retard the progress of this mighty power--a power which may alter the destinies of half the world. The hostility, therefore, of persons who cannot hope by their united opposition to effect the slightest change in the system, becomes contemptible.

It is a wise proverb which recommends us not to show our teeth unless we can bite. To expose the defects of steamers, may produce their remedy; but to denounce them altogether, is equally useless and unwise, since, however inconvenient they may be, no person, with whom despatch is an object, will hesitate to prefer them to a sailing-vessel; while every officer, who takes the Queen's or the Company's pay, should consider it to be his duty to uphold the service which tends to promote the interests of his country.

CHAPTER IX.
BOMBAY.

Contrast between landing at Bombay and at Calcutta--First feelings those of disappointment--Aspect of the place improves--Scenery of the Island magnificent, abounding with fine Landscapes--Luxuriance and elegance of the Palms--Profusion and contrast of the Trees--Multitude of large Houses in Gardens--Squalid, dirty appearance of the Native Crowd--Costume of the Natives--Inferior to the Costume of Bengal--Countenances not so handsome--The Drive to the Fort--The Burrah Bazaar--Parsee Houses--"God-shops" of the Jains--General use of Chairs amongst the Natives--Interior of the Native Houses--The Sailors' Home--The Native Town--Improvements--The Streets animated and picturesque--Number of Vehicles--The Native Females--The Parsee Women--The Esplanade--Tents and Bungalows--The Fort--The China Bazaar--A Native School--Visit to a Parsee Warehouse--Seal ornamental China-ware--Apprehension of Fire in the Fort--Houses fired by Rats--Illumination of Native Houses--Discordant noise of Native Magic--The great variety of Religions in Bombay productive of lamp-lighting and drumming.

The bunder, or pier, where passengers disembark upon their arrival in Bombay, though well-built and convenient, offers a strong contrast to the splendours of Chandpaul Ghaut in Calcutta; neither are the bunder-boats at all equal in elegance to the budgerows, bohlias, and other small craft, which we find upon the Hooghley. There is nothing to indicate the wealth or the importance of the presidency to be seen at a glance; the Scottish church, a white-washed building of no pretensions, being the most striking object from the sea.

Landward, a range of handsome houses flank so dense a mass of buildings, occupying the interior of the Fort, as to make the whole appear more like a fortified town than a place of arms, as the name would denote. The tower of the cathedral, rising in the centre, is the only feature in the scene which boasts any architectural charm; and the Esplanade, a wide plain, stretching from the ramparts to the sea, is totally destitute of picturesque beauty.

The first feelings, therefore, are those of disappointment, and it is not until the eye has been accustomed to the view, that it becomes pleased with many of the details; the interest increasing with the development of other and more agreeable features, either not seen at all, or seen through an unfavourable medium. The aspect of the place improved, as, after crossing the Esplanade or plain, the carriage drove along roads cut through palm-tree woods, and at length, when I reached my place of destination, I thought that I had never seen any thing half so beautiful.

The apartments which, through the kindness of hospitable friends, I called my own, commanded an infinite variety of the most magnificent scenery imaginable. To the left, through a wide vista between two hills, which seemed cleft for the purpose of admitting the view, lay the placid waters of the ocean, land-locked, as it were, by the bold bluff of distant islands, and dotted by a fairy fleet of fishing-boats, with their white sails glittering in the sun. In front, over a beautifully-planted foreground, I looked down upon a perfect sea of palms, the taller palmyras lifting their proud heads above the rest, and all so intermingled with other foliage, as to produce the richest variety of hues. This fine wood, a spur of what may be termed a forest further to the right, skirted a broad plain which stretched out to the beach, the bright waters beyond expanding and melting into the horizon, while to the right it was bounded by a hilly ridge feathered with palm-trees, the whole bathed in sunshine, and forming altogether a perfect Paradise.

Every period of the day, and every variation in the state of the atmosphere, serve to bring out new beauties in this enchanting scene; and the freshness and delicious balm of the morning, the gorgeous splendour of mid-day, the crimson and amber pomps of evening, and the pale moonlight, tipping every palm-tree top with silver, produce an endless succession of magical effects. In walking about the garden and grounds of this delightful residence, we are continually finding some new point from which the view appears to be more beautiful than before. Upon arriving at the verge of the cleft between the two hills, we look down from a considerable elevation over rocky precipitous ground, with a village (Mazagong) skirting the beach, while the prospect, widening, shows the whole of the harbour, with the high ghauts forming the back-ground.

Turning to the other side, behind the hill which shuts out the sea, the landscape is of the richest description--roads winding through thick plantations, houses peeping from embowering trees, and an umbrageous forest beyond. The whole of Bombay abounds with landscapes which, if not equal to that from Chintapooglee Hill, which I have, vainly I fear, attempted to describe, boast beauties peculiarly their own, the distinguishing feature being the palm-tree. It is impossible to imagine the luxuriance and elegance of this truly regal family as it grows in Bombay, each separate stage, from the first appearance of the different species, tufting the earth with those stately crowns which afterwards shoot up so grandly, being marked with beauty. The variety of the foliage of the coco-nut, the brab, and others, the manner of their growth, differing according to the different directions taken, and the exquisite grouping which continually occurs, prevent the monotony which their profusion might otherwise create, the general effect being, under all circumstances, absolutely perfect. Though the principal, the palm is far from being the only tree, and while frequently forming whole groves, it is as frequently blended with two species of cypress, the peepul, mango, banian, wild cinnamon, and several others.

In addition to the splendour of its wood and water, Bombay is embellished by fragments of dark rock, which force themselves through the soil, roughening the sides of the hills, and giving beauty to the precipitous heights and shelving beach. Though the island is comparatively small, extensively cultivated and thickly inhabited, it possesses its wild and solitary places, its rains deeply seated in thick forests, and its lonely hills covered with rock, and thinly wooded by the eternal palm-tree; hills which, in consequence of the broken nature of the ground, and their cavernous recesses, are difficult of access. It is in these fastnesses that the hyenas find secure retreats, and the Parsees construct their "towers of silence."

There is little, or indeed nothing, in the scenery that comes under the denomination of jungle, the island being intersected in every part with excellent roads, macadamized with the stone that abounds so conveniently for the purpose. These roads are sometimes skirted by walls of dark stone, which harmonize well with the trees that never fail to spread their shade above; at others, with beautiful hedgerows, while across the flats and along the Esplanade, a water-course or a paling forms the enclosures.

The multitude of large houses, each situated in the midst of gardens or ornamented grounds, gives a very cheerful appearance to the roads of Bombay; but what the stranger on his first arrival in India is said to be most struck with is, the number and beauty of the native population. Probably, had I never seen Bengal, I might have experienced similar delight and astonishment; but with the recollections of Calcutta fresh in my mind, I felt disappointed.

Accustomed to multitudes of fine-looking well-dressed people, with their ample and elegant drapery of spotless white muslin, I could not help contrasting them with the squalid, dirty appearance of the native crowd of Bombay. Nor is it so easy at first to distinguish the varieties of the costume through the one grand characteristic of dirt; nor, with the exception of the peculiar Parsee turban, which is very ugly, the Persian cap, and the wild garb of the Arab, do they differ so widely as I expected. For instance; the Hindus and Mohamedans are not so easily recognized as in Bengal. The vest in ordinary wear, instead of being fitted tightly to the figure, and having that peculiarly elegant cut which renders it so graceful, seems nothing more than a loose bed-gown, coarse in materials and tasteless in shape: this forms the most common costume. The higher classes of Parsees wear an ample and not unbecoming dress; the upper garment of white cambric muslin fits tightly to the waist, where it is bound round with a sash or cummurbund of white muslin; it then descends in an exceedingly full skirt to the feet, covering a pair of handsome silk trowsers. A Parsee group, thus attired, in despite of their mean and unbecoming head-dress, make a good appearance.

The Arabs wear handkerchiefs or shawls, striped with red, yellow, and blue, bound round their heads, or hanging in a fanciful manner over their turbans. The Persian dress is grave and handsome, and there are, besides, Nubians, Chinese, and many others; but the well-dressed people must be looked for in the carriages, few of the same description are to be seen on foot, which gives to a crowd in Bengal so striking an appearance. In fact, a Bengallee may be recognized at a glance by his superior costume, and in no place is the contrast more remarkable than in the halls and entrances of Anglo-Indian houses. The servants, if not in livery--and it is difficult to get them to wear one, the dignity of caste interfering--are almost invariably ill-dressed and slovenly in their appearance. We see none of the beautifully plaited and unsullied white turbans; none of the fine muslin dresses and well-folded cummurbunds; the garments being coarse, dirty, scanty, and not put on to advantage. Neither are the countenances so handsome or the forms so fine; for though a very considerable degree of beauty is to be found of person and feature amid many classes of Parsees, Jews, Hindus, and Mohamedans, it is not so general as in Bengal, where the features are usually so finely cut, and the eyes so splendid.

Nevertheless, although my admiration has never been so strongly excited, and I was in the first instance greatly disappointed, every time I go abroad I become more reconciled to this change, and more gratified by the various objects which attract my attention; and there are few things that please me more than a drive to the Fort.

It is very difficult, perhaps impossible, to convey any idea of the lively scene which is presented in this excursion, or the great variety of features which it embraces. Enclosures sprinkled over with palm-trees, and filled with a herd of buffaloes, occur close to a farm-house, which looks absolutely English; then we come to a cluster of huts of the most miserable description, occupying some low situation, placed absolutely on the ground, and scantily thatched with palm branches; stately mansions now arise to view, and then there is a row of small but apparently comfortable dwellings, habitations being thickly scattered over fields and gardens, until we reach what has been denominated the Black Town, but which is now generally known as the Burrah Bazaar. This is now a broad street, and, without exception, one of the most curious places I have ever beheld. It is said to have been much improved during late administrations, and, forming the high road to the Fort, is the avenue most frequented in the native town by Europeans. The buildings on either side are very irregular, and of various descriptions; some consist of ranges of small shops, with a story above in a very dilapidated and tumble-down condition. Then comes a row of large mansions of three floors, which look very much like the toy baby-houses constructed for children in England, the windows being so close together, and the interiors so public; others intervene, larger, more solid, and irregular, but exceedingly picturesque.

Most of the better kind of houses are ascended by a flight of steps, which leads to a sort of verandah, formed by the floor above projecting over it, and being supported by wooden pillars or other frame-work in front. In the Parsee houses of this kind, there is usually a niche in this lower portion for a lamp, which is kept always burning. In some places, the houses are enclosed in courtyards, and at others a range of dwellings, not very unlike the alms-houses in England, are divided from the road by a low wall, placed a few yards in the front, and entered at either end by gateways. These houses have a very comfortable appearance, and the shading of a few palm-trees completes a rather pretty picture. There are two mosques, one on either side of this street, which are handsomely constructed, and would be great embellishments to the scene, were they not so painfully whiter-washed.

A peculiar class of Hindus, the Jains, have also what have not been inappropriately termed "god-shops," for they certainly have not the slightest appearance of temples. These pagodas, if they may be so styled, are nothing more than large houses, of three floors, with balconies running in front, the heavy wooden framework that supports them being painted a dark dingy red, and the walk adorned with representations of deities, executed in a variety of colours, and of the most nondescript character. The interiors appear to be decorated in the same manner, as they are seen through the open windows and by the light of many lamps suspended from the ceilings. The ringing of bells, and the full attendance of priests and worshippers of an evening, show the purpose to which these houses are dedicated, and superstition is here exhibited in its most revolting aspect, for there is no illusion to cheat the fancy--no beautiful sequestered pagoda, with its shadowing trees and flower-strewed courts, to excite poetical ideas--all being coarse, vulgar, and contemptible.

Great numbers of artizans are to be seen at work in their respective shops in this bazaar, copper-smiths particularly, who seem an industrious race, toiling by lamp-light long after the day has completely closed. There are also **caravanserais** and **cafes**, where the country and religion of the owner may be known by the guests congregated about his gate. Groups of Persians are seen seated on the outside smoking; the beautiful cats, which they have brought down for sale, sporting at their feet. A few yards farther on, the Arab horse-dealers, in front of their stables, are equally conspicuous, and it is easy to perceive, by the eager glances with which some of these men survey the English carriages bearing fair freights of ladies along, that they have never visited an European settlement before.

My former visit to India enabling me to observe the differences between two of our presidencies, I was particularly struck, on my arrival at Bombay, with the general use of chairs among the natives; none but the very meanest description of houses seem to be entirely destitute of an article of furniture scarcely known in the native habitations of Bengal; and these seats seem to be preferred to the more primitive method of squatting on the ground, which still prevails, the number of chairs in each mansion being rather circumscribed, excepting in the best houses, where they abound. Sofas and divans, though seen, are not so common as in Egypt, and perhaps the divan, properly speaking, is not very usual.

The cheapness of oil, and in all probability the example shown by the Parsees, render lamps very abundant. The common kind of hall-lamp of England, of different sizes and different colours, is the prevailing article; these are supplied with a tumbler half-filled with water, having a layer of oil upon the top, and two cotton-wicks. As I lose no opportunity whatever of looking into the interiors of the native houses, I have been often surprised to see one of these lamps suspended in a very mean apartment of a cottage, boasting few other articles of furniture, which, nevertheless, in consequence of its cleanliness, and the excellence of the light afforded, possessed an air of comfort. In fact, many of the houses, whose exteriors are anything but promising, are very well fitted up in the inside; many of the apartments are panelled with wood, handsomely carved, and have ceilings and floors of the same, either painted of a dark colour, or highly polished. In the evening, the windows being all open, and the lamps lighted, a foil view may be obtained of these apartments.

Many of the houses appear to be kept entirely for show, since in all my peregrinations I have never seen any human being in the upper chambers, although illuminated every night. In others, there can be no doubt concerning the fact of their having inhabitants, since the owners do not scruple to go to bed with the windows open and the lamps burning, not disturbed in their repose by the certainty of being seen by every passer-by, or by the noise and bustle of the street.

The bazaar ends at the commencement of the Esplanade, in a large building, wooden-fronted, of a circular form, and not unhandsome, which is decorated with a flag upon the roof, and is called "The Sailors' Home." Its verandahs and open windows often display our jovial tars enjoying themselves in an asylum which, though evil has been spoken against it, is said to be well-conducted, and to prevent a very thoughtless class of persons from falling into worse hands.

The native town extends considerably on either side of the principal avenue, one road leading through the coco-nut gardens, presenting a great variety of very interesting features; that to the left is more densely crowded, there being a large and well-frequented cloth bazaar, besides a vast number of shops and native houses, apparently of considerable importance. Here the indications shown of wealth and industry are exceedingly gratifying to an eye delighting in the sight of a happy and flourishing population. There are considerable spaces of ground between these leading thoroughfares, which, by occasional peeps down intersecting lanes, seem to be covered with a huddled confusion of buildings, and, until the improvements which have recently taken place, the whole of the town seems to have been nearly in the same state.

The processes of widening, draining, pulling down, and rebuilding, appear to have been carried on very extensively; and though much, perhaps, remains to be done in the back settlements, where buffaloes may be seen wading through the stagnant pools, the eye is seldom offended, or the other senses disagreeably assailed, in passing through this populous district. The season is, however, so favourable, the heat being tempered by cool airs, which render the sunshine endurable, that Bombay, under its present aspect, may be very different from the Bombay of the rains or of the very hot weather. The continual palm-trees, which, shooting up in all directions, add grace and beauty to every scene, must form terrible receptacles for malaria; the fog and mist are said to cling to their branches and hang round them like a cloud, when dispersed by sun or wind elsewhere; the very idea suggesting fever and ague.

Though, as I have before remarked, the contrast between the muslined millions of Bengal and the less tastefully clad populace of Bombay is unfavourable, still the crowds that fill the streets here are animated and picturesque. There is a great display of the liveliest colours, the turbans being frequently of the brightest of yellows, crimsons, or greens.

The number of vehicles employed is quite extraordinary, those of the merely respectable classes being chiefly bullock-carts; these are of various descriptions, the greater number being of an oblong square, and furnished with seats across (after the fashion of our taxed carts), in which twelve persons, including women and children, are frequently accommodated. It is most amusing to see the quantity of heads squeezed close together in a vehicle of this kind, and the various contrivances resorted to in order to accommodate a more than sufficient number of personages in other conveyances, not so well calculated to hold them. Four in a buggy is a common complement, and six or nine persons will cram themselves into so small a space, that you wonder how the vehicle can possibly contain the bodies of all the heads seen looking out of it. The carts are chiefly open, but there are a few covered *rhuts*, the conveyances probably of rich Hindu or Mohamedan ladies, who do not content themselves, like the Parsees, with merely covering their heads with the veil.

Young Parsee women of the better class are frequently to be seen in carriages with their male relations, nor do they object to appear publicly in the streets following wedding processions. They are the only well-dressed or nice-looking women who drive or walk about the streets or roads. The lower classes of females in Bombay are the most unprepossessing people I ever saw. In Bengal, the *saree*, though rather too scanty, is a graceful costume, and at a little distance appears to be a modest covering. Here it is worn very differently, and without the slightest attempt at delicacy or grace, the drapery being in itself insufficient, and rendered more offensive by the method of its arrangement.

The Parsee women are, generally speaking, of fair complexions, with small features, and a very sweet expression of countenance; many of them are exceedingly pretty, and they all dress gracefully and becomingly. Very respectable females of this class are to be seen walking about, showing by their conduct that propriety of behaviour does not consist in seclusion, or the concealment of the face.

There is an innate delicacy and refinement about Parsee women which commands respect, and their value is known and acknowledged by their male relatives, who treat them with a degree of deference and consideration which is highly creditable to both parties. Though the men are found in service in every European family, they do not allow their wives and daughters to become domestics to foreigners, and they are only permitted to become servants to their own people. The higher classes of natives have adopted European equipages, and are the owners of the handsomest carriages and horses in Bombay. Chariots, barouches, britschkas, and buggies, appear in great numbers, filled with Mohamedan, Hindu, or Parsee gentlemen. The less fashionable use the palanquin carriage, common in Bengal, but which at this place is called a ***shigram***; these are often crammed full of servants and children.

Upon emerging from the bazaar, we enter upon the wide plain called the Esplanade. To the left, across an extensive parade-ground, appears the Fort, which is seen to the best advantage from this point; the walls are low, and afford an ample view of a range of three-storied houses, having verandahs all the way up, called Rampart Row, and from which one or two very splendid mansions stand out conspicuously. To the right, there is a whole encampment of tents, these canvas dwellings being the sole refuge for the destitute. They may be hired in any number and of every degree of elegance, none, however, quite reaching to the refinements of Bengal, or being supplied with glass doors and windows. Beyond the tents, and quite close to the beach, is the space allotted for the temporary bungalows erected during the cold season--singular places, which will be more fully described under the head of Anglo-Indian residences. In front, and close to the warf or bunder, are immense irregular piles of cotton in bales, which at a distance appear like fortifications, and upon a nearer approach assume somewhat of a picturesque air.

The Fort is surrounded on the land-side with a moat, and is entered through some very shabby gateways. The interior of this extensive work presents a busy, bustling scene; its numerous houses being arranged with some degree of regularity in streets and open places. Those who content themselves, however, with driving through the European portion, will have very little idea of the true character of the place. Rampart Row--the avenues leading into a large open space, in which stand the cathedral, the town-hall, the mint, a cavalry barrack, &c.--and the immediate environs, are composed of lofty, well-constructed houses, some standing a little apart in courtyards, and others with a narrow platform in front, ascended by steps, and roofed by the story above. This, as I have previously stated, is the general method of building in Bombay. These streets have somewhat of an European, though not an English, air, but are for the most part tenanted by natives, who may be seen at the windows of every floor, and who apparently are better lodged, at least according to our idea, than the same class in Calcutta. In this part of the Fort there are several shops, or rather warehouses, for the sale of European goods--dingy places, having a melancholy assortment of faded articles in dim glass cases, freshness and variety in the merchandize depending upon shipping arrivals.

Earthenware, glass, and cutlery, are abundant; but, altogether, there is nothing at present to compare with the first-rate establishments of Calcutta--such as Tulloh's, for instance--the whole style being dirty and slovenly. A very civil native, named Muncherjee, who calls himself a milliner, has, I am informed, very frequently well-chosen investments to dispose of, but upon my visits I have seen nothing wearable in the shape of bonnets and caps. An English milliner resides in his neighbourhood, who possesses both skill and taste, and makes up her silks and gauzes after the best French models; but necessarily, perhaps, the purchases made at her rooms are rather expensive.

There is quite enough of bustle and animation in this quarter of the Fort to engage the attention, but it seems silent and deserted when compared with the crowd of the more exclusively native portions. Here the streets literally swarm with life--men, women, children, and bullocks, filling them almost to suffocation. Ranges of open shops appear on each side, raised a foot or two from the ground, the occupant being seated upon a ledge in front, in the midst of his wares. Here, too, immense quantities of English glass and crockery-ware are exhibited, which may be purchased at a much cheaper rate than in shops styled, **par distinction**, European.

One or two opportunities offering for a visit to what is called the China Bazaar, I gladly availed myself of them, and was much amused, as the carriage made its slow way through the multitudes that thronged the streets, to observe the employments of the people, buying, selling, manufacturing their goods, or, for want of something else to do, dragging little children in carts, which, by some contrivance, ran back across the floor of the narrow apartment, and were then impelled forward again by means of a string. This I found to be a favourite occupation, and I never in any place saw more fondness manifested towards children by their parents than in Bombay, or a greater desire to associate them in all their amusements. At length, the carriage stopped at a gateway, and upon alighting, I found myself in the midst of a crowd of little children--an infant school, in fact, composed indiscriminately of boys and girls. They were, generally speaking, very pretty, and all well-dressed, many being adorned with very handsome jewels.

The pedagogue--a Parsee, and rather a young man--with the barbarity common to his class, was in the act of inflicting corporal punishment upon a poor little creature, whom he beat upon the feet (ornamented, by the way, with rich anclets) with a rod of split bamboo. I commanded him to forbear, but speaking half in English and half in Hindustanee, made myself better understood by look and gesture than by words. The unhappy infant seemed to know that I interfered in its behalf, for it gazed upon me with a piteous but grateful expression; it could not have been more than three years old, and was really very pretty and interesting in its tears. It was evidently the child of wealthy parents, being dressed in a silk shirt embroidered and trimmed with silver, a cap of the same upon its head, and numerous jewels besides. The whole of the Lilliputian assembly uttered their lesson as I passed, all raising their voices at the same time, and rendering it, I imagine, rather difficult to determine whether each pupil repeated his or her part correctly.

I would fain have lingered for a few minutes, but my attendants officiously showing the way, I walked across a paved yard and up two flights of steps to the shop of which I came in search, which was kept by a good-looking Parsee. The trade of this person was designated as that of a ***bottlee wallah***, which being literally rendered means 'bottle-fellow,' but, according to a more free translation, a dealer in glass, lamps, candlesticks, preserved meats in tin-cases, &c. &c. I found a vast stock of the articles most in request in Indian housekeeping, such as wall-shades, and all descriptions of earthen and hard-ware, all of which he sold at very moderate prices, but having executed the part of my commission which related to candlesticks, I was unable to find the more *recherche* articles of which I came in quest.

I had been told that a great variety of ornamental china, the real product of the Celestial Empire, was to be seen in the native shops in Bombay. Though showy in appearance, this sort of china is of little value, except to mark how much the manufacture has degenerated since Europeans have learned to make their own teacups. I wished to obtain a few specimens, but could not succeed. My friend, the bottlee wallah, though very civil, could not afford me the information I required, nor have I yet been able to obtain it. I have seen some handsome jars, plates such as are used in England for the deposit of visitors' cards, &c., which were purchased for a few annas, and have been told that I might procure any quantity I pleased, but the where is still a mystery.

All the information obtainable in Bombay must be fished out in an extraordinary manner, both natives and Europeans seeming to make it a rule never to commit themselves by a direct reply to any question; in every single instance, up to the present time, I have always, upon making an inquiry, been referred to somebody else. Neither do I find the same zeal manifested in the servants, which amounts to officiousness on the other side of India. I have sent them to purchase the china, but can get nothing but rubbish, knowing all the while that there are plenty of a better description to be had.

Upon my return, the bottlee wallah accompanied me to the carriage in waiting, and as I paused to notice some of the children in the school, introduced me to a group of his own sons and daughters, well decked out in jewels, and otherwise richly dressed. The instruction given at these schools I understood to be merely oral, the repetition of a few verses, intended rather to pass away the time and keep the children out of mischief, than as a foundation of more useful studies. I hope that the system will be improved, for the pupils seemed to be extremely intelligent, and capable of better things.

Returning home, I passed several shops, in which the artizans of a very beautiful manufacture, peculiar to Bombay, were at work. Desks, dressing-cases, work-boxes, card-cases, ink-stands, and a variety of other ornamental fancy articles, are made of sandal-wood, covered and inlaid with ivory, ebony, and a material resembling silver. They copy the best patterns, and produce exceedingly elegant appendages for the drawing or dressing-room tables. A desk, handsomely fitted up and lined with velvet, is sold for seven or eight pounds; large ink-stands and blotting books for twenty rupees, and card-cases for six or eight.

It is impossible, while perambulating the Fort of Bombay, to avoid a feeling of apprehension concerning a catastrophe, which sooner or later seems certain to happen, and which nothing short of a miracle appears to prevent from taking place every night; I mean the destruction of the whole by fire. All the houses are constructed of the most combustible materials, and the greater number belonging to the native quarter are thatched. Though contrary to law, many of the warehouses contain gunpowder, while the immense quantity of oil and spirits stored up in them would render a conflagration, once commenced, most fearful. Few or no precautions seem to be taken by the natives against fire. There are lights burning in every room of every house, fires are continually made outside, whence a single spark might set the whole in flames; and added to these dangers, are the prejudices of the great number of the inhabitants, whose religious feelings would prevent them from making the slightest endeavour to stay the progress of the element which they worship. Nor would the destruction of property be the sole danger. It is terrible to think of the fearful risk of life in a place in which escape would be so difficult. The gates of the Fort are few in number, and of narrow dimensions; a new one is now constructing, probably with some view to an emergence of the kind. The natives, upon the occasion of its proposal, evinced their readiness to assist in the execution of a plan so advantageous to the place of their abode, and immediately advanced half the sum which this necessary improvement would cost--namely, thirty thousand rupees--which were subscribed and paid into the treasury in the course of a week.

In 1803 or 1804, a very destructive conflagration actually took place in the Fort of Bombay, and upon that occasion, in order to save the castle, which did then, and does now, contain an immense quantity of gunpowder, the authorities were obliged to bring out cannon to batter down the surrounding houses, for the purpose of arresting the progress of the flames. When the place was rebuilt, many salutary regulations were made to prevent the recurrence of so great a calamity, and could all the plans of Government have been accomplished, the danger which now threatens Bombay would have been very considerably lessened; but it was found impossible to carry out all the objects contemplated, in consequence of the great value of the property which they would affect.

The land within the walls of the Fort has become in a great measure private property, and the convenience of its contiguity to the harbour is so great, and the natives entertain so strong an idea of security in a residence in a fortified place, however disqualified to resist a hostile force, that nothing would prevail upon them to relinquish their houses. The higher classes are well aware of the hazards they incur, but, like the dwellers in the neighbourhood of a volcano, are unwilling to quit a place endeared to them by long residence, though they know not the hour in which they may be buried beneath its smoking ruins. There are only a few Europeans who continue to inhabit the Fort, but it must contain a very considerable portion of the property of those merchants who have their offices and warehouses within its walls. The British authorities have taken all the precautions in their power, the fire-engines have been placed in a state of greater efficiency than heretofore, while, should an extensive fire take place, everything that European strength and skill could accomplish would be attempted.

Amongst the various accidents to which houses in Bombay are subjected, the one to be most apprehended, that of fire, is often brought about by rats. They will carry off a lighted candle at every convenient opportunity, setting fire to dwellings by this means. They have been also known to upset tumblers containing oil, which is thus spread abroad and likely to be ignited by the falling wick. It is, perhaps, impossible totally to exterminate this race of vermin, which in the Fort set cats completely at defiance, but something might be done to keep the population down. I have been told that there are places in the more crowded portion rendered perfectly impassable at night in consequence of the effluvia arising from the immense quantities of musk rats, which, together with the common sort, and bandicoots of an incredible size, abound, the narrow close lanes being apparently built for the purpose of affording accommodation to vermin of every description. Nevertheless, some of the native houses of the Fort would form very agreeable residences to persons accustomed to the utmost refinement. Being exceedingly lofty, the upper apartments have the advantage of every breeze that blows, while the views both of sea and land are splendid.

The immense size of these houses, and the elegance of their decorations, evince the spirit and wealth of their owners; they become absolutely beacons at night, in consequence of the frequency and the extent of their illuminations. Numerous are the occasions, either of holidays or other rejoicings, in which the natives of Bombay light up their houses; rows of lamps hung along the wide fronts of the verandahs, upon every floor, produce a good effect, which is often heightened by the flood of light poured out of apartments decorated with chandeliers and lamps of every description.

In passing through the bazaar at night, every third or fourth house is lit up upon some festive occasion; one favourite and very pretty method consists of a number of small lamps, arranged to resemble bunches of grapes, and hung up in the trees of a court-yard. Sometimes in the evening, a sort of market is held in the native town beyond the Esplanade, and every stall is profusely lighted; the hawkers, who carry about their goods in a more humble way upon their heads in baskets, have them stuck with candles, and the wild shadowy effects produced, amid the quaint buildings thus partially lighted, afford a continual phantasmagoria.

They must be destitute of imagination, indeed, who cannot find pleasure in the contemplation of the night-scenes of Bombay, either from its native crowds, or the delicious solitudes of its sylvan shades. The ear is the only organ absolutely unblest in this sunny island, the noises being incessant, and most discordant; the shrieking of jackals by night is music compared to that from native instruments, which, in the most remote places, are continually striking up: the drums, trumpets, bells, and squeaking pipes, of a neighbouring village, are now inflicting their torments upon my distracted brain in the most barbarous manner possible. The exertions of the performers never appear to relax, and by night or day, it is all the same; they make themselves heard at any distance, parading along the roads for the sole purpose, it should seem, of annoying the more peaceable inhabitants. Certainly, the sister arts of music and painting have yet to make their way in India, the taste for both being at present perfectly barbarous.

The European bands, when playing on the Esplanade, attract a very considerable number of natives; but whether congregated for the purpose of listening to the music, or merely for the sake of passing the time, seems very doubtful. A few, certainly, manifest a predilection for "concord of sweet sounds," and no difficulty is experienced by band-masters in recruiting their forces from natives, the boys learning readily, and acquitting themselves very well upon instruments foreign to the country. There is, however, no manifestation at present of the spread of a refined taste, and many years will probably elapse before any thing like good music will be common in this part of Asia.

The great variety of religions extant in Bombay, each being distinguished by numerous festivals, all celebrated in the same manner--that is, by noise and illuminations--sufficiently accounts for the perpetual recurrence of lamp-lighting and drumming in all directions. Every week brings round the anniversary of some day of rejoicing of the Mohamedans, Hindus, Parsees, Jews, Roman Catholics, or Armenians, and Bombay may therefore be said to present one universal holiday. Passing the other evening one of the handsomest pagodas in the island, an oblong square building of yellow stone, with a mitre-shaped tower at one end, I was surprised by the number of European carriages in waiting. The exterior had all the air of a Christian church, the situation beautiful, a platform of rock overlooking the sea; and I could not help indulging the hope, that the substitution of chariots and buggies for palanquins and ***rhuts*** would lead to the introduction of a purer and better creed.

CHAPTER X.
BOMBAY--(Continued).

Bombay the rising Presidency--Probability of its becoming the Seat of Government--The Anglo-Indian Society of Bombay--Style of Living--The Gardens inferior to those of Bengal--Interiors of the Houses more embellished--Absence of Glass-windows an evil--The Bungalows--The Encamping-ground--Facility and despatch of a change of residence--Visit to a tent entertainment--Inconveniences attending a residence in tents--Want of Hotels and Boarding-houses--Deficiency of public Amusements in Bombay--Lectures and **Conversaziones** suggested, as means of bringing the native community into more frequent intercourse with Europeans--English spoken by the superior classes of natives--Natives form a very large portion of the wealth and intelligence of Bombay--Nothing approaching the idea of a City to be seen--The climate more salubrious than that of Bengal--Wind blows hot and cold at the same time--Convenience a stranger finds in so many domestic servants speaking English--Their peculiar mode of speaking it--Dress of servants--Their wages--The Cooks--Improved by Lord Clare--Appointments of the tables--The Ramoosee Watchmen--Their vociferations during the night--Fidelity of the natives--Controversy concerning their disregard of truth.

Comparisons are so frequently both unfair and invidious, that I had determined, upon my arrival at Bombay, to abstain from making them, and to judge of it according to its own merits, without reference to those of the rival presidency. It was impossible, however, to adhere to this resolution, and being called upon continually to give an opinion concerning its claims to superiority over Calcutta, I was reluctantly compelled to consider it in a less favourable point of view than I should have done had the City of Palaces been left out of the question.

That Bombay is the rising presidency there can be no doubt, and there seems to be every probability of its becoming the seat of the Supreme Government; nothing short of a rail-road between the two presidencies can avert this catastrophe; the number of days which elapse before important news reaching Bombay can be known and acted upon by the authorities of Calcutta rendering the measure almost imperative. Bengal, too proudly triumphing in her greatness, has now to bear the mortifications to which she delighted to subject Bombay, a place contemptuously designated as "a fishing village," while its inhabitants, in consequence of their isolated situation, were called "the Benighted."

Steam-communication brought the news to Bombay of the accession of Queen Victoria to the throne of England, and this event was celebrated at the same time that the Bengallees were toasting the health of William the Fourth at a dinner given in honour of his birth-day. "Who are the Benighted now?" was the universal cry; and the story is told with great glee to all new arrivals.

Concerning the Anglo-Indian society of Bombay, I do not pretend to know any thing, or to give opinions which must necessarily be premature and presumptuous. A round of dinner parties affords little opportunity of making acquaintance; they are much the same everywhere, and when a large company is assembled, their agreeability must entirely depend upon the persons who occupy the neighbouring chairs.

Bombay is accused, with what degree of justice I cannot determine, of being a place much addicted to scandal and gossip. If this charge be well founded, it is one which it must share in common with all limited circles. The love of detraction is unhappily a thoroughly English vice, flourishing under all circumstances, and quite as prevalent, though not, perhaps, equally hurtful, in great cities as in the smallest village. The same people who in London delight in the perusal of newspapers of the most libellous description, and who read with avidity every publication which attacks private character, will, when removed into a congenial sphere, pick their neighbours to pieces; an amusement which cannot be enjoyed in the metropolis, where happily we do not know the names of the parties who occupy the adjoining houses.

We are proud of our virtues, not unjustly giving ourselves credit for many that elevate and refine the human character; but even the most solid and the most dazzling can scarcely compensate for that one universal sin, that want of charity, which leads English people upon all occasions to undervalue and disparage their most intimate acquaintance. How few will scruple to point out to others the follies and foibles of their dearest friends, weaknesses which they have discovered during long and familiar intercourse; and how few will hesitate to impute the very worst motives for actions which may spring from a laudable source, or be merely the result of thoughtlessness! In our most Christian country, the spirit of the Christian religion is still to be sought, and until we see stronger proofs of its influence than can at present be shown throughout the United Kingdom, we must not single out a remote colony as a specimen of the indulgence of a vice common to us all.

The great evil, which Bombay must share with other communities similarly constituted, is the want of family ties, and the consequent loss of all the gentle affections which spring amid a wide domestic circle. Neither the very old nor the very young are to be found in an Indian colony; there are few connecting links to bind the sojourners of a foreign land together; each has a separate interest, and the result is seen in a general want of sympathy; no one seems to enter into the views, feelings, hopes, or objects of another. I employ the word **seems**, since, as a stranger, I can only give my first impressions upon the subject.

The style of living is more easily described, and its relative advantages determined. The Anglo-Indian residents of Bombay are, for the most part, scattered all over the island, living in very comfortable houses, of no great pretensions to exterior elegance, yet having for the most part an air of home enjoyment, which suggests pleasing ideas. One feature is very striking, the porticoes and verandahs of many being completely covered with luxuriant flowering creepers, which in Bengal are never suffered to be near the house, in consequence of the harbour they are supposed to give to insects and reptiles. The approach to these beautiful screens is, however, frequently through a cabbage-garden, the expedience of planting out the unsightly but useful vegetables destined for the kitchen not having been as yet considered; neither can the gardens at this period of the year, the cold season, compare with those of Bengal, the expense of irrigation preventing the inhabitants from devoting so much time and attention to their improvement, while as yet the natives have not been encouraged to fill the bazaars with European vegetables. Pease are spoken of as not being uncommon, but I have only seen them once, even at the best tables. Neither have cauliflowers, French beans, or asparagus, made their appearance--vegetables common at Christmas all over the Bengal presidency.

The interiors of the houses are, generally speaking, more embellished than those of Calcutta; the greater part have handsome ceilings, and the doorways and windows are decorated with mouldings, and otherwise better finished. The walls also are coloured, and often very tastefully picked out with white or some other harmonizing tint. The reception-rooms, therefore, have not the barn-like air which detracts from the magnitude of those of Bengal, and the furniture, if not always equally splendid, is shown off to greater advantage; but here I should say the superiority ends.

Some of the small bungalows are very neatly fitted up with boarded ceilings, a great improvement upon the cloth which conceals the rafters in those of Bengal; others, however, are canopied with cloth, and some there are which appear more like summer-houses than habitations intended for Europeans throughout the year, being destitute of glass windows, and open to all the winds of heaven.

The frequent changes of the atmosphere which occur in Bombay, and the danger of a touch of the land-wind, render the absence of glass windows a very serious evil; they are, however, unknown in the temporary bungalows erected upon the Esplanade, which seem to be favourite residences of people who could lodge themselves more substantially if they pleased. The barn-like thatched roofs of these dwellings make them rather unsightly objects, though some are redeemed by a thick drapery of creepers; but the interiors of many are of a very pavilion-like description, and the singularity of all renders them interesting to a stranger.

These houses usually consist of two or more principal apartments, united with each other by means of verandahs, and formed chiefly of wooden frame-work panelled with canvas, with here and there a partition of wattle and dab. They have generally large porticoes of trellice-work in front, sufficiently spacious to allow a carriage to drive under them, which is thus screened from the sun; these porticoes being mantled with flowering creepers of many beautiful kinds. A sort of garden is also formed by plants in tubs, and there is sometimes a cultivated oval or circular space, which, in such a climate, a very few weeks will render luxuriant. The fronts of these bungalows face the sea, and have all the benefit of its breezes, while the intervening space between the fort forms the parade-ground of the garrison, and the most esteemed evening drive.

Those who inhabit these bungalows, and who do not rise before the sun, are subjected to all the inconveniences attending upon field practice, the firing of musquetry and the war of cannon close to their ears, and though favourite residences, they seem better suited to persons well accustomed to all the vicissitudes of Anglo-Indian life than to a stranger. For my own part, I confess a prejudice in favour of brick and mortar, glass windows, and chimneys; and though perfectly content, while travelling, to put up with any accommodation that may offer, would never willingly settle down for a season in a mansion of canvas, mat, and bamboo, where the rats have free ingress, and the atmosphere is filled with innumerable winged insects.

Before the general setting-in of the rains, these bungalows, I am informed, assume a very damp and tatterdemalion appearance, and when the skies open their flood-gates, they are obliged to be taken down and warehoused until the following year. Some of these bungalows are private property, others are erected by the natives and let to their tenants at a monthly rent. In some, the sleeping and sitting apartments are under different roofs; all have a considerable piece of ground enclosed round them, the allotments to each party being made by Government, and appertaining to certain appointments in the service.

Beyond these bungalows is the encamping ground, in which certain temporary sojourners in Bombay either pitch or hire a tent or tents, the accommodation differing according to the expense incurred. The superior tents--such, for instance, as that engaged by the late admiral--are spacious and convenient; a handsome suite of apartments, consisting of ante-room, drawing-room, and dining-room, partitioned off by canvas curtains, which could be rolled up at pleasure, were lighted by chandeliers suspended from the cross-poles and girandoles against those that supported the roof; the walls were handsomely lined, the floors covered with thick mats and carpets; nothing being wanted to render this canvas dwelling equal in comfort and elegance to the tents of Bengal, excepting glass doors.

The weather, during the cold season in this part of India, is not nearly so inclement as in Calcutta and the north-western provinces; nevertheless, it is very desirable to shut out the keen and cutting wind, which frequently blows during the night. The people here, however, seem fond of living in tents, and it often happens that gentlemen especially, who have had good houses of their own over their heads, go to very considerable expense for the purpose of enjoying the free air of a camp.

I had an opportunity of seeing the facility and despatch with which such a change of residence is managed in Bombay. Driving one evening round the foot of a conical hill overlooking the sea, we met a party of gentlemen who said that they were looking out for a good place to pitch their tents, and invited us to dine with them on the following evening at seven o'clock. As the hill was in our neighbourhood, we ascertained at eleven o'clock the next morning that there was not a symptom of habitation upon it; however, we were determined to keep our engagement, and accordingly arrived at the appointed hour at the point of the road at which a rude pathway opened.

It was perfectly dark, but we found the place indicated by a cluster of lamps hanging like a bunch of grapes from a tree; a palanquin was also in waiting to carry the ladies up the hill in turn. I preferred walking; and though my shoes and the hem of my gown were covered with prickles and thorns, which interweaved themselves in an extraordinary manner through a satin dress, I enjoyed the walk amazingly. A man with a lanthorn led the way, a precaution always taken in Bombay, on account of the alleged multitude of the snakes, and at every three or four yards' distance, another cluster of lamps suspended from a tree pointed out the way.

In a few minutes we arrived at a platform of table-land on the summit of the hill, prettily sprinkled with palm-trees, and came upon a scene full of life, picture, and movement. The white outline of the smaller tents had a sort of phantom look in the ambiguous light, but the open doors of the principal one showed a strong illumination. A table, which we might have supposed to be raised by the hand of an enchanter, gleaming with silver, cut glass, and wax candles, was absolutely framed in by the darkness around. Two or three horses picketed under the trees with their grooms, cowering over fires made upon the ground, looked very like unearthly chargers, just emerged with their grim attendants from some subterranean kingdom; while the red glare from the cooking tents, and the dusky figures moving about, could scarcely be recognised as belonging to human and every-day life--the whole scene having a supernatural air.

The interior of the tents was extremely picturesque, fitted up with odds and ends of foreign products, and looking very like the temporary haunt of some pirate; tiger skins, rich soft thick rugs of Persian manufacture, interspersed with Indian mats, covered the floors; the tents were lined with flags, favouring the notion that the corsair's bark lay anchored in some creek below; while daggers, and pistols, and weapons of all kinds, helped out a fanciful imagination to a tale of wild adventure. The butler of our host had enacted more wonders than a man; under such circumstances, a repast of fish and curry might have been considered a great achievement, but we had the three regular courses, and those, too, of a most **recherche** kind, with a dessert to match, all sent up to the point of perfection.

After coffee, I went out to look upon the sea, which lay like a mirror below the perpendicular height on which I stood; and as my eyes became accustomed to the darkness of a moonless night, I saw under new aspects the sombre outlines of those soft hills, whose purple loveliness I had admired so much during the day.

I spent several pleasant evenings in these tents, which were engaged by a young nobleman upon his travels for the purpose of escaping from the annoyances of the Fort, and who, during his short residence under canvas, had the advantage of the companionship of a friend, to whose experienced servants he was indebted for the excellence of the arrangements.

When it is considered that these tents were pitched upon a lonely spot, upwards of four miles from Bombay and from the bazaars, the celerity and success with which every thing was managed will appear quite wonderful. The tents were found to be so cold, that a gentleman who afterwards joined the party slept in his palanquin; they were subsequently removed, and now the palm-tree waves its broad leaves over the lonely hill, and the prowling jackal seeks his meal elsewhere. Tents such as those now described form the rarer and brighter specimens, their usual character being very different.

On the Esplanade we step at once from the ground upon a settrinjee, which bears all the marks of having been well trodden by sandy feet; an opening at the farther extremity shows the sea, glaring on the eye with a hot dazzle; a table, a few chairs, with some books and papers, perhaps, upon the ground, complete the arrangements that are visible; while, if proceeding farther, we find ourselves in a room fitted up as a bed-chamber, nearly as small and inconvenient as the cabin of a ship, with a square aperture in the thin canvas wall for a window.

These tents are dreadfully warm during the day, and exceedingly cold at night; they are, moreover, notwithstanding their proximity to the sea, and the benefit of its breezes, filled with mosquitoes, or sand-flies, which are equally troublesome. Persons who contemplate a long residence in them, keep out of the cold and heat by erecting a chopper, or roof, formed of thatch, over them; but, in my opinion, they are but uncomfortable residences. Many strangers, however, arriving at Bombay, have no alternative, there being no other place where they can find equally good accommodation.

An hotel, it appears, has been established in the Fort, but not of a description to suit private families or ladies; the constant arrival of steamers full of passengers fills the houses of the residents with a succession of guests, who would gladly put up at an hotel or boarding-house, if such could be found, while there are besides many ladies now in Bombay, whose husbands are in the army, living uncomfortably either alone or going about from friend to friend's houses, who would rejoice to be quietly and comfortably established in a respectable boarding-house. Nothing of the kind, however, appears to be at present in contemplation, and Bombay can never, with any degree of justice, presume to call itself England, until it can offer suitable accommodation to the vast numbers of strangers who land upon its shores.

European foreigners, who visit Bombay in a commercial capacity, find it exceedingly *triste*; independently of private society, there is absolutely no amusement--no play, no concert, no public assembly of any kind; nor would it be advisable to attempt to establish an entertainment of this nature, since there would be no chance of its support. There is a fine building, the Town Hall, well adapted for the purpose, but its most spacious saloon is suffered to remain empty and unfurnished; the expense which must be incurred in the purchase of chandeliers proving sufficient to deter the community from an undertaking which would serve to add gaiety to a sombre scene.

Those who have visited the Town Hall of Calcutta, and who retain a recollection of the brilliance of its re-unions, with all their gay variety of concert, opera, and acted charade, cannot help seeing that Bombay lags very far behind; it is, therefore, unwise to provoke comparisons, and the society here should rather pride itself upon what it will do, than upon what it has done. It is, perhaps, little to be lamented that merely frivolous amusements should be wholly confined to the private circles of social life, but there are others which might be cultivated with infinite advantage to the community at large, and for which the great room at the Town Hall seems to be most admirably adapted.

Whether the native ear is sufficiently refined to relish the superior performances of music, seems doubtful; but when we see so large a portion of the society of Bombay composed of Parsee, Hindu, and Mohamedan gentlemen, we cannot help wishing that some entertainment should be provided for them which would attract and interest, while it expanded the mind. A series of lectures upon popular subjects, illustrated by entertaining experiments, might, I should think, be introduced with good effect. The wonders of the microscope, laid open to the eyes of intelligent persons who perfectly understand and speak English, could scarcely fail to delight and instruct, while the secrets of phantasmagoria, the astonishing effects produced by electricity, the movements of the heavenly bodies exhibited in an orrery, and, indeed, all the arcana of science, agreeably laid open, would furnish inexhaustible funds of amusement, and lead to inquiries of the most useful nature. Lectures, also, upon horticulture, floriculture, &c., might be followed by much practical good; and as there are many scientific men at the presidency who could assist one or more lecturers engaged for the purpose, the expense of such an institution would be materially lessened, while, if it were once established, the probabilities are in favour of its being supported by contributions of the necessary models, implements, &c., from the capitals of Europe.

It is certainly very pleasing to see the numbers of native gentlemen of all religious persuasions, who enter into the private society of Bombay, but I could wish that we should offer them some better entertainment than that of looking on at the eternal quadrille, waltz, or galoppe. They are too much accustomed to our method of amusing ourselves to view it in the light in which it is looked upon in many other parts of India; still, they will never, in all probability, reconcile it to their ideas of propriety, and it is a pity that we do not show ourselves capable of something better. Conversation at these parties is necessarily restricted to a few commonplaces; nothing is gained but the mere interchange of civility, and the native spectators gladly depart, perhaps to recreate themselves with more debasing amusements, without having gained a single new idea.

If meetings once a fortnight, or once a month, could be held at the Town Hall, for the purpose of diffusing useful knowledge in a popular manner, they would not only afford amusement at the time, but subjects also of conversation for the future. Such meetings would give no offence to that part of the community who are averse, upon religious principles, to cards and dancing, or dramatic amusements; and if not rendered too abstruse, and consequently tiresome and incomprehensible to the general auditor, must necessarily become a favourite method of passing time now too frequently lost or mis-spent.

The literary and scientific *conversaziones* given by Lord Auckland, in Calcutta, afford a precedent for an institution of the kind; the successful features might be copied, and if there should have been any failures, the experience thus gained would prevent similar hazards. There seems to be no good reason why ladies should be excluded, since the more general and extensive a plan of the kind could be made, the greater chance there would be of a beneficial exercise of its influence over society.

There is a very good library attached to the Town Hall, and the germ of a museum, which would furnish materials for much intellectual entertainment; and there can be little doubt that, if the proposition were judiciously made, and properly supported, the wealthy portion of the native community would subscribe very liberally towards an establishment so eminently calculated to interest and amuse the youth of their families. The greater number of the sons of respectable natives are now receiving their education at the Elphinstone College, and these young people would understand and appreciate the advantages of a literary and scientific institution, for the discussion and illustration of subjects intimately connected with the end and aim of their studies. In the course of a few years, or even less, many of these young men would be qualified to take a leading part in the establishment, and perhaps there would be no greater incentive to the continuation of studies now frequently abandoned too early, for the sake of some money-getting pursuit, than the hope that the scientific acquirements attained at college might be turned to useful account.

A small salary would allure many natives, who, in consequence of the necessity which they are under of gaining their own bread, are obliged to engage in some, perhaps not very lucrative, trade, and who, engrossed in the gathering together o petty gains, lose all the advantages they might otherwise have derived from a liberal education. The difficulties which in other parts of our Asiatic territories stand in the way of the participation of natives in the studies and amusements of Anglo-Indian residents, in consequence of the difference of language, are not felt in Bombay.

All the superior classes of natives speak excellent English, the larger portion expressing themselves with great fluency, and even elegance. English is spoken in every shop frequented by Europeans, and there are generally one or two servants in every family who can make themselves understood in it. The natives form, in fact, a very large portion of the wealth and intelligence of Bombay, and become, consequently, an important part of its society. They are the owners of nearly all the best houses in the island, which are not commonly either built or purchased, as in Calcutta, by their European tenants.

Many rich native merchants, who reside usually in the Fort, possess splendid country mansions, to which they retire occasionally, or which are used merely for the purpose of giving parties to their friends. These mansions are to be recognised by the abundance of ornament, by gateways surmounted by nondescript monsters, after the fashion of the lions or bears of carved stone, which are sometimes seen at the entrance of a nobleman's grounds in England. At others, they are gaily painted in a variety of colours, while a profusion of many-coloured lamps, hanging in the verandah and porticoes on the occasion of every fete, shed great brilliance on the evening scene. These residences are scattered all over Bombay, the interiors being all richly furnished, and many fitted up with infinite taste and elegance.

Although, as I have before remarked, these scattered houses impart an air of rural enjoyment to the island, yet their being spread over its whole surface prevents Bombay from appearing to be so important a place as it is in reality. There is nothing approaching to the idea of a city to be seen, nothing solid or substantial to indicate the presence of wealth or of extensive commerce. Calcutta, on the contrary, offers to the stranger's eye an aspect so striking and imposing, brings so strongly to the mind the notion that its merchants are princes, and that it ranks crowned heads amongst its vassals and its tributaries, that we see at once that it must be the seat of a powerful and permanently established government. Nor does it seem possible, even in the event of Bombay taking the ascendance as the capital of British India, that the proud City of Palaces shall upon that account dwindle and sink into decay. Stranger things, and even more melancholy destinies, have befallen the mighty Babylons of the earth; but with all its faults of situation and of climate, I should at least, for one, regret the fate that would render the glories of a city so distinct in its character, and so proudly vying with the capitals of Europe, a tale of the past. A new direction in the course of the Ganges may reduce it to a swamp, and its palaces and pleasant places may be left to desolate creatures, but it will never be rivalled by any modern creation. The days of Anglo-Indian magnificence are gone by, and though we may hope for all that is conveyed by the words ***comfort*** and ***prosperity***, splendour will no longer form a feature in the scene.

The climate of Bombay is said to be superior in point of salubrity to that of Bengal; what is termed the cold season, however, can scarcely merit the name, there being nothing like the bracing weather experienced at the same period of the year in the neighbouring presidency. One peculiarity of Bombay consists in the wind blowing hot and cold at the same time, so that persons who are liable to rheumatic pains are obliged to wrap themselves up much more warmly than is agreeable. While enduring a very uncomfortable degree of heat, a puff of wind from the land or the sea will produce a sudden revulsion, and in these alternations the whole day will pass away, while at night they become still more dangerous. It is said that the hot season is not so hot as in Bengal, and the absence of punkahs in the drawing-rooms and bed-chambers favours the statement; but if the atmosphere be much more sultry in the hot season than it is in what is by courtesy called cold, it must be rather difficult to bear.

To a stranger in Bombay, it is a great convenience to find so many persons who speak English, the objection to the engagement of domestic servants who have acquired the language of their Christian masters not existing to the same extent here as in Bengal, where, in most cases, it is a proof of utter worthlessness. Numbers of very respectable servants, who are found in old established families at this presidency, speak English, and the greater portion take a pride in knowing a little of their masters' language. These smatterers are fond of showing off their acquirements upon all occasions, replying in English, as far as they are able, to every question asked in Hindostanee, and delivering their messages in all the words that they can muster. With few exceptions, the pronunciation of the language they have acquired is correct; these exceptions consist in the prefix of *e* to all words beginning with an *s*, and the addition of the same letter to every termination to which it can be tacked. Thus they will ask you to take some ***fowlee-stew;*** and if you object to any thing, say they will bring you ***anotheree***. Though very respectful when addressing their superiors in their native language, the same degree of propriety is not maintained under the disadvantage of an incompetent acquaintance with English. Instead of the ***khana tear hi***, 'dinner is ready,' they will very unintentionally substitute an abrupt summons. I was much amused one day, when, being rather late at my toilette, a servant made his appearance at the door of my apartment, just as I was quitting it, and said, "You come to dinner." He had been sent to tell me that it was served, and had not the least idea that he had not delivered his message with the greatest propriety.

Though, generally speaking, well-behaved and attentive, the domestics of a Bombay establishment are very inferior in style and appearance to those of Bengal, the admixture of Portuguese and Parsees, with Mohammedans and Hindus, forming a motley crew, for all dress in their national costume, it being impossible to prevail upon people having so many and such different religious prejudices to assume the same livery. The Parsees who engage as domestic servants seldom dress well; the ugly chintz cap will always be a disfigurement, and it is not often redeemed by the ample robe and handsome shawl which distinguish the better classes.

The Mohammedans do not wear the beautifully plaited turbans and well-fitting vests so common in Bengal, while the sailors' jackets and trowsers, almost universally worn by the Portuguese, a few only assuming the swallow-tailed coat, are any thing rather than handsome or becoming. The inferiority of dress exhibited is the more inexcusable, since the wages of servants in Bombay are much higher than those of the same class in Bengal, while the difference in point of number does not make up for the difference in the rate. The youngest table-servant demands twelve rupees a month, no one will engage as a butler under twenty, and the remainder are in proportion. The ayahs' wages are also very high, amounting to from fifteen to twenty rupees a month; they are certainly, however, more efficient than the same class of persons in Bengal, undertaking to wash silk stockings, lace, and fine muslin; they are, generally speaking, well-conducted and respectable. The dirzees or tailors are very inferior to their brethren of Bengal, though paid at a much higher rate, fifteen rupees a month being the common demand. Whenever a Bengal tailor happens to come round, he is eagerly seized upon, the reputation of workmen from the rival presidency being deservedly high. Tailors are indiscriminately Parsees, Mohammedans, or Hindus, the latter-named being the least desirable, as they will neither eat, drink, nor cook in a European manner, and are always eager to get away by half-past four in the afternoon.

The cooks of Bombay are, for the most part, well acquainted with the culinary art, an advantage for which, according to common report, they are indebted to Lord Clare. Upon the arrival of that nobleman at the seat of his government, it is said that he started with horror at the repast which the hospitality of the island had provided for him. At this substantial dinner, the ponderous round jostled the sirloin of beef, saddles and haunches of mutton *vis-a-vis'd* with each other, while turkey and ham, tongue and fowls, geese and ducks, filled up the interstices.

Lord Clare had either brought a French cook in his train, or sent for one with the least possible delay, and this accomplished person not only reformed the *cuisine* at Government House, but took pupils, and instructed all who chose to pay for the acquirement in the mysteries of his art. He found his scholars a very teachable race, and it is only now necessary to describe the way in which any particular method should be practised, in order to secure success. They easily comprehend the directions given, and, what is of equal consequence, are not above receiving instructions. Through the exertions of these praiseworthy persons, the tables of Bombay are frequently exceedingly well served, and nobody is actually obliged to dine upon the huge joints which still make their appearance.

Turkey maintains its high position, and is, with its accompaniment of ham, considered indispensable; rounds of boiled salt-beef, plentifully garnished with carrots, are apparently in high esteem, the carrots being an importation from England, coming out hermetically sealed in tin cases. What are considered the dainties of the table consist chiefly of fresh salmon, preserved by the patent process, Highland mutton, partridges stuffed with truffles, &c., these things, in consequence of their rendering the dinner more expensive as well as more *recherche*, being in great request.

Although the high prices of provisions are adduced as the reason of the high rate of servants' wages, as compared with those of Bengal, this increased expenditure, according to the observations I have been able to make, relates more to the commodities of the native bazaars than those consumed by Europeans. The necessity of bringing in supplies from a distance for the consumption of the island occasions the increase of the price of grain, &c, while probably the demand for beef, mutton, fowls, &c. not being go great as in Calcutta, these articles are sold at a lower rate. Buffalo meat is occasionally eaten by Europeans, a thing unheard of in Bengal; but it is not in any esteem.

The tables in Bombay are handsomely appointed, though not with the same degree of splendour that prevails in Bengal, where the quantity of plate makes so striking a display. The large silver vases, in which butter and milk are enclosed in a vessel filled with saltpetre, which give to the breakfast-tables of Calcutta an air of such princely grandeur, are not in use here.

The servants are summoned by the exclamation of "Boy" instead of the ***Qui hi?*** which is so Indian-like in its expression, and has afforded a distinguishing ***soubriquet*** to the Bengallees. The word ***boy*** is said to be a corruption of ***bhaee***, 'brother,' a common mode of salutation all over the East. As it is now employed, it is often very absurdly answered by a grey-bearded man, who has long lost all title to the appellation.

Notwithstanding the strength and acknowledged efficiency of the Bombay police, it is considered expedient in every house to engage a Ramoosee or watchman, who, while himself a professional thief, is bound in honour to protect his employer from the depredation of his brethren. Though, in virtue of this implied compact, the house ought to be considered sacred, and the Ramoosee entitled to receive his wages for the protection that his name affords, some there are who insist upon the display of their watchfulness in a very unwelcome manner.

Occasionally the Ramoosee, more peaceably inclined, settles himself quietly down to sleep in the verandah, and leaves the family to the enjoyment of repose; but there are others who disdain thus to eat the bread of idleness, and who make it a point to raise an alarm every hour in the night. Personal courage or strength of body is by no means essential in a Ramoosee, all that is required of him being powerful lungs; this qualification he cultivates to the utmost, and any thing more dreadful than the sounds emitted in the dead of the night close to the window nearest the head of my bed I never heard. I have started up in the most horrible state of apprehension, fancying that the world was at an end, while, after calming down all this perturbation, just as I have been going to sleep again, the same fearful shout has brought on new alarm. Vainly have I remonstrated, vainly endeavoured to convince the Ramoosee that his duty to his employers would be better performed by making these shocking outcries at the road-side; he is either inflexibly silent, or waging war against my repose; for I believe that he selects the side of the house devoted to the visit or for the exercise of his extraordinary faculty; I cannot in any other way account for the small disturbance he gives to the rest of the family.

The absolute necessity of paying one of these men, in order to secure the forbearance of his colleagues, is illustrated by an anecdote commonly told. It appears that two friends were living together, one of whom had engaged a Ramoosee, while the other, not imagining it to be incumbent upon him to incur the same expense, neglected this precaution. One night, every thing belonging to this unfortunate chum was stolen. The Ramoosee was summoned, and accused of not having performed his duty. He boldly denied the charge. "All master's property is safe," he said; "when master lose any thing, I will account for it."

The fidelity with which the greater number of natives, however corrupt in other respects, fulfil all their engagements, the few instances in which a pledge once given is forfeited, if taken into grave consideration, would do much towards settling the point at issue between the Bishop of London and Sir Charles Forbes. The word of a native, generally speaking, if solemnly given, is a bond never to be broken, while an oath is certainly not equally binding.

In accusing the natives of a deliberate crime in the commission of perjury, we do not sufficiently reflect upon the difference of the religious principles which actuate Christians, and the heinous nature in their eyes of the sin of calling upon a God of purity to witness their falsehoods. If we could administer an oath to a native, the profanation of which would fill him with equal horror, we should find that he would speak the truth. A case in point occurred lately at Aden. There are a class of Mohammedans who are great knaves, many being addicted to cheating and theft: the evidence of these men cannot be depended upon, since for the value of the most trifling sum they would swear to any thing. Nevertheless, although they do not hesitate to call upon God and the Prophet to witness the most flagrant untruths, they will not support a falsehood if put to a certain test. When required to swear by a favourite wife, they refuse to perjure themselves by a pledge which they esteem sacred, and will either shrink altogether from the ordeal or state the real fact.

The following occurrence is vouched for by an eye-witness: "A Somali had a dispute with a Banian as to the number of komasies he had paid for a certain article, swearing by God and the Prophet that he had paid the price demanded of him for the article in question; but no sooner was he called upon to substantiate his assertions by swearing by his favourite wife, than he threw down the article contended for, and took to his heels with all speed, in order to avoid the much dreaded oath." It will appear, therefore, that there is scarcely any class of persons in India so utterly destitute of principle, as to be incapable of understanding the obligation of an oath, or the necessity of speaking truth when solemnly pledged to do so, the difficulty being to discover the asseveration which they consider binding.

In nearly every transaction with servants in India we find them most unscrupulous respecting the truth of any account which they give, and yet at the same time they will fulfil every engagement they enter into with a conscientiousness almost unknown in Christian countries. The lowest servant of the establishment may be trusted with money, which will be faithfully appropriated to the purpose for which it was intended, but certainly they entertain little or no respect for abstract truth.

The controversy at home concerning the general disregard to accuracy manifested by the natives of India has caused much consternation here, and will, I trust, be productive of good. It will show at least to the large portion of the native community, who can understand and appreciate the value of the good opinion of the country of which they are fellow-subjects, the necessity of a strict adherence to veracity, in order to maintain their pretensions to morality, and it will evince the superiority of that religion which, as one of its precepts, teaches a regard for truth.

Willing as I feel to bear testimony to many excellent points in the native character, I regret to say, that, although they do not deserve the sweeping accusations brought against them, the standard by which they are guided is very low. At the same time it must be said, that the good faith which they observe, upon occasions in which persons guided by superior lights would be less scrupulous, shows that they only require a purer religious system to regard truth as we have been taught to regard it.

CHAPTER XI.
BOMBAY--(Continued.)

Residences for the Governor--Parell--Its Gardens--Profusion of Roses--Receptions at Government-house--The evening-parties--The grounds and gardens of Parell inferior to those at Barrackpore--The Duke of Wellington partial to Parell--Anecdotes of his Grace in India--Sir James Mackintosh--His forgetfulness of India--The Horticultural Society--Malabar Point, a retreat in the hot weather--The Sea-view beautiful--The nuisance of fish--Serious effects at Bombay of the stoppage of the trade with China--Ill-condition of the poorer classes of Natives--Frequency of Fires--Houses of the Parsees--Parsee Women--Masculine air of the other Native Females of the lower orders who appear in public--Bangle-shops--Liqueur-shops--Drunkenness amongst Natives not uncommon here, from the temptations held out--The Sailors' Home--Arabs, Greeks, Chinamen--The latter few and shabby--Portuguese Padres--Superiority of the Native Town of Bombay over that of Calcutta--Statue of Lord Cornwallis--Bullock-carriages--High price and inferiority of horses in Bombay--Hay-stacks--Novel mode of stacking.

There are three residences for the accommodation of the Governor of Bombay; one, the Castle, situated within the Fort, has been long disused, and appropriated to government-offices; a second, at Malabar Point, is intended as a retreat for the hot weather; Parell, the third, being the mansion most usually occupied.

Though not built in a commanding position, Parell is very prettily situated in the midst of gardens, having a rich back-ground of wood, while, from the upper windows, the eye, after ranging over these luxuriant groves, catches a view of the sea, and is carried away to more remote regions by the waving outline of distant hills, melting into the soft haze until it effaces all their details.

Parell was originally a college of Jesuits, and, after so many alterations and improvements, that its original occupants would be puzzled to recognise it, is now rendered worthy of the purpose to which it is dedicated. The house is an irregular structure, without pretension to architectural design or ornament, but having something noble in its appearance, which is helped out by a fine portico and battlemented roof. The interior is handsome and convenient; two flights of marble stairs, twelve feet broad, lead into a very spacious drawing-room, with galleries on either side, and three smaller drawing-rooms beyond. The terrace over the portico, at the other end, separated from this suite of apartments by a verandah, is easily convertible into a fourth reception-room, it being roofed in by an awning, and furnished with blinds, which in the day-time give a very Italian air to the whole building.

Though I have never been in Italy, the acquaintance gained of it through the medium of illustrating pens and pencils makes me fancy that the island of Bombay, and Parell especially, at this season of the year (the cold weather), may bear a strong resemblance to that fair and sunny land.

The gardens of Parell are perfectly Italian, with their fountains and cypress trees; though regular, they are not sufficiently symmetrical to offend the eye, the nature of the ground and of the building, which runs out at right angles, preventing the formality from being carried beyond its just limit. Price, the most judicious of landscape-gardeners, would scarcely have desired to alter arrangements which have quite enough of the varied and the picturesque to satisfy those who do not contend for eternal labyrinthine mazes and perpetually waving lines. There is one straight avenue in front, but the principal carriage-road has just the kind of curve most desirable, sweeping round some fine trees which group themselves for the purpose of affording an agreeable diversity.

A broad terrace, overlooking a large tank, runs along one side of the garden, and beyond, upon a rising hill, are seen the New Horticultural Gardens, and a part of the picturesque village of Metunga, while the rest is laid out in small lawns, interspersed with rounds and ovals, fountains in the centre, surrounded by flower-beds, and flanked by tall, slender cypresses, and the more rare, delicate, and elegant species of palms: all this is set off by clumps of mangoes, now covered with blossoms of dark gold burnishing their green leaves.

It is, indeed, a fair and stately garden, enriched with many native and foreign productions, both of tree and flower, of great beauty. In one place, two large trees, on either side a broad gravel walk, are united by a splendid festoon, formed by a creeper, which bears in the greatest profusion bell-shaped flowers, at least four inches long, and of the most beautiful pearly whiteness and fragrant scent. I regret that my want of botanical knowledge incapacitates me from giving its name and family. That species of palm which is called the Travellers' Tree, and which, growing in sandy places, contains in its leaves an ample supply of fresh water, is to be found here. It resembles the banana or plantain, in its broad leaves, springing immediately from the stem, but attains a much greater height, and is altogether very striking and singular in its appearance.

The wealth of roses at the gardens of Parell seems to exceed all computation, bushels being collected every day without any apparent diminution; indeed it may be questioned whether there is in any part of the world so great a consumption of this beautiful flower as in Bombay. The natives cultivate it very largely, and as comparatively few employ it in the manufacture of rose-water, it is gathered and given away in the most lavish profusion. At Parell, every morning, one of the gardeners renews the flowers which decorate the apartments of the guests; bouquets are placed upon the breakfast-table, which, though formal, are made up after the most approved Parisian fashion, the natives being exceedingly skilful in the arrangement of flowers. Vases filled with roses meet the eye in every direction, flowers which assume their supremacy over all other daughters of Flora, though there are many beautiful specimens, the common productions of the gardens, which are rarely found even in hothouses in England.

The society of Bombay enjoys the great advantage arising from the presence of the ladies of the Governor's family, who have rendered themselves most deservedly popular by the frequency and the agreeableness of their entertainments, and the kind attention which they pay to every invited guest. The slight forms that are kept up at Government-house are just sufficient to give a somewhat courtly air to these parties without depriving them of their sociability. Morning visitors are received once a-week, and upon these occasions Parell assumes a very gay appearance.

The band, which is an excellent one, is stationed in the hall below, playing occasionally the most popular compositions of the day, while its pillared verandah is filled with liveried servants, handsomely dressed in scarlet, white, and gold. The ample staircases are lined with flowers, and as the carriages drive up, the aide-de-camps and other military resident guests are in readiness to receive the visitors, and to usher them up stairs, and introduce them to the ladies of the family.

The morning reception lasts from eleven until two, and the numerous arrivals from distant stations, or from England, officers continually coming down from the army or the dominions of foreign princes, give occasion to conversations of great interest, while it forms a rallying-point to the whole of Bombay. The evening parties are distinguished for the excellence of the music, the band having improved greatly under the stimulating influence of the ladies of the Governor's family, who are all delightful performers, one especially excelling. In addition, therefore, to their own talents, all the musical genius of Bombay is put into requisition, and the result is shown in some very charming episodes between the dancing.

At these evening parties, the brilliance of the lights, and the beauty of the flowers, which in the supper-room especially are very tastefully displayed, render the scene extremely attractive. One very pleasing feature must not be omitted; in the ante-room is placed a large silver salver, filled with bouquets, which are presented, according to the Oriental custom, to every guest. The number and variety of the uniforms, and the large proportion of native gentlemen, add much to the gaiety of the appearance of these parties, and the eye most accustomed to European splendour may find pleasure in roaming over these spacious, well-filled, and brilliantly illuminated apartments.

Nor is it the interior alone that attracts; on the still moonlight nights, which are so beautiful in India, the scenery viewed from the windows assumes a peculiar and almost magical appearance, looking more like a painting than living reality. The trees, so motionless that not a leaf stirs, present a picture of such unbroken repose, that we can scarcely imagine it to be real; the sky seems to be drawn closer to us, while the whole breathes of divine art, suggesting poetry and music and thoughts of Paradise.

In England I remember feeling a longing desire to breathe the delicious balm, and gaze upon the exquisite effects of an Indian night again, with its tone of soft beauty and the silvery mystery of its atmosphere, which adds so great a charm to the rich magnificence of the foliage; and now I fancy that I can never sufficiently drink in a scene, not only lovely in itself, but peculiarly delightful from its contrast to the glare of the day.

The grounds and gardens of Parell, in extent and splendour, will bear no comparison with those of Barrackpore, which are, perhaps, some of the finest in the world, and which must be explored in carriages or on horseback, while the plantations and parterres at this place offer nothing more than agreeable walks, which perhaps, after all, afford superior gratification; at least to those who prefer a feeling of home to the admiration elicited by great splendour.

Not one of the least pleasing sensations excited by a residence at Parell, is the recollection of the distinguished persons who have inhabited the same chambers, and sat in the same halls. The Duke of Wellington is said frequently to have expressed a partiality for Parell, and to look back to the days of his sojourn within its walls with pleasure. Here he reposed after those battles in which he laid the foundation of his future glory, and to which, after long experience, and so many subsequent triumphs as almost to eclipse their splendour, he recurs with peculiar satisfaction. So far from underrating, as is the fashion with many of the military servants of the Crown, the merits of a successful campaign in India, the great captain of the age, than whom there can be no better judge, rates the laurels that he gathered in his earliest fields as highly as those wrested from the soldiers of France, glorying in the title given him by Napoleon, of "the Sepoy General."

Few things can be more agreeable than listening to anecdotes told at the dinner-table at Parell of the Duke of Wellington by officers who have formerly sat at the same board with him, who have served under his command in India, and who delight in recording those early traits of character which impressed all who knew him with the conviction that he was destined to become the greatest man of the age. The Duke of Wellington, though wholly unacquainted with the language spoken in India, was always held in the highest esteem by the natives, with whom, generally speaking, in order to become popular, it is absolutely necessary to be able to converse in their own tongue. He obtained, however, a perfect knowledge of their modes of feeling, thinking, and acting, and by a liberal policy, never before experienced, endeared himself to all ranks and classes. It is recollected at this day that, in times of scarcity, he ordered all the rice sent up for the subsistence of the troops to be sold, at a moderate price, to the starving multitude; and that, while more short-sighted people prophesied the worst results from this measure, it obtained for him abundant supplies, together with a name that will never be forgotten.

A re-perusal at Parell of the "Life of Sir James Mackintosh" also affords interest, though of a different kind. The house which Sir James designates as large and convenient, with two really good rooms, has been much improved since his time. It could not be expected that a man like Sir James Mackintosh would employ many words in the description of a mansion chiefly interesting on account of its former occupants; but that he should have dismissed the whole of the presidency in as summary a manner, seems perfectly unaccountable.

It does not appear that the importance and value of British India ever made any strong impression upon Sir James Mackintosh, who seems to have looked upon its various inhabitants with a cold and careless eye; to have done nothing in the way of making the people of England better acquainted with their fellow-subjects in the East, and never to have felt any desire to assist in the work of their improvement, or to facilitate its progress. During his subsequent career, India appears to have been totally forgotten, or remembered only as the scene of an exile, in which he had found nothing to compensate for the loss of literary society and the learned idling away of time, from which so much was expected, and which produced so little.

The eloquence of Sir James Mackintosh, if exerted in favour of British India, might, years before, have excited that interest in its behalf, which remained dormant until Bishop Heber created a new feeling upon the subject; and in this place especially, I cannot help regretting that the powers of so great a mind should not have been devoted to the promotion of the welfare of a country dependant upon England for intellectual and moral improvement, and which, in the eyes of all reflecting persons, must be looked upon as the strongest support of England's ancient glory.

The garden of the Horticultural Society, which occupies a convenient space of ground near Parell, is yet in an infant state, but bids fair in a short time to add very considerably to the pleasures of those persons who take delight in the cultivation of flowers and fruits. Many gentlemen are stimulating their gardeners to make great exertions for the prizes, which it is expected will be chiefly carried away at the ensuing meeting by exhibitors from the Deccan. Though there are several very good gardens in the island, they are, according to all accounts, greatly excelled in other parts of the presidency.

The system of cultivation carried on by the Horticultural Society will, no doubt, tend very considerably to their improvement, while the new method of conveying plants to and from distant places, in boxes covered with glass, will soon enrich all the gardens, both in India and at home, with interesting exotics. Several of these cases, filled with bulbous and other roots, under the inspection of Messrs. Loddiges, have arrived at Parell, and been planted out in pots; the eases will be returned, filled with equally valuable specimens of Indian products; and thus a continual interchange may be kept up.

I wished much to enrich the collection of foreign plants making by the Royal Botanical Society of London, by some of the most interesting specimens of Indian growth, feeling deeply interested in the success of this institution; but not being a practical gardener myself, I have as yet been unable to fulfil my intentions. I calculated, perhaps, too strongly upon the desire of scientific people in Bombay to promote objects of general utility at home, and see little chance, unless I do every thing relating to the collecting, planting, packing, and transmitting the plants with my own hands, of succeeding in sending any thing to England. Indeed, I find a difficulty in procuring a **_hortus siccus_**.

As every body, who can possibly get away, leaves Bombay during the hot weather and the rains, the residence at Malabar Point, intended as a retreat in the sultry season, is seldom tenanted by the Governor's family. The house, however, is not very often empty, being generally occupied by some great person and his suite, such as newly-arrived commanders-in-chief, who are accommodated at this establishment until they can provide for themselves. The principal residence, and several bungalows attached to it, are erected on the side of a hill overlooking and washed by the sea. The views are beautiful, the harbour affording at all times a scene of great liveliness and interest, while the aerial summits of the hills in the distance, and their purple splendours, complete the charm. The numerous fairy-like skiffs, with their white sails, catching the sunlight, give life and movement to the picture, while the cottages of the fishermen are often placed with happy effect upon the neighbouring shore.

There are, unfortunately, serious drawbacks to the enjoyment which the eye derives from the gliding boats and palm-crowned huts; the amusement of ***yachting*** being seriously impeded by the method of spreading nets, for the purpose of capturing the finny tribes, while, in consequence of the immense quantity which is caught, the whole island occasionally smells of fish. The fishermen have certain places secured to them by law, in which they drive immense stakes, usually the trunks of palm-trees, and between these stakes they fasten their nets, any damage done to them by passing boats being punishable by a fine; the navigation of the harbour, to those who wish to visit its beautiful islands, is, in consequence, rather difficult, and would scarcely admit of being carried on by those small steamers, which render every place in the neighbourhood of Calcutta so accessible.

The boats here, with the exception of private yachts, which are not numerous, are a disgrace to a civilized place. Nothing can be easily imagined to be worse than the pattamars usually employed for the conveyance of troops and travellers to distant points; they are dirty, many so low in the roof that the passengers cannot stand upright in them, and filled with insects and vermin.

The abundance and cheapness of fish render it the common food of the lower classes, and consequently its effluvia sometimes pervade the whole atmosphere. The smell of frying fish, with its accompaniment of oil, is sufficiently disagreeable; but this is not all; a much more powerful odour arises from fish drying for future use, while, as it is commonly spread over the fields and employed as manure, the scents wafted by the breezes upon these occasions breathe any thing but perfume.

There are many very delicate kinds of fish, which are held in great esteem, to be seen at European tables; but, to a stranger, the smell of the refuse allowed to decay is quite enough, and habit must reconcile the residents of Bombay to this unpleasant assailant of the olfactory nerves, before they can relish the finest specimens of pomfret or other favourite. As it can always be purchased freshly caught, fish appears at dinner as well as at the breakfast-table in Bombay; the list of shell-fish includes oysters, which, though not so tempting in their appearance as those of England, are of excellent quality.

The fishermen, like those of Europe, leave the sale of their fish to their wives, who are said to be a busy, bustling, active race, quite equal to the tasks which devolve upon them, and, in consequence of the command which their occupation gives them over the pecuniary receipts of the house, exerting a proportionate degree of authority.

Fishermen's huts, though very picturesque, are not usually remarkable for their neatness or their cleanliness, and those of Bombay form no exception to their general appearance. They are usually surrounded by a crowd of amphibious animals, in the shape of tribes of children, who for the most part are perfectly free from the incumbrance of drapery. Many, who have not a single rag to cover them, are, notwithstanding, adorned with gold or silver ornaments, and some ingeniously transform a pocket-handkerchief into a toga, or mantle, by tying two ends round the throat, and leaving the remainder to float down behind, so that they are well covered on one side, and perfectly bare on the other. Amid the freaks of costume exhibited at Bombay, an undue preference seems to be given to the upper portion of the person, which is frequently well covered by a warm jacket with long sleeves, while the lower limbs are entirely unclad.

There is said to be cotton goods to the amount of a million sterling lying in the godowns and warehouses of Bombay, unemployed, in consequence of the stoppage of the China trade, and it seems a pity that the multitudes who wear gold chains about their necks, and gold ear-rings in their ears, could not be prevailed upon to exchange a part of this metal for a few yards of covering of some kind or other, of which apparently they stand much in need.

Great numbers of the poorer classes seem to be ill-fed, ill-lodged, and worse clothed; yet scantiness in this particular is certainly not always the result of poverty, as the redundance of precious ornaments above mentioned can witness. Neither does the wretched manner in which many belonging to the lower orders of Bombay shelter themselves from the elements appear to be an absolute necessity, and it is a pity that some regulations should not be made to substitute a better method of constructing the sheds in which so many poor people find a dwelling-place. The precaution of raising the floor even a few inches above the ground is not observed in these miserable hovels, and their inhabitants, often destitute of bedsteads, sleep with nothing but a mat, and perhaps not even that, between them and the bare earth.

At this season of the year, when no rain falls, the palm-branches with which these huts are thatched are so carelessly placed, as to present large apertures, which expose the inmates to sun-beams and to dews, both of which, so freely admitted into a dwelling, cannot fail to produce the most injurious effects. Were these houses raised a foot or two from the ground, and well roofed with the dry palm-branches, which seem to supply so cheap and efficient a material, they would prove no despicable abodes in a country in which only at one season of the year, the rains, very substantial shelter is required.

As it may be supposed, conflagrations are frequent in these hovels; they are fortunately seldom attended with loss of life, or even of much property, since the household furniture and wardrobes of the family can be easily secured and carried off, while the people themselves have nothing to do but to walk out. On these occasions, the rats are seen to decamp in large troops, and gentlemen, returning home from drives or parties, are often arrested by a fire, and by the instructions they afford, do much towards staying the progress of the flames, while the greater number of natives, Parsees in particular, look quietly on, without offering to render the slightest assistance. Whole clusters of huts are in this manner very frequently entirely consumed; the mischief does not spread farther, and would be little to be lamented should it lead to the entire demolition of dwelling-places equally unsightly, and prejudicial to health.

Much to my astonishment, I have seen, in the midst of these very wretched tenements, one superior to the rest placed upon a platform, with its verandah in front, furnished with chairs, and surrounded by all the dirt and rubbish accumulated by its poverty-stricken neighbours, miserable-looking children picking up a scanty subsistence, and lean cats groping about for food. Such houses are, besides, exposed to all the dangers of fire originating in the adjoining premises; but apparently this circumstance has been overlooked, together with the expediency of building a little apart from the horrors of the surrounding abominations. This is the more remarkable, from the contrast it affords to the air of comfort which is so often manifest in the inferior dwellings of the natives of Bombay.

I often, in my drives, come upon a small patch of ground, well cultivated, and boasting vegetables, fruits, and flowers, with a small low-roofed house of unbaked mud in one corner, having a verandah all round, well tiled and supported on bamboos. It is difficult under this sloping roof to get a peep at the interior, but my efforts have been rewarded by the sight of floors cleanly swept, bedsteads, and those articles of furniture which can scarcely be dispensed with without suffering considerable privation.

As yet, I have not been able to discover to what class of persons these kind of dwellings belong, but I suspect that they are tenanted chiefly by Parsees, a money-getting and luxurious race of people, who are sufficiently industrious to exert themselves, with great perseverance, to gain a living, and have the spirit to spend their money upon the comforts and conveniences of life. They are accused of extravagance in this particular, and perhaps do occasionally exceed; but, generally speaking, their style of living is more commendable than that of the Hindus, who carry their thrift and parsimony to an outrageous height.

Near their houses very graceful groups of Parsee women and children are to be seen, who, upon the encouragement afforded by a smile, **salaam** and smile again, apparently well-pleased with the notice taken of them by English ladies. These women are always well-dressed, and most frequently in silk of bright and beautiful colours, worn as a **saree** over a tight-fitting bodice of some gay material. The manner in which the saree is folded over the head and limbs renders it a graceful and becoming costume, which might be imitated with great propriety by the Hindu women, who certainly do not appear to study either taste or delicacy in their mode of dress.

I may have made the remark before, for it is impossible to avoid the recurrence of observations continually elicited by some new proofs of the contrast between the women upon this side of India, and their more elegant sisters on the banks of the Hooghly. Here all the women, the Parsees excepted, who appear in public, have a bold masculine air; any beauty which they may have ever possessed is effaced, in the very lower orders, by hard work and exposure to the weather, while those not subjected to the same disadvantages, and who occupy a better situation, have little pretensions to good looks. Many are seen employed in drawing water, or some trifling household work, wearing garments of a texture which shews that they are not indebted to laborious occupation for a subsistence; and while the same class in Bengal would studiously conceal their faces, no trouble whatever of the kind is taken here. They are possibly Mahrattas, which will account for their carelessness; but I could wish that, with superior freedom from absurd restraint, they had preserved greater modesty of demeanour.

The number of shops in the bazaars for the sale of one peculiar ornament, common glass rings for bracelets, and the immense quantities of the article, are quite surprising; all the native women wear these bangles, which are made of every colour. The liqueur-shops are also very common and very conspicuous, being distinguished by the brilliant colours of the beverage shown through bottles of clear white glass. What pretensions this rose and amber tinted fluid may have to compete with the liqueurs most esteemed in Europe, I have not been able to learn. Toddy-shops, easily recognised by the barrels they contain upon tap, and the drinking-vessels placed beside them, seem almost as numerous as the gin-palaces of London, arguing little for the sobriety of the inhabitants of Bombay. In the drive home through the bazaar, it is no very uncommon circumstance to meet a group of respectably-dressed natives all as tipsy as possible.

It is on account of the multitude of temptations held out by the toddy-shops, that the establishment I have mentioned as the Sailors' Home is so very desirable, by affording to those who really desire to live comfortably and respectably, while on shore, the means of doing both. Here they may enjoy the advantages of clean, well-ventilated apartments, apparently, according to what can be seen through the open windows, of ample size; and here they may, if they please, pass their time in rational employment or harmless amusement. Groups of sun-burnt tars, with their large straw hats and honest English faces, are often to be seen mingled with the crowd of Asiatics, of whom every day seems to show a greater variety.

I saw three or four very remarkable figures last evening; one was an extremely tall and handsome Arab, well dressed in the long embroidered vest, enveloping an ample quantity of inner garments, which I have so often seen, but of which I have not acquired the name, and with a gaily-striped handkerchief placed above the turban, and hanging down on either side of his face. This person was evidently a stranger, for he came up to the carriage and stared into it with the strongest expression of surprise and curiosity, our dress and appearance seeming to be equally novel and extraordinary to this child of the desert. Shortly afterwards, we encountered a Greek, with luxuriant black ringlets hanging down from under a very small scarlet and gold cap; the others were Jews, very handsome, well-dressed men, profusely enveloped in white muslin, and with very becoming and peculiar caps on their heads.

I regret to see my old friends, the China-men, so few in number, and so shabby in appearance; yet they are the only shoemakers here, and it ought to be a thriving trade. Their sign-boards are very amusing; one designating himself as "Old Jackson," while a rival, close at hand, writes "Young Jackson" upon his placard; thus dividing the interest, and endeavouring to draw custom from the more anciently established firm.

The Portuguese padres form striking and singular groups, being dressed in long black gowns, fitting tightly to the shape, and descending to their feet. They seem to be a numerous class, and I hope shortly to see the interiors of some of their churches. A very large, handsome-looking house was pointed out to us by one of the servants of whom we made the inquiry, as belonging to a Portuguese padre; it was situated near the cloth bazaar, and I regretted that I could not obtain a better view of it.

My predilection for exploring the holes and corners of the native town is not shared by many of the Anglo-Indian residents of Bombay, who prefer driving to the Esplanade, to hear the band play, or to a place on the sea-shore called the Breach. I hope, however, to make a tour of the villages, and to become in time thoroughly acquainted with all the interesting points in the island, the variety and extent of the rides and drives rendering them most particularly attractive to a traveller, who finds something interesting in every change of scene.

I have accomplished a second drive through the coco-nut gardens on the Girgaum road, a name by which this quarter of the native town is more commonly known; the view thus obtained only excited a desire to penetrate farther into the cross-lanes and avenues; but as I do not ride on horseback, I have little chance of succeeding, since I could not see much from a palanquin, and taun-jauns, so common in Calcutta, are scarcely in use here. The more I see of what is called the Native Town in Bombay, the more satisfied I am of its great superiority over that of Calcutta; and I gladly make this admission, since I have found, and still continue to find, so great a falling-off in the style of the dress, whether it relates to form, material, or cleanliness. I have lately observed a very handsome turban, which seems worn both by the Mohammedans and Hindus, of red muslin, with gold borders, which is an improvement.

A taste for flowers seems universal, plants in pots being continually to be seen on the ledges of the porticoes and verandahs; these are sometimes intermingled with less tasteful ornaments, and few things have struck me as more incongruous than a plaster bust of a modern English author, perched upon the top of a balustrade over the portico of a house in the bazaar; mustachios have been painted above the mouth, the head has been dissevered from the shoulders, and is now stuck upon one side in the most grotesque manner possible, looking down with half-tipsy gravity, the attitude and the expression of the countenance favouring the idea, upon the strange groups thus oddly brought into juxta-position. The exhibition is a droll one; but it always gives me a painful feeling: I do not like to see the effigy of a time-honoured sage abased.

The statue of Lord Cornwallis, on the Esplanade--which, being surrounded by sculptured animals, not, I think, in good taste, might be mistaken for Van Amburgh and his beasts--is close to a spot apparently chosen as a hackney-coach stand, every kind of the inferior descriptions of native vehicles being to be found there in waiting.

Some of the bullock-carriages have rather a classical air, and might, with a little brushing up and decoration, emulate the ancient triumphal car. They are usually dirty and shabby, but occasionally we see one that makes a good picture. The bullocks that draw it are milk-white, and have the hanging dewlap, which adds so greatly to the appearance of the animal; the horns are painted blue, and the forehead is adorned with a frontlet of large purple glass beads, while bouquets of flowers are stuck on either side of the head, after the manner of the rosettes worn by the horses in Europe.

A very small pair of milk-white bullocks, attached to a carriage of corresponding dimensions, merely containing a seat for two persons, is a picturesque and convenient vehicle, which will rattle along the roads at a very good pace. These bullocks usually have bells attached to their harness, which keep up a perpetual and not disagreeable jingle. The distances between the European houses are so great, and the horses able to do so little work, that it seems a pity that bullocks should not be deemed proper animals to harness to a shigram belonging to the **saib logue**: but fashion will not admit the adoption of so convenient a means of paying morning visits, and thus sparing the horses for the evening drive.

Great complaints are made about the high price and the inferiority of the horses purchaseable in Bombay, a place in which the Arab is not so much esteemed as I had expected. Some difficulty was experienced in obtaining very fine specimens of this far-famed race for the Queen, who gave a commission for them. I had the pleasure of seeing four that are going home in the *Paget*, destined for her Majesty's stables.

The Imaum of Muscat lately sent a present of horses to Bombay, but they were not of high caste; those I have mentioned, as intended for the Queen, being of a much finer breed. They are beautiful creatures, and are to be put under the care of an English groom, who has the charge of some English horses purchased in London for a native Parsee gentleman. From the extent of the Arab stables, and the number of Arab horse-merchants in Bombay, it would appear easy to have the choice of the finest specimens; but this is not the case, while various circumstances have combined to reduce the numbers of native horses, which were formerly readily procurable. Thus, the fine breed of Kattywar is not now attainable, and the same value does not appear to be set upon horses from Kutch and the Deccan, which in other parts of India are esteemed to be so serviceable. Persian horses are little prized; and those imported from England, though very showy and handsome, will not do much work in this climate, and are therefore only suited to rich people, who can keep them for display. The stud-horses bred near Poonah do not come into the market so freely as in the Bengal presidency, where they are easily procurable, and are sought after as buggy and carriage horses. Old residents, I am told, prefer the Arabs, the good qualities of these celebrated steeds requiring long acquaintance to be justly appreciated, while persons new to the country can see nothing but faults in them.

A novel feature in Bombay, to persons who have only visited the other side of India, is found in the hay-stack, the people having discovered the advantage of cutting and drying the grass for future use. Immense numbers of carts, drawn by bullocks and loaded with hay, come every day into the island; this hay is stacked in large enclosures built for the purpose, and can be purchased in any quantity. There are large open spaces, near tanks or wells, on the road-side, which give the idea of a hay-market; the carts being drawn up, and the patient bullock, always an accompaniment to an Indian rural scene, unyoked, reposing on the ground. The drivers, apparently, do not seek the shelter of a roof, but kindle their cooking-fires on the flats on the opposite side of the road, and sleep at night under the shelter of their carts. The causeway which unites the island of Bombay with its neighbour, Salsette, affords a safe and convenient road, greatly facilitating the carriage of supplies of various kinds necessary for the consumption of so populous a place.

The villagers at Metunga, and other places, make as much hay as their fields will supply for their own use, and have hit upon a singular method of stacking it. They choose some large tree, and lodge the hay in its branches, which thus piled up, assumes the appearance of an immense bee-hive. This precaution is taken to preserve the crop from the depredations of cattle, and, if more troublesome, is less expensive than fencing it round. From the miserably lean condition of many of the unfortunate animals, which their Hindu masters worship and starve, it would appear that, notwithstanding its seeming abundance, they are very scantily supplied with hay. It is a pity that some agriculturist does not suggest the expedience of feeding them upon fish, which, as they are cleanly animals, they would eat while fresh.

CHAPTER XII.
BOMBAY--(Continued).

The Climate of Bombay treacherous in the cold season--The land-wind injurious to health--The Air freely admitted into Rooms--The Climate of the Red Sea not injurious to Silk dresses--Advice to lady-passengers on the subject of dress--The Shops of Bombay badly provided--Speculations on the site of the City, should the seat of Government be removed hither--The Esplanade--Exercise of Sailors on Shore and on Ship-board--Mock-fight--Departure of Sir Henry Fane--Visit to a fair in Mahim Wood--Prophecy--Shrine of Mugdooree Sahib--Description of the Fair--Visit to the mansion of a Moonshee--His Family--Crowds of Vehicles returning from the Fair--Tanks--Festival of the *Duwallee*--Visit to a Parsee--Singular ceremony--The Women of India impede the advance of improvement--They oppose every departure from established rules--Effect of Education in Bombay yet superficial--Cause of the backwardness of Native Education.

Every day's experience of the climate of Bombay assures me that, in what is called the cold season, at least, it is the most treacherous in the world; and that, moreover, its dangers are not sufficiently guarded against by the inhabitants. Cold weather, such as takes place during the period from November to March, in all parts of Bengal, is not felt here, the days being more or less sultry, and tempered only by cold, piercing winds.

The land-wind, which blows alternately with the sea-breezes, comes fraught with all the influences most baneful to health; cramps, rheumatic pains, even headaches and indigestion, brought on by cold, are the consequences to susceptible persons of exposure to this wind, either during the day or the night: so severe and so manifold are the pains and aches which attend it, that I feel strongly inclined to believe that Bombay, and not "the vexed Bermoothes," was the island of Prospero, and that the plagues showered upon Caliban still remain. Though the progress of acclimation can scarcely fail to be attended by danger to life or limb, the process, when completed, seems to be very effectual, since little or no pains are taken by the old inhabitants to guard against the evil.

Some of the withdrawing-rooms of Bombay are perfectly open at either end, and though the effect is certainly beautiful--a charming living landscape of wood and water, framed in by the pillars at the angles of the chamber--yet it is enjoyed at too great a risk. Dining-rooms are frequently nearly as much exposed, the aim of everybody apparently being to admit as great a quantity of air as possible, no matter from what point of the compass it blows. Strangers, therefore, however guarded they may be in their own apartments, can never emerge from them without incurring danger, and it is only by clothing themselves more warmly than can be at all reconciled with comfort, that they can escape from rheumatic or other painful attacks.

These land-winds are also very destructive to the goods and chattels exposed to them; desks are warped and will not shut, leather gloves and shoes become so dry that they shrink and divide, while all unseasoned wood is speedily split across. It is said that the hot weather is never so fierce in Bombay as in Bengal, the sea-breezes, which sometimes blow very strongly, and are not so injurious as those from the land, affording a daily relief.

It may be necessary, for the advantage of succeeding travellers, to say that, in passing down the Red Sea, in the autumn and winter months, no danger need be apprehended from the effects of the climate upon coloured silks. It was not possible for me to burthen myself with tin cases, and I was obliged to put my wearing apparel, ribbons, &c, into portmanteaus, with no other precaution than a wrapper of brown paper. Nothing, however, was injured, and satin dresses previously worn came out as fresh as possible: a circumstance which never happens in the voyage round the Cape.

And now, while upon the subject of dress, I will further say, that it is advisable for ladies to bring out with them to Bombay every thing they can possibly want, since the shops, excepting immediately after the arrival of a ship, are very poorly provided, while the packs, for few have attained to the dignity of tin boxes, brought about by the hawkers, contain the most wretched assortment of goods imaginable. The moment, therefore, that the cargo of a vessel hag been purchased by the retail dealers, all that is really elegant or fashionable is eagerly purchased, and the rejected articles, even should they be equally excellent, when once consigned to the dingy precincts of a Bombay shop, lose all their lustre. The most perfect bonnet that Maradan ever produced, if once gibbeted in one of Muncherjee's glass-cases, could never be worn by a lady of the slightest pretensions. Goods to the amount of L300 were sold in one morning, it is said, in the above-mentioned worthy's shop, and those who were unable to pay it a visit on the day of the opening of the cases, must either content themselves with the leavings, or wait the arrival of another ship.

It is but justice to Miss Lyndsay, the English milliner, to say that she always appears to be well provided; but as her establishment is the only one of the kind in Bombay, there must necessarily be a sameness in the patterns of the articles made up. The want of variety is the evil most strongly felt in Anglo-Indian toilets; and, therefore, in preparing investments, large numbers of the same pieces of silk ribbons should be avoided, nobody liking to appear in a general uniform, or livery.

The stoppage of the China trade has cut off one abundant source of supply, of which the ladies of Bombay were wise enough to avail themselves. It is difficult now to procure a morsel of China silk in the shops, and there appears to be little chance of any goods of the kind coming into the market, until the present differences between Great Britain and the Celestial Empire shall be adjusted. With the exception of the common and trifling articles brought about by hawkers, every thing that is wanted for an Anglo-Indian establishment must be sent for to the Fort, from which many of the houses are situated, four, five, or six miles.

As there are populous villages at Bycullah, Mazagong, &c, it seems strange that no European bazaars have been established at these intermediate places for the convenience of the inhabitants, who, with the exception of a few fowls, do not usually keep much in the way of a farmyard. With an increase in the number of inhabitants, of course shops would start up in the most eligible situations, and should the anticipated change take place, and Bombay become the seat of the Supreme Government, the demands of the new establishment would no doubt be speedily supplied.

It is impossible, however idle the speculation may be, not to busy the mind with fancies concerning the site of the city which it is supposed would arise in the event of the Governor-general being instructed to take up his abode at Bombay. The Esplanade has been mentioned as the most probable place, although in building over this piece of ground the island would, in a great measure, be deprived of its lungs, and the enjoyment of that free circulation of air, which appears to be so essential to the existence of Anglo-Indians, who seem to require the whole expanse of heaven in order to breathe with freedom. The happy medium between the want of air and its excess will not answer the demand, and accordingly the Esplanade, no matter how strongly the wind blows, is a favourite resort. Although its general features are unattractive, it occasionally presents a very animated scene; the review of the troops in the garrison is seen to great advantage, and forms a spectacle always interesting and imposing.

This mustering of the troops is occasionally varied by military exercises of a more novel nature. The sailors of the flag-ship are brought on shore, for the purpose of perfecting themselves in the manual and platoon exercise, and in the performance of such military evolutions as would enable them to co-operate successfully with a land force, or to act alone with greater efficiency upon any emergency. Though not possessing much skill in military affairs, I was pleased with the ease and precision with which they executed the different movements, their steadiness in marching, and the promptness with which the line was dressed. They brought field-pieces on shore with them, which, according to my poor judgment, were admirably worked. These parades were the more interesting, in consequence of the expected war with China, a war in which the sailors of the **Wellesley** will, no doubt, be actively engaged.

I had also an opportunity of witnessing from the deck of that vessel, when accompanying the Governor's party on board, the manoeuvring of the ship's boats while landing a force. The mock fight was carried on with great spirit, and the most beautiful effect; the flashing from the guns in the bows of the boats and the musketry, amid the exquisite blue smoke issuing from the smaller species of artillery, producing fire-works which, in my opinion, could not be excelled by any of the most elaborate construction. The features of the landscape, no doubt, assisted to heighten the effect of the scene--a back-ground of lovely purple islands--a sea, like glass, calmly, brightly, beautifully blue--and the flotilla of boats, grouped as a painter would group them, and carrying on a running fire, which added much to the animation of their evolutions, the smoke occasionally enveloping the whole in vapour, and then showing the eager forms of men, as it rolled off in silvery clouds towards the distant hills.

As I gazed upon this armament, and upon the palm-woods that fringed the shore, I could not help calling to mind the lawless doings of the buccaneers of old, and the terror spread through towns and villages by the appearance of a fleet of boats, manned by resolute crews, and armed with the most deadly weapons of destruction. The sight realized also the descriptions given in modern novels of the capture of towns, and I could easily imagine the great excitement which would lead daring men to the execution of deeds, almost incredible to those who have never felt their spirits stirred and their arms nerved by danger, close, imminent, and only to be mastered by the mightiest efforts.

When any *tamasha*, as the natives call it, is going on upon the Esplanade, near the beach, they add very considerably to the effect of the scene, by grouping themselves upon the bales of cotton, piled near the wharf for exportation: those often appear to be a mass of human beings, so thickly are they covered with eager gazers. Upon the occasion of the departure of Sir Henry Fane to England, there appeared to be a general turn-out of the whole of Bombay, and the effect was impressive and striking. The road down to the Bunder, or place of embarkation, was lined with soldiers, the bands of the different regiments playing while the *cortege* passed. All the ladies made their appearance in open carriages, while the gentlemen mounted on horseback, and joined the cavalcade. A large party of native gentlemen assembled on foot at the Bunder, for the purpose of showing a last mark of respect to a distinguished officer, about to leave the country for ever.

Sir Henry, accompanied by his staff, but all in plain clothes, drove down the road in a barouche, attended by an escort of cavalry, and seemed to be much affected by the tokens of esteem which he received on every hand. He left the shore amidst the waving of handkerchiefs, and a salute of seventeen guns, and would have been greeted with hearty cheers, did military discipline allow of such manifestation of the feelings.

Sights and scenes like these will, of course, always attract numerous spectators, while on the evenings in which the band plays, there is a fair excuse for making the

Esplanade the object of the drive; but Bombay affords so many avenues possessing much greater beauty, that I am always delighted when I can diversify the scene by a visit to places not nearly so much in request, but which are to me infinitely more interesting, as developing some charm of nature, or displaying the habits and manners of the people of the country. With these views and feelings, I was much pleased at receiving an invitation to accompany some friends to a fair held in Mahim Wood--that sea of palm-trees, which I had often looked down upon from Chintapootzlee Hill with so much pleasure.

The fair was held, as is usual in oriental countries, in honour of a saint, whose canonized bones rest beneath a tomb apparently of no great antiquity, but which the people, who are not the best chronologists in the world, fancy to be of very ancient date. The name of the celebrated person thus enshrined was Mugdooree Sahib, a devotee, who added the gift of prophecy to his other high qualifications, and amongst other things has predicted that, when the town shall join the wood, Bombay shall be no more. The accomplishment of what in his days must have appeared very unlikely ever to take place--namely, the junction of inhabited dwellings with the trees of Mahim--seems to be in rapid course of fulfilment; the land has been drained, many portions formerly impassable filled up, and rendered solid ground, while the houses are extending so fast, that the Burruh Bazaar will in no very long period, in all probability, extend to Mahim. Those who attach some faith to the prophecy, yet are unwilling to believe that evil and not good will befal the "rising presidency," are of opinion that some change of name will take place when it shall be made the seat of the Supreme Government: thus the saint's credit will be saved, and no misfortune happen to the good town of Bombay. The superstitious of all persuasions, the Christians perhaps excepted--though many of the Portuguese Christians have little more than the name--unite in showing reverence to the shrine of the saint, while Mugdooree Sahib is held quite as much in estimation by the Hindus as by the followers of he own corrupted creed, the Mohammedans of Bombay being by no means orthodox.

Many respectable natives have built houses for themselves at Mahim, on purpose to have a place for their families during the time of the fair, while others hire houses or lodgings, for which they will pay as much as twenty rupees for the few days that it lasts. A delightful drive brought us to the confines of the wood; the whole way along, we passed one continuous string of bullock-carriages, filled with people of all tribes and castes, while others, who could not afford this mode of conveyance, were seen in groups, trudging on foot, leading their elder children, and carrying their younger in their arms. The road wound very prettily through the wood, which at every turn presented some charming bits of forest scenery, shown to great advantage in the crimson light of evening, which, as it faded, produced those wild, shadowy illusions, which lend enchantment to every view. Parasitical plants, climbing up the trunks of many of the trees, and flinging themselves in rich garlands from bough to bough, relieved the monotony of the tall, straight palm-trees, and produced delicious green recesses, the dearest charm of woodland scenery.

I have frequently felt a strong desire to dwell under the shade of forest boughs, for there is something in that sylvan kind of life so redolent of the hunter's merry horn, the mating song of birds, and the gurgling of secret rills, as to possess indescribable charms to a lover of the picturesque. Now, however, experience in sober realities having dispelled the illusions of romance, I should choose a cottage in some cleared space by the wood-side, though at this dry season of the year, and mid the perpetual sunshine of its skies, the heart of Mahim Wood would form a very agreeable residence.

The first house we came to was very comfortable, and almost English in its appearance; a small, neat mansion, with its little court-yard before it, such as we should not be surprised to see in some old-fashioned country village at home. Straggling huts on either side brought us to the principal street of Mahim, and here we found the houses lighted, and lamps suspended, in imitation of bunches of grapes, before all that were ambitious of making a good appearance.

After passing the shops belonging to the village--the grain-sellers, the pan-sellers, and other venders of articles in common demand--we came to a series of booths, exactly resembling those used for the same purpose in England, and well supplied with both native and foreign products. The display was certainly much greater than any I had expected to see. Some of the shops were filled with French, English, and Dutch toys; others with China and glass ornaments; then came one filled with coloured glass bangles, and every kind of native ornament in talc and tinsel, all set off with a profusion of lights. Instead of gingerbread, there were immense quantities of *metai*, or sweetmeats, of different shapes and forms, and various hues; sugar rock-work, pink, white, and yellow, with all sorts and descriptions of cakes. The carriage moved slowly through the crowd, and at length, finding it inconvenient to proceed farther in it, we alighted.

Our party had come to Mahim upon the invitation of a very respectable moonshee, who had his country-house there, and who was anxious to do the honours of the fair to the English strangers, my friends, like myself, being rather new to Bombay. We met the old gentleman at an opening in the village, leading to the tomb of the saint, and his offer to conduct us to the sacred shrine formed a farther inducement to leave the carriage, and venture through the crowd on foot.

The tomb, which was strongly illuminated, proved to be a white-washed building, having a dome in the centre, and four minarets, one at each angle, standing in a small enclosure, the walls of which were also newly white-washed, and approached by a flight of steps, leading into a portico. Upon either side of the avenue from the village were seated multitudes of men and women, who, if not beggars by profession, made no scruple to beg on this occasion.

I felt at first sorry that I had neglected to bring any money with me, but when I saw the crowd of applicants, whom it would have been impossible to satisfy, and recollected that my liberality would doubtless have been attributed to faith in the virtues of the saint, I no longer regretted the omission. The steps of the tomb were lined with these beggars, all vociferating at once, while other religious characters were singing with all the power of their lungs, and a native band, stationed in the verandah of the tomb, were at the same time making the most hideous discord by the help of all kinds of diabolical instruments.

Having a magistrate of our party, we were well protected by the police, who, without using any rudeness, kept the people off. So far from being uncivil, the natives seemed pleased to see us at the fair, and readily made way, until we came to the entrance of the chamber in which, under a sarcophagus, the body of the saint was deposited. Here we were told that we could proceed no farther, unless we consented to take off our shoes, a ceremony with which we did not feel disposed to comply, especially as we could see all that the chamber contained through the open door, and had no intention to pay homage to the saint. The sarcophagus, according to custom, was covered with a rich pall, and the devout pressed forward to lay their offerings upon it. These offerings consisted of money, cloths, grain, fruit, &c. nothing coming amiss, the priests of the temple being quite ready to take the gifts which the poorest could bestow. The beggars in the porch were more clamorous than ever, the *maam sahibs* being especially entreated to bestow their charity.

Having satisfied my curiosity, I was glad to get away into the fair, where I found many things more interesting. Convenient spaces in the wood were filled with merry-go-rounds, swings, and other locomotive machinery, of precisely the same description as those exhibited in England, and which I had seen in Hyde Park at the fair held there, in honour of Queen Victoria. Mahim Wood boasted no theatres or wild-beast shows, neither were we treated with the sight of giants or dwarfs; but there was no want of booths for the purpose of affording refreshment. One of these *cafes*, the front of which was entirely open, was most brilliantly illuminated, and filled with numerous tables, covered with a multitude of good things. That it was expected to be the resort of English guests was apparent, from an inscription painted in white letters, rather askew, upon a black board, to the following effect: "Tea, Coffee, and Pastry-House."

We were invited to enter this splendid establishment by the moonshee, who had evidently ordered a refection to be prepared for the occasion. Being unwilling to disappoint the old gentleman, we took the seats offered to us, and ate the cakes, and drank the coffee, presented by some respectable-looking Parsees, the owners of the shop, which they had taken pains to set off in the European style. Although the natives of India will not eat with us, as they know that we do not scruple to partake of food prepared for their tables, they are mortified and disappointed at any refusal to taste the good things set before us; the more we eat, the greater being the compliment. I was consequently obliged to convey away some of the cakes in my handkerchief, to avoid the alternatives of making myself ill or of giving offence.

When we were sufficiently rested and refreshed, we followed the moonshee to his mansion. The moon was at the full, and being at this time well up, lighted us through the less thronged avenues of the village, these tangled lanes, with the exception of a few candles, having no other illumination. Here, seated in corners upon the ground, were the more humble traders of the fair, venders of fruit, the larger kind being divided into slices for the convenience of poor customers. In one spot, a group of dissipated characters were assembled round bottles and drinking-vessels (of which the contents bore neither the colour nor the smell of sherbet), who were evidently determined to make a night of it over the fermented juice of the palm. From what I have seen, I am inclined to believe sobriety to be as rare a virtue in Bombay as in London; toddy-shops appear to be greatly upon the increase, and certainly in every direction there are already ample means of gratifying a love of spirituous liquors. In other places, the usual occupation of frying fish was going on, while a taste for sweet things might be gratified by confectionary of an ordinary description compared with that exhibited in the shops.

As we receded from the fair, the bright illumination in the distance, the twinkling lights in the fore-ground, dimly revealing dusky figures cowering round their fires, and the dark depths of the wood beyond, with now and then a gleam of moon-shine streaming on its tangled paths, made up a landscape roll of scenic effects. Getting deeper and deeper into the wood, we came at last to a small modest mansion, standing in the corner of a garden, and shadowed by palm-trees, through which the moon-beams chequered our path. We did not enter the house, contenting ourselves with seats in the verandah, where the children of our host, his wife or wives not making their appearance, were assembled. The elder boys addressed us in very good English, and were, the moonshee told us, well acquainted with the Guzerattee and Mahratta languages; he had also bestowed an education upon his daughters, who were taught to read in the vernacular.

The old man told us that he was born in Mahim Wood at the time of the festival, and, though a Hindu, had had the name of Mugdooree, that of the saint, bestowed upon him, for a good omen. Having a great affection for his native place, he had, as soon as he could command the means, built the house which we now saw, and in which he always resided during the fair, which was called **oories**, or the Mugdooree Sahib's **oories**, at Mahim. After sitting some time with the old man, and admiring the effect of the moonlight among the palm-trees, we rose to depart. In taking leave of the spot, I could not repress a wish to see it under a different aspect, although it required very slight aid from fancy to picture it as it would appear in the rains, with mildew in the drip of those pendant palm branches, green stagnant pools in every hollow, toads crawling over the garden paths, and snakes lurking beneath every stone.

Returning to the place in which we had left the carriage, we found the fair more crowded than ever, the numbers of children, if possible, exceeding those to be seen at English places of resort of the same nature. The upper rooms of the superior houses, many of which seemed to be large and handsome, were well lighted and filled with company, many of the most respectable amongst the Hindus, Mohammedans, and Parsees, repairing to Mahim, to recreate themselves during the festival. The shops had put on even a gayer appearance, and though there was no rich merchandize to be seen, the character of the meeting being merely that of a rustic fair, I was greatly surprised by the elegance of some of the commodities, and the taste of their arrangement.

It was evident that all the purchasers must be native, and consequently I could not help feeling some astonishment at the large quantities of expensive European toys with which whole booths were filled. Dolls, which were to me a novelty in my late visit to Paris, with real hair dressed in the newest fashion, were abundant; and so were those excellent representations of animals from Germany, known by the name of "Barking toys." The price of these things, demanded of our party at least, was high. I had wished to possess myself of something as a remembrance of this fair, but as the old moonshee was the only individual amongst us who carried any money about him, I did not like him to become my banker on this occasion, lest he should not permit me to pay him again, and I should by this means add to the disbursements already made upon our account.

Upon leaving the fair, we found some difficulty in steering our way through the bullock-carriages which almost blocked up the road, and as we drove along the grand thoroughfare towards Girgaum, a populous portion of the native town, the visitants seemed to increase; cart followed upon cart in quick succession, all the bullocks in Bombay, numerous as they are, appearing to have been mustered for the occasion.

In the different drives which I have taken through the island, I have come upon several fine tanks, enclosed by solid masonry of dark-coloured stone; but, with the exception, in some instances, of one or two insignificant pillars or minarets, they are destitute of those architectural ornaments which add so much splendour to the same works in Bengal. The broad flights of steps, the richly decorated temple, or the range of small pagodas, so frequently to be seen by the side of the tanks and bowlies in other parts of India, are here unknown; the more ancient native buildings which

I have yet examined being, comparatively speaking, of a mean and paltry description, while all the handsome modern houses are built after the European manner. There is one feature, however, with which I am greatly pleased--the perpetual recurrence of seats and ledges made in the walls which enclose gentlemen's gardens and grounds, or run along the roads, and which seem to be intended as places of repose for the wayfarer, or as a rest to his burthen.

It is always agreeable to see needful accommodation afforded to the poor and to the stranger; public benefits, however trifling, displaying liberality of mind in those who can give consideration to the wants and feelings of multitudes from whom they can hope for no return. These seats frequently occur close to the gate of some spacious dwelling, and may be supposed to be intended for the servants and dependants of the great man, or those who wait humbly on the outside of his mansion; but they as frequently are found upon the high roads, or by the side of wells and tanks.

The festival of the **Duwallee** has taken place since my arrival in Bombay, and though I have seen it celebrated before, and more splendidly in one particular--namely, the illuminations--I never had the same opportunity of witnessing other circumstances connected with ceremonies performed at the opening of the new year of the Hindus. When I speak of the superiority of the illuminations, I allude to their taste and effect; there were plenty of lights in Bombay, but they were differently disposed, and did not mark the outline of the buildings in the beautiful manner which prevails upon the other side of India, every person lighting up his own house according to his fancy. Upon the eve of the new year, while driving through the bazaar, we saw preparations for the approaching festival; many of the houses were well garnished with lamps, the shops were swept and put into order, and the horns of the bullocks were garlanded with flowers, while fire-works, and squibs and crackers, were going off in all directions.

On the following evening, I went with a party of friends, by invitation, to the house of a native gentleman, a Parsee merchant of old family and great respectability, and as we reached the steps of his door, a party of men came up with sticks in their hands, answering to our old English morice-dancers. These men were well clad in white dresses, with flowers stuck in their turbans; they formed a circle somewhat resembling the figure of **moulinet**, but without joining hands, the inner party striking their sticks as they danced round against those on the outer ring, and all joining in a rude but not unmusical chorus. The gestures of these men, though wild, were neither awkward nor uncouth, the sticks keeping excellent time with the song and with the action of their feet. After performing sundry evolutions, and becoming nearly out of breath, they desisted, and called upon the spectators to reward their exertions. Having received a present, they went into the court-yard of the next mansion, which belonged to one of the richest native merchants in Bombay, and there renewed their dance.

We found in the drawing-room of our host's house a large company assembled. The upper end was covered with a white cloth, and all round, seated on the floor against the walls, were grave-looking Parsees, many being of advanced years. They had their books and ledgers open before them, the ceremony about to be commenced consisting of the blessing or consecration of the account-books, in order to secure prosperity for the ensuing year. The officiating priests were brahmins, the custom and the festival--of which Lacshmee, the goddess of wealth, is the patroness--being purely Hindu.

The Parsees of India, sole remnant of the ancient fire-worshippers, have sadly degenerated from that pure faith held by their forefathers, and for which they became fugitives and exiles. What persecution failed to accomplish, kindness has effected, and their religion has been corrupted by the taint of Hinduism, in consequence of their long and friendly intercourse with the people, who permitted them to dwell in their land, and to take their daughters in marriage. Incense was burning on a tripod placed upon the floor, and the priests muttering prayers, which sounded very like incantations, ever and anon threw some new perfume upon the charcoal, which produced what our friend Dousterswivel would call a "suffumigation." These preliminaries over, they caused each person to write a few words in the open book before him, and then threw upon the leaves a portion of grain. After this had been distributed, they made the circle again, and threw gold leaf upon the volumes; then came spices and betel-nut, cut in small pieces, and lastly flowers, and a profusion of the red powder (abeer) so lavishly employed in Hindu festivals. More incense was burned, and the ceremony concluded, the merchants rising and congratulating each other. Formerly, when our host was a more wealthy man than, in consequence of sundry misfortunes, he is at present, he was in the habit of disbursing Rs. 10,000 in gifts upon this day: everybody that came to the house receiving something.

The custom of blessing the books, after the Hindu manner, will in all probability shortly decline among the Parsees, the younger portion being already of opinion that it is a vain and foolish ceremony, borrowed from strangers; and, indeed, the elders of the party were at some pains to convince me that they merely complied with it in consequence of a stipulation entered into with the Hindus, when they granted them an asylum, to observe certain forms and ceremonies connected with their customs, assuring me that they did not place any reliance upon the favour of the goddess, looking only for the blessing of God to prosper their undertakings.

This declaration, however, was somewhat in contradiction to one circumstance, which I omitted to mention, namely, that before the assembled Parsees rose from the floor, they permitted the officiating brahmins to mark their foreheads with the symbol of the goddess, thus virtually admitting her supremacy. The lamps were then lighted, and we were presented with the usual offering of bouquets of roses, plentifully bedewed with ***goolabee panee***, or the distilled tears of the flower, to speak poetically; and having admired the children of the family, who were brought out in their best dresses and jewels, took our leave. The ladies, the married daughters and daughters-in-law of our host, did not make their appearance upon this occasion; for, though not objecting to be seen in public, they are not fond of presenting themselves in their own houses before strangers.

It is the women of India who are at this moment impeding the advance of improvement; they have hitherto been so ill-educated, their minds left so entirely uncultivated, that they have had nothing to amuse or interest them excepting the ceremonies of their religion, and the customs with which it is encumbered. These, notwithstanding that many are inconvenient, and others entail much suffering, they are unwilling to relinquish. Every departure from established rule, which their male relatives deem expedient, they resolutely oppose, employing the influence which women, however contemned as the weaker vessel, always do possess, and always will exert, in perpetuating all the evils resulting from ignorance. The sex will ever be found active either in advancing or retarding great changes, and whether this activity be employed for good or for evil, depends upon the manner in which their intellectual faculties have been trained and cultivated.

It appears to me that, although education is making great progress in Bombay, all it has yet accomplished of good appears upon the surface, it not having yet wrought any radical change in the feelings and opinions of the people, or, excepting in few instances, directing their pursuits to new objects. I give this opinion, however, with great diffidence--merely as an impression which a longer residence in Bombay may remove; meanwhile, I lose no opportunity of acquainting myself with the native community, and I hope to gather some interesting information relative to the probable effects of the system now adopting at the different national schools.

As far as I can judge, a little of Uncle Jonathan's fervour in progressing is wanting here; neither the Anglo-Indian or native residents seem to manifest the slightest inclination to "go ahead;" and while they complain loudly of the apathy evinced at home to all that concerns their advantage and prosperity, are quite content to drowze over their old ***dustoors*** (customs), and make no attempt to direct the public attention in England to subjects of real importance.

Though unwilling to indulge in premature remarks, these are pressed upon me by the general complaints which I hear upon all sides; but though everybody seems to lament the evil, no one exerts himself to effect a remedy, and while much is talked of individually, little is done by common consent. One great bar to improvement consists, I am told, of the voluminous nature of the reports upon all subjects, which are heaped together until they become so hopelessly bulky, that nobody can be prevailed upon to wade through them. In England, at all public meetings, a great deal of time and breath are wasted in superfluous harangues; but these can only effect the remote mischief threatened by Mr. Babbage, and produce earthquakes and other convulsions in distant lands, in distant centuries; whereas the foolscap is a present and a weighty evil, and has probably swamped more systems of improvement, and more promising institutions, than any other enemy, however active.

The intellectual community of India seems yet to have to learn the advantage of placing all that relates to it in a clear, succinct, and popular form, and of bringing works before the British public which will entertain as well as instruct, and lead those who are employed in legislating for our Eastern territories to inquire more deeply into those subjects which so materially affect its political, moral, and commercial prosperity.

www.bookjungle.com *email: sales@bookjungle.com fax: 630-214-0564 mail: Book Jungle PO Box 2226 Champaign, IL 61825*

The Codes Of Hammurabi And Moses
W. W. Davies

QTY

The discovery of the Hammurabi Code is one of the greatest achievements of archaeology, and is of paramount interest, not only to the student of the Bible, but also to all those interested in ancient history...

Religion   ISBN: *1-59462-338-4*   Pages:132
                                     MSRP $12.95

The Theory of Moral Sentiments
Adam Smith

QTY

This work from 1749. contains original theories of conscience amd moral judgment and it is the foundation for systemof morals.

Philosophy   ISBN: *1-59462-777-0*   Pages:536
                                     MSRP $19.95

Jessica's First Prayer
Hesba Stretton

QTY

In a screened and secluded corner of one of the many railway-bridges which span the streets of London there could be seen a few years ago, from five o'clock every morning until half past eight, a tidily set-out coffee-stall, consisting of a trestle and board, upon which stood two large tin cans, with a small fire of charcoal burning under each so as to keep the coffee boiling during the early hours of the morning when the work-people were thronging into the city on their way to their daily toil...

Childrens   ISBN: *1-59462-373-2*   Pages:84
                                     MSRP $9.95

My Life and Work
Henry Ford

QTY

Henry Ford revolutionized the world with his implementation of mass production for the Model T automobile. Gain valuable business insight into his life and work with his own auto-biography... "We have only started on our development of our country we have not as yet, with all our talk of wonderful progress, done more than scratch the surface. The progress has been wonderful enough but..."

Biographies/   ISBN: *1-59462-198-5*   Pages:300
                                       MSRP $21.95

www.bookjungle.com *email: sales@bookjungle.com fax: 630-214-0564 mail: Book Jungle PO Box 2226 Champaign, IL 61825*

The Art of Cross-Examination
Francis Wellman

QTY

I presume it is the experience of every author, after his first book is published upon an important subject, to be almost overwhelmed with a wealth of ideas and illustrations which could readily have been included in his book, and which to his own mind, at least, seem to make a second edition inevitable. Such certainly was the case with me; and when the first edition had reached its sixth impression in five months, I rejoiced to learn that it seemed to my publishers that the book had met with a sufficiently favorable reception to justify a second and considerably enlarged edition. ...

Reference ISBN: *1-59462-647-2* Pages:412 MSRP *$19.95*

On the Duty of Civil Disobedience
Henry David Thoreau

QTY

Thoreau wrote his famous essay, On the Duty of Civil Disobedience, as a protest against an unjust but popular war and the immoral but popular institution of slave-owning. He did more than write—he declined to pay his taxes, and was hauled off to gaol in consequence. Who can say how much this refusal of his hastened the end of the war and of slavery ?

Law ISBN: *1-59462-747-9* Pages:48 MSRP *$7.45*

Dream Psychology Psychoanalysis for Beginners
Sigmund Freud

QTY

Sigmund Freud, born Sigismund Schlomo Freud (May 6, 1856 - September 23, 1939), was a Jewish-Austrian neurologist and psychiatrist who co-founded the psychoanalytic school of psychology. Freud is best known for his theories of the unconscious mind, especially involving the mechanism of repression; his redefinition of sexual desire as mobile and directed towards a wide variety of objects; and his therapeutic techniques, especially his understanding of transference in the therapeutic relationship and the presumed value of dreams as sources of insight into unconscious desires.

Psychology ISBN: *1-59462-905-6* Pages:196 MSRP *$15.45*

The Miracle of Right Thought
Orison Swett Marden

QTY

Believe with all of your heart that you will do what you were made to do. When the mind has once formed the habit of holding cheerful, happy, prosperous pictures, it will not be easy to form the opposite habit. It does not matter how improbable or how far away this realization may see, or how dark the prospects may be, if we visualize them as best we can, as vividly as possible, hold tenaciously to them and vigorously struggle to attain them, they will gradually become actualized, realized in the life. But a desire, a longing without endeavor, a yearning abandoned or held indifferently will vanish without realization.

Self Help ISBN: *1-59462-644-8* Pages:360 MSRP *$25.45*

www.bookjungle.com email: sales@bookjungle.com fax: 630-214-0564 mail: Book Jungle PO Box 2226 Champaign, IL 61825

QTY

- [ ] **The Rosicrucian Cosmo-Conception Mystic Christianity** by *Max Heindel* ISBN: *1-59462-188-8* **$38.95**
  The Rosicrucian Cosmo-conception is not dogmatic, neither does it appeal to any other authority than the reason of the student. It is; not controversial, but is; sent forth in the, hope that it may help to clear... *New Age/Religion Pages 646*

- [ ] **Abandonment To Divine Providence** by *Jean-Pierre de Caussade* ISBN: *1-59462-228-0* **$25.95**
  "The Rev. Jean Pierre de Caussade was one of the most remarkable spiritual writers of the Society of Jesus in France in the 18th Century. His death took place at Toulouse in 1751. His works have gone through many editions and have been republished... *Inspirational/Religion Pages 400*

- [ ] **Mental Chemistry** by *Charles Haanel* ISBN: *1-59462-192-6* **$23.95**
  Mental Chemistry allows the change of material conditions by combining and appropriately utilizing the power of the mind. Much like applied chemistry creates something new and unique out of careful combinations of chemicals the mastery of mental chemistry... *New Age Pages 354*

- [ ] **The Letters of Robert Browning and Elizabeth Barret Barrett 1845-1846 vol II** ISBN: *1-59462-193-4* **$35.95**
  by *Robert Browning* and *Elizabeth Barrett* *Biographies Pages 596*

- [ ] **Gleanings In Genesis (volume I)** by *Arthur W. Pink* ISBN: *1-59462-130-6* **$27.45**
  Appropriately has Genesis been termed "the seed plot of the Bible" for in it we have, in germ form, almost all of the great doctrines which are afterwards fully developed in the books of Scripture which follow... *Religion/Inspirational Pages 420*

- [ ] **The Master Key** by *L. W. de Laurence* ISBN: *1-59462-001-6* **$30.95**
  In no branch of human knowledge has there been a more lively increase of the spirit of research during the past few years than in the study of Psychology, Concentration and Mental Discipline. The requests for authentic lessons in Thought Control, Mental Discipline and... *New Age/Business Pages 422*

- [ ] **The Lesser Key Of Solomon Goetia** by *L. W. de Laurence* ISBN: *1-59462-092-X* **$9.95**
  This translation of the first book of the "Lernegton" which is now for the first time made accessible to students of Talismanic Magic was done, after careful collation and edition, from numerous Ancient Manuscripts in Hebrew, Latin, and French... *New Age/Occult Pages 92*

- [ ] **Rubaiyat Of Omar Khayyam** by *Edward Fitzgerald* ISBN: *1-59462-332-5* **$13.95**
  Edward Fitzgerald, whom the world has already learned, in spite of his own efforts to remain within the shadow of anonymity, to look upon as one of the rarest poets of the century, was born at Bredfield, in Suffolk, on the 31st of March, 1809. He was the third son of John Purcell... *Music Pages 172*

- [ ] **Ancient Law** by *Henry Maine* ISBN: *1-59462-128-4* **$29.95**
  The chief object of the following pages is to indicate some of the earliest ideas of mankind, as they are reflected in Ancient Law, and to point out the relation of those ideas to modern thought. *Religion/History Pages 452*

- [ ] **Far-Away Stories** by *William J. Locke* ISBN: *1-59462-129-2* **$19.45**
  "Good wine needs no bush, but a collection of mixed vintages does. And this book is just such a collection. Some of the stories I do not want to remain buried for ever in the museum files of dead magazine-numbers an author's not unpardonable vanity..." *Fiction Pages 272*

- [ ] **Life of David Crockett** by *David Crockett* ISBN: *1-59462-250-7* **$27.45**
  "Colonel David Crockett was one of the most remarkable men of the times in which he lived. Born in humble life, but gifted with a strong will, an indomitable courage, and unremitting perseverance... *Biographies/New Age Pages 424*

- [ ] **Lip-Reading** by *Edward Nitchie* ISBN: *1-59462-206-X* **$25.95**
  Edward B. Nitchie, founder of the New York School for the Hard of Hearing, now the Nitchie School of Lip-Reading, Inc, wrote "LIP-READING Principles and Practice". The development and perfecting of this meritorious work on lip-reading was an undertaking... *How-to Pages 400*

- [ ] **A Handbook of Suggestive Therapeutics, Applied Hypnotism, Psychic Science** ISBN: *1-59462-214-0* **$24.95**
  by *Henry Munro* *Health/New Age/Health/Self-help Pages 376*

- [ ] **A Doll's House: and Two Other Plays** by *Henrik Ibsen* ISBN: *1-59462-112-8* **$19.95**
  Henrik Ibsen created this classic when in revolutionary 1848 Rome. Introducing some striking concepts in playwriting for the realist genre, this play has been studied the world over. *Fiction/Classics/Plays 308*

- [ ] **The Light of Asia** by *sir Edwin Arnold* ISBN: *1-59462-204-3* **$13.95**
  In this poetic masterpiece, Edwin Arnold describes the life and teachings of Buddha. The man who was to become known as Buddha to the world was born as Prince Gautama of India but he rejected the worldly riches and abandoned the reigns of power when... *Religion/History/Biographies Pages 170*

- [ ] **The Complete Works of Guy de Maupassant** by *Guy de Maupassant* ISBN: *1-59462-157-8* **$16.95**
  "For days and days, nights and nights, I had dreamed of that first kiss which was to consecrate our engagement, and I knew not on what spot I should put my lips..." *Fiction/Classics Pages 240*

- [ ] **The Art of Cross-Examination** by *Francis L. Wellman* ISBN: *1-59462-309-0* **$26.95**
  Written by a renowned trial lawyer, Wellman imparts his experience and uses case studies to explain how to use psychology to extract desired information through questioning. *How-to/Science/Reference Pages 408*

- [ ] **Answered or Unanswered?** by *Louisa Vaughan* ISBN: *1-59462-248-5* **$10.95**
  Miracles of Faith in China *Religion Pages 112*

- [ ] **The Edinburgh Lectures on Mental Science (1909)** by *Thomas* ISBN: *1-59462-008-3* **$11.95**
  This book contains the substance of a course of lectures recently given by the writer in the Queen Street Hall, Edinburgh. Its purpose is to indicate the Natural Principles governing the relation between Mental Action and Material Conditions... *New Age/Psychology Pages 148*

- [ ] **Ayesha** by *H. Rider Haggard* ISBN: *1-59462-301-5* **$24.95**
  Verily and indeed it is the unexpected that happens! Probably if there was one person upon the earth from whom the Editor of this, and of a certain previous history, did not expect to hear again... *Classics Pages 380*

- [ ] **Ayala's Angel** by *Anthony Trollope* ISBN: *1-59462-352-X* **$29.95**
  The two girls were both pretty, but Lucy who was twenty-one who supposed to be simple and comparatively unattractive, whereas Ayala was credited, as her Bombwhat romantic name might show, with poetic charm and a taste for romance. Ayala when her father died was nineteen... *Fiction Pages 484*

- [ ] **The American Commonwealth** by *James Bryce* ISBN: *1-59462-286-8* **$34.45**
  An interpretation of American democratic political theory. It examines political mechanics and society from the perspective of Scotsman James Bryce. *Politics Pages 572*

- [ ] **Stories of the Pilgrims** by *Margaret P. Pumphrey* ISBN: *1-59462-116-0* **$17.95**
  This book explores pilgrims religious oppression in England as well as their escape to Holland and eventual crossing to America on the Mayflower, and their early days in New England... *History Pages 268*

www.bookjungle.com *email: sales@bookjungle.com fax:* 630-214-0564 *mail: Book Jungle PO Box 2226 Champaign, IL 61825*

QTY

The Fasting Cure *by Sinclair Upton* **ISBN:** *1-59462-222-1* **$13.95**
In the Cosmopolitan Magazine for May, 1910, and in the Contemporary Review (London) for April, 1910, I published an article dealing with my experiences in fasting. I have written a great many magazine articles, but never one which attracted so much attention... New Age/Self Help/Health Pages 164

Hebrew Astrology *by Sepharial* **ISBN:** *1-59462-308-2* **$13.45**
In these days of advanced thinking it is a matter of common observation that we have left many of the old landmarks behind and that we are now pressing forward to greater heights and to a wider horizon than that which represented the mind-content of our progenitors... Astrology Pages 144

Thought Vibration or The Law of Attraction in the Thought World **ISBN:** *1-59462-127-6* **$12.95**
by William Walker Atkinson *Psychology/Religion Pages 144*

Optimism *by Helen Keller* **ISBN:** *1-59462-108-X* **$15.95**
Helen Keller was blind, deaf, and mute since 19 months old, yet famously learned how to overcome these handicaps, communicate with the world, and spread her lectures promoting optimism. An inspiring read for everyone... Biographies/Inspirational Pages 84

Sara Crewe *by Frances Burnett* **ISBN:** *1-59462-360-0* **$9.45**
In the first place, Miss Minchin lived in London. Her home was a large, dull, tall one, in a large, dull square, where all the houses were alike, and all the sparrows were alike, and where all the door-knockers made the same heavy sound... Childrens/Classic Pages 88

The Autobiography of Benjamin Franklin *by Benjamin Franklin* **ISBN:** *1-59462-135-7* **$24.95**
The Autobiography of Benjamin Franklin has probably been more extensively read than any other American historical work, and no other book of its kind has had such ups and downs of fortune. Franklin lived for many years in England, where he was agent... Biographies/History Pages 332

Name	
Email	
Telephone	
Address	
City, State ZIP	

☐ Credit Card   ☐ Check / Money Order

Credit Card Number	
Expiration Date	
Signature	

Please Mail to: Book Jungle
PO Box 2226
Champaign, IL 61825
or Fax to: 630-214-0564

ORDERING INFORMATION

web: *www.bookjungle.com*
email: *sales@bookjungle.com*
fax: *630-214-0564*
mail: *Book Jungle PO Box 2226 Champaign, IL 61825*
or PayPal *to sales@bookjungle.com*

Please contact us for bulk discounts

DIRECT-ORDER TERMS

20% Discount if You Order Two or More Books
Free Domestic Shipping!
Accepted: Master Card, Visa, Discover, American Express

www.ingramcontent.com/pod-product-compliance
Lightning Source LLC
Chambersburg PA
CBHW081836170426
43199CB00017B/2750